For Ronnie Bellew

The Road to Croker

Eamonn Sweeney was born in 1968 in Sligo and lives in West Cork. He is the author of two novels, *Waiting for the Healer* and *The Photograph*; two sports books, *There's Only One Red Army* and *Munster Hurling Legends*; and a play, *Bruens Twist*. He is the father of one daughter, Emily.

CONTENTS

Introduction

Tipp Transvestites, Down Geezers
and Nervous Corkmen

Back in 1988 myself, my best friend and my brother set off for Croke Park to see the All-Ireland hurling final between Galway and Tipperary. My best friend was from Galway and the affection me and my brother had for the Tribesmen could be accounted for by the parentage rule. With Sligo completely in the doldrums, having a Galway mother and a Kilkenny father was a boon to a young GAA fan who might otherwise never have had any real partisan interest in what transpired in Croke Park.

Our trips to Dublin in those days, for matches, for concerts, for the pure hell of it, were supremely disorganised. Never did we do anything as prosaic as book a B & B or even ring someone to tell them that we might be coming up and would appreciate a berth on their floor. Instead, we just presumed that, at some stage, we would meet an acquaintance who'd dig us out. This meant that we often spent the early hours of the morning wandering around the centre of Dublin and working out how many hours it was until somewhere serving breakfast opened its doors. Strangely enough, this didn't bother us.

That particular Saturday night ran true to form. Somewhere along the way, we had met two women but neither of them was in a position to provide lodgings. One of them was up from Kerry and the other lived at home with her parents. An enterprising young man from Dublin did try to sell us drugs but he couldn't

1

help out with accommodation. There was nothing for it but to kill a couple more hours in a nightclub.

This was not as easy as it sounds. Dublin in the eighties was not the orgiastic late-night temple of arcane delights that it is today. All pubs closed well before midnight and there were no more than a dozen nightclubs near the city centre. Hardly any of them served beer and you were forced to splash out on warm bottles of wine while a bouncer hovered over you to make sure it was being drunk quickly. Had Copper Face Jacks been open back then, it would have been regarded as the classiest club in town. OK, there was the Pink Elephant but that prided itself on an elitist door policy. We had more chance of spending the night on Charlie Haughey's couch than getting in to the Pink.

Having been turned away from both the Mont Clare Hotel, where we thought we might be able to sneak in for a drink in the residents' bar, and the truly horrible Club Nasty on Nassau Street, we stumbled across a newly opened club called Sides.

One of the great current hobbies of my generation is false nostalgia. The problem we have is that our time was on the cusp of the old, repressive Ireland and the new anything-goes model that exists today. So the country's thirty-somethings suffered the agony of knowing they should be cool and liberated while being born just too early to carry it off. We compensate for this by lying about our past, spoofing on about the last days of disco, the punk explosion, teenage sexual adventures and recreational drug use as though we'd been brought up in Greenwich Village or somewhere else these things actually happened. In reality, we were more like characters from a John McGahern short story than a Brett Easton Ellis novel.

So myself, my brother and my best friend were awed by the immense coolness of Sides. Instead of bouncers, it had trendy youngsters in MA 1 flying jackets and colourful scarves doing the door; instead of chart music, it played the kind of tunes you heard during the club scenes in *Shaft's Big Score* and, shocker, some of the clientele were obviously gay, something as exotic to us at the time as the Amazonian anteater. Of course, we knew there were probably gays in the West of Ireland. We just never imagined that they'd venture out in public.

Most impressive of all was a long-haired gent of androgynous mien who didn't look dissimilar to Pete Burns of Dead or Alive. He wore, shock two, make-up, had painted fingernails and, to top it all, wore a long dress. In the right light, you could have mistaken him for a good-looking woman. Not that any of us admitted this for a long time afterwards.

Near the end of the night, myself and my friend found ourselves siphoning the python at the Sides stalls. In came the Pete Burns lookalike, hiked up his dress and began to relieve himself. There was that stolid silence which usually attends men pissing in unison. Pete broke the ice.

'Are ye up for the match, lads?'

'We are.'

'I don't think there's any way Conor Hayes will hold Nicky English. And Tipp will be too strong at midfield as well. I'm from Tipp.'

So commenced ten minutes of hurling speculation. Two country lads put the case for Galway, a neophyte drag queen argued for Tipperary. The GAA, you see, affects almost everybody in Ireland and there's no such thing as a typical follower.

It was only when we'd left the club that we decided there was something terribly wrong with our cross-dressing friend.

Conor Hayes was well able for Nicky English and anyone could see that Galway had the stronger midfield duo.

Galway won that final and it was the last game I'd see live for a while. The year after, I hit for London and, for a couple of years, just about the only time I saw the championship was when I came home on holidays. Just about because the All-Ireland semi-finals and finals were shown in a cinema in Hammersmith. It was something else to see Corkmen and Meathmen abusing each other in a West London Tube station after the 1990 football decider.

My most memorable GAA year in London was 1991. That was when an intrepid satellite broadcasting company started beaming matches to Irish pubs in the city. You didn't have to trek to Hammersmith anymore, the games were down the road in your local. And they didn't just show the later stages of the championship, we got *The Sunday Game* every week so you could follow the ebb and flow as though you were at home.

The pub I drank in wasn't particularly Irish but the landlord was from Galway and there were enough Paddies there to ensure that no one complained about *The Sunday Game* being turned up full blast in the public bar every Sunday night. But there was one very unlikely supporter. The guy was known as Chelsea Mick. He was a fanatical Chelsea fan whose arms were emblazoned with tattoos proclaiming his loyalty to that club and to England. He was never short of stories about his involvement in terrace mayhem and, during the 1990 World Cup, rarely left the pub without singing 'Rule Britannia'. He seemed like the embodiment of the Bulldog Spirit that laid continental city centres to waste.

On the opening night of the 1991 championship, Chelsea Mick strolled into the pub, looked at the television and said confidently, 'Daaan's gonna win that.'

'What did you say, Mick?'

'Daaan's gonna win that coz Daaan's got the best footballers in Ireland. Sean O'Neill, Paddy Doherty, Jim McCartan, they all come from Daaan. So the geezers from Daaan's gonna win that. Up Daaan.'

It turned out that Chelsea Mick's father came from Down and that he'd been brought up on tales of the county's invincible sides of the sixties. He joined us every Sunday and we decided to break the news to him that, though the geezers from Daaan had once been a powerful force, those days were long gone. Meath, Cork, Kerry, Dublin, counties like that were on top now. It would be a cold week in hell before Down, or any Ulster team, made an impression on the big sides from Munster and Leinster.

'Naaah, mate. Daaan's gonna win that.'

Even when Down only scraped a draw with a far from mighty Derry in their first game, Chelsea Mick was not discouraged. And he became ever more certain of the correctness of his beliefs when Down, complete outsiders at the start of the season, beat Donegal to win the Ulster title. Still, there wasn't much chance of them beating a resurgent Kerry team in the All-Ireland semi.

'You don't know wot you're talkin abaaht, mate. Daan ain't never lost to Kerry.'

This was true and, to the amazement of all but one of the pub audience, Down duly hammered the Kingdom to reach the All-Ireland final against Meath.

When I walked in to the pub on the last Sunday in September, it looked like the terrace at a county ground. Chelsea Mick was there, with his father, his mother, his brother, nephews, nieces and grandchildren. They were wearing Down colours, waving Down flags, roaring encouragement as the Down team came out onto the field. The only pity was that their team hadn't a hope. Meath had been heroic in disposing of Dublin after four games and must have been one of the hottest favourites to ever play in a football final. We prepared Mick for the inevitable, tried to let him down gently.

'That's bollocks mate. Daaan doesn't lose finals. Everyone knows that.'

Chelsea Mick was right and we were wrong. And as he and his family did a jog of joy round the public bar there were tears in his eyes.

'You see that bloke with the cup, the Sam Maguire, innit? That's Paddy O'Rourke. He's from my old man's manor.'

Up Daaan.

* * *

5

In 1999, I was writing about the GAA for the *Irish Examiner*. One Tuesday night, I fetched up in Killeagh, a small East Cork village near Youghal, which would have been totally unremarkable had it not produced Mark Landers (captain) and Joe Deane (top scorer) of the Cork team that was to play Kilkenny in the following Sunday's All-Ireland hurling final. What made this all the more remarkable was that the Killeagh club had not in its entire history ever had a player in a senior final.

When I arrived in the village, most people were in the village hall at the draw for final tickets. I ducked into a pub called Kennedys, one of those thousands all over the country with GAA photos on the wall and club colours behind the bar. Two worn-looking gents were silent when I came in and then one of them turned to the other and said with considerable fervour, 'Wouldn't it be great all the same? Wouldn't it be unbelievable?'

His voice was full of the enormity of what was happening to the little village. In it was the realisation that, this time next week, Killeagh might be the centre of the hurling universe but also the knowledge that the dream might well not come true. He sounded like a man who had just heard five of his Lotto numbers come up and was waiting for the sixth to be announced. He'd either know joy beyond his wildest dreams or horror at coming so close but falling short.

A hundred yards away, Crowley's pub was packed with people who'd been at the draw. The premises was humming the way rural bars do only at Christmastime and on St Patrick's Day. One man told me it had been like this every night since the semi-final.

'I tell myself I'll stay home tonight but then I start thinking about the match and I have to go out and talk to someone about it.'

Everyone else seemed to have the same idea. Killeagh had been totally taken over by the thought of the final. Nothing else mattered. I met Deane's brother, the man who'd brought Landers to Croke Park for the first time, Deane's father and mother,

Landers' brother-in-law, the man who'd travelled to matches w.
the captain's late father, the man who'd trained Deane at U-12
level and a hundred other people who felt intimately connected
with Cork's fortunes in the final because they'd known the two
local players before they'd ever picked up a hurl.

Cork won that final and the night the Liam McCarthy Cup
came to Killeagh, the celebrations attained a South American level
of passion. There was such a crowd that Cork captain Brian
Corcoran had to be rescued from the crush by guards and took
shelter in the back room of a local pub. There mustn't have been
any place better to be in Ireland that night. The entire village had
won the Lotto.

One of the greatest strengths of the GAA is that it can make
ordinary places extraordinary. If you'd passed through Killeagh
any other week of the year, it wouldn't have looked any different
from a hundred other hamlets. But the achievements of Landers
and Deane mean that, from now on, whenever Killeagh is
mentioned, GAA fans will nod their heads knowingly and say, 'Ah
yeah. Joe Deane and Mark Landers' homeplace.'

Two thousand and three was the summer of Cork and Kilkenny,
Armagh and Tyrone, and it was also the summer of The Thrills
who'll probably become the biggest Irish rock band since U2.
Everywhere I went, I seemed to be followed by the group's soft
harmonies and jangly guitars, their take-off of a West Coast
American-style that seemed peculiarly appropriate for the hottest
summer in memory. And there was one line from a song that
stuck with me. 'Hanging around in a one-horse town does nothing
for your state of mind.'

And it probably doesn't. I should know, I was born in a one-
horse town and I live just outside another one. But what makes the
one-horse towns of Ireland bearable is the GAA.

It thrives in small places that have never had a lot going for
them, places where there is nothing happening but the GAA.

Hurling and football keep the one-horse towns alive, practically give them a reason to be. That's why our attachment to the games is so profound and so different from the way other sports are followed.

That's my theory anyway, but I'm not going to start clattering you over the head with sociological observation so here are two stories that illustrate the notion that, unless you know what the GAA means in this country, your knowledge of Ireland is seriously deficient.

The first is taken from Breandán Ó hEithir's *Over the Bar*, the finest book ever written about the GAA. It tells of how the great Connemara writer Máirtín Ó Cadhain, a neighbour of my mother's in An Spidéal, travelled to an IRA convention on the morning of an All-Ireland football final between Galway and Kerry in the forties. Seán MacBride, later to become a renowned jurist and peacenik, was head of the IRA at the time and, when a debate on some aspect or other of republican policy began to drag on, the delegates began to become restless. Ó Cadhain caught MacBride's attention and explained to him that it was getting near match time and the volunteers wanted to head for Croke Park. MacBride was furious and started haranguing the delegates about their notion that some football match was more important than the sacred republican struggle.

'It was then,' said Ó Cadhain, 'that I knew the IRA would never get anywhere because our leader had no understanding of the Irish people.'

In the eighties, a leader of a different hue, Garret FitzGerald, was travelling the country during a general-election campaign. He arrived in Cork as the natives were celebrating victory in some big match or other and, puzzled, asked one of his aides why there were so many red-and-white flags being waved.

'Is it a tribute to the Solidarity movement in Poland?' Garret wondered.

Since then, my attitude to Fine Gael has been something akin to Máirtín Ó Cadhain's view of the Seán MacBride IRA. Like I said, not knowing the GAA means you don't fully know this country.

One more thing before we set off on our championship journey. On the Friday before Kilkenny met Tipperary in last year's eagerly awaited All-Ireland hurling semi-final, I got several text messages from my father, the gist of which was that his nerves were destroyed waiting for Sunday's game.

These would have been unremarkable sentiments had it not been for the fact that the man was battling cancer. Several months of strenuous radiotherapy having failed to eradicate the unwelcome guest from his body, he was embarking on a course of chemotherapy. My father was being fed through a bag attached to his stomach, his speech was almost incomprehensible because of tubes inserted in his throat and he had to take a bewildering and seriously debilitating amount of drugs every day. You might imagine he wouldn't have been particularly worried about how his home county did against Tipperary. Yet he was genuinely bothered about the possibility that Kilkenny's long lay-off since the Leinster final would leave them susceptible to an ambush from their old rivals.

Sport isn't a matter of life and death but it does enable us to forget the harsher realities of existence. A great championship match can make every member of the crowd believe for those seventy minutes that nothing is more immediately important. Like art, sport takes us out of ourselves, helps us soar momentarily. To dismiss an All-Ireland hurling or football final as 30 men chasing a bag of wind around the place is as foolishly reductive as to describe *Hamlet* as just a load of old paper and ink, the *Mona Lisa* as a bit of paint thrown on some cloth. Sport matters to people not because they're deluded but because it appeals to a part of their soul that would otherwise remain dormant.

Anyway, this is the story of what happened when I decided to follow the 2003 All-Ireland championships, getting to at least one game every week, talking to people who were centrally, or peripherally, involved, trying to capture the essence of what makes the GAA summer so special. En route, I think I learned things about the GAA I hadn't known before, I definitely saw lots of fine hurling and football, I met some incredibly nice people without whose acquaintance I'd be a poorer man and, above all, I had a lot of fun. If this book is half as much fun to read as it was to research, we're flying it.

And now, the last notes of the national anthem have died away and it's time for the ball to be thrown in.

1

I'm a Loser Baby, So Why
Don't You Kill Me?

25 May: Munster Football Championship First Round
Walsh Park, Waterford
Tipperary 0–18; Waterford 1–12

The journey is the essence of the All-Ireland championships. A team starts in its own backyard and sets its eyes on Croke Park. The counties are Dick Whittingtons, dreaming about arriving in the big city to make their name.

GAA fans are prone to read the championships in teleological fashion. Whoever wins the Sam Maguire or the Liam McCarthy was destined to win it from Day One. As James Joyce, writing about geniuses in *Ulysses*, said, 'even their errors are volitional'. The eventual champions have done everything right; everyone else has lost the plot at some stage. Even a team that loses the final by a point is considered to be miles behind its conquerors.

The championship picks up a fearsome momentum as it goes on. By September, the happenings of May seem impossibly distant and trivial, not part of the campaign at all. Even losing provincial finalists, unless they've redeemed themselves in the back-door section, can be written off quickly enough. The season ends on, is defined by and was always heading towards those two fateful September Sundays.

But, back in May, I decided to start my journey in Waterford, home of a team who are the antithesis of success. The Waterford footballers weren't dreaming of Croke Park glory in front of 80,000 spectators, they were just hoping to beat Tipperary in the first round of the Munster championship. That, in itself, would be an achievement of enormous magnitude for the team because the county has not won a single championship match since 1988. Not a single one. The Waterford footballers cannot win one game when it really matters. Because the championship is all that really matters in the GAA season. It would be unthinkable for a player to go through his career without experiencing victory at least once in the competition. Except that this is precisely what happened to Waterford's Liam Dalton who played 13 years for his county without ever knowing what it felt like to win a meaningful game – trapped in a nightmare from which there was no waking.

This book will end at the very pinnacle of GAA success, but it begins at the bottom, which was definitely where Waterford were situated before the 2003 championship got underway. When the years didn't bring merciless maulings by the big two of Cork and Kerry, they brought beatings by fellow minnows Clare, Tipperary and Limerick, confirming that Waterford are, literally, the lowest of the low – losers of a quite spectacular stripe.

This wasn't the first championship weekend, but there's a nice symmetry – from the very bottom to the top – which appealed to me, so it was where I decided to start. There'd already been three eye-catching results in the first couple of weeks. All-Ireland football champions Armagh had, unbelievably, been beaten by Monaghan and saddled with the indignity of having to negotiate the back-door system; a Tipperary hurling side, which had been many people's choice as potential champions, had been humiliated by Clare; and Limerick had made a historic breakthrough by knocking Cork out of the Munster football championship. Though Limerick would never regain anything like the form they showed that day, it was still an achievement of some magnitude. The other two results, however, proved to be absolutely meaningless.

My championship odyssey started inauspiciously. I'd chosen Dungarvan as my base for the weekend and, after walking the town, discovered there wasn't a spare bed in it. This wasn't the first time this had happened to me. In 2001, I'd travelled on spec to the All-Ireland football quarter-final between Roscommon and Galway in Castlebar. After the match, I discovered that every hotel, B & B, and room over the pub in the home of Pee Flynn had been booked out. Weeks ago. A friendly taxi driver volunteered to drive me around the outer suburbs of Castlebar but the story was the same there and I began to realise how Joseph and Mary felt when they were trying to get their heads down in Bethlehem. One hotelier did reveal the reason for the accommodation famine, Pierce Brosnan was getting married locally so the world's press had decided to kip in the Castlebar area.

'Not to worry,' said the driver. 'We'll go as far as Claremorris.'

We drove into the Mayo night, through Manulla and Balla, into Claremorris. It was like being in a Paul Durcan poem. All Claremorris had to offer us though was a big no. Through Brickeens and Bekan into Ballyhaunis. By this stage, we'd been travelling for nearly an hour but there was no more sympathy in Ballyhaunis than anywhere else. I pictured happy paparazzi snug in their rooms listening to the death notices and Big Tom records on Midwest Radio. If I'd been the driver, I'd have slung me out to take my chances on the mean Ballyhaunis streets. But he kept going and, just outside Knock, we found a place where I had the most grateful sleep of my life.

As you can see, the experience marked me deeply and I had no wish to go hunting for hospitality with some West Waterford Travis Bickle. My horror at such a prospect was obviously written all over my face because the landlady at my final port of call, after informing me that she, too, was booked out, mentioned that she did have a bed made up in a converted garage out the back. This suited me fine and I booked in before heading to the hotel to find out what it was like to play for the biggest losers in Gaelic football.

The landlord of the B & B handed me a copy of the local paper, which laid out in gruesome detail the various failures by Waterford to break their duck over the last decade and a half. Then he told me that they had actually beaten tomorrow's opposition in the league.

'So, they have a great chance tomorrow then?'

'Not at all. What happened was that Declan Browne injured himself in the warm-up. I know a man who was at the match and the minute he saw Browne go down, he raced to the bookies and put a rake of money on, got there just before the start.'

Declan Browne is arguably the best forward in Ireland. Though stranded by geographical misfortune in Tipperary, he has nevertheless managed to terrify the defences of Cork and Kerry. What he might possibly do against Waterford didn't bear thinking about, something with which the bookies seemed to agree. The landlord told me Waterford were 5/2 to win the following day. He didn't think anyone would be having any of that.

I waited for Gary Hurney, who I'd been informed was the best footballer in Waterford and a player, like Browne, who could have shone for a major county. It was Communion Day in Dungarvan and the bar was packed. What struck me was that no one was actually passing much heed on the Communion kids. Instead, and this was two in the day, the bar was lined with soused adults in states of edgy drunkenness. Men in their fifties who still sported earrings and tattooes would beckon youngsters over, clap them on the back, point at an equally drunk acquaintance and slur, 'You see this man, this man here, this man is a gennelman, so he is. Don't forget that now, this man is a gennelman.'

It was a pretty dispiriting sight. The bar rang with the shouts of mothers and grannies trying to control kids who were tearing round the place out of sheer boredom while their elders got stuck into the booze.

One kid hurtled into a barman who was transporting a plate of sandwiches to a table. The mite's mother got hold of him.

'Mind the man.'

'Mind the man? Fuck the man.'

It was at this point that Gary Hurney arrived. There are young men who, even if you happened to see them loping towards you across the Gobi Desert, are immediately identifiable as Gaelic footballers. They are the ideal shape and build for the game, between six-one and six-three, weighing in at around a trim 14 stone, loose limbed and agile. Every decent club in the country has a lad like this playing midfield. Gary Hurney was one of these and he smiled as we sat down amid the chaos of Communion Day in Dungarvan.

'Is there much excitement around about tomorrow's game?'

'No. People are more bothered about going to see *Matrix Reloaded.*'

Gary didn't have many illusions about the grip of Waterford football on his fellow townspeople (he plays with Dungarvan club Ballinacourty) but he seemed absurdly hopeful about the county's chances against Tipperary.

'I definitely think we have a realistic chance. Like we do a savage lot of work and it has to pay off sometime. We're on the go since last November, we had six hard weeks trying to get fit. Since January, we've been training two nights a week with a game at the weekends, sometimes it's been three nights. We do put it in, the same as any other county.'

But why do it for Waterford football?

'That's a hard question to answer. I just know for myself that I love to play football and I love training. There will never be a transfer system in the GAA because everyone wants to play for their own county. It would be hard to look back at the end of your career and have no medals to show it, but we're trying to make a difference. I live and die for the game, I really love it. And we've had some good days too.'

The most famous of all Waterford football's good days came in 1957 when they defeated a Kerry team that had been All-Ireland champions only two years previously. Kerry had, perhaps understandably, gone into the game in a somewhat over-confident frame of mind and travelled without several players. They completed their team by dragging a couple of supporters out of the crowd. Waterford played the game of their lives and won by 2–5 to 0–10. But they lost the Munster final against Cork by 11 points and haven't reached one since. Still, there had been signs of recovery in recent years. The county junior team won the All-Ireland in 1999 and, a year later, the U-21s dumped Kerry out of the Munster championship before losing narrowly to Limerick in the provincial final. The thought of those games was keeping Hurney going.

'There were 8,000 people from Waterford at that junior final. Waterford people love the GAA but we only get a few hundred people at our games. I suppose we haven't given them much encouragement. If we could win tomorrow, we could make a start. It's our All-Ireland because it would make such a difference. I know we've been written off already but we've been written off all our lives.'

Yet Waterford were struggling against a considerable handicap. Three of the best forwards in the county – Shane Walsh, Michael Walsh and Conan Watt – had left the panel. The reason? They were wanted by the county hurling panel. None of them were likely to make a significant contribution in the championship but hurling trumps football in Waterford and it always will. Tipperary has the same problem, so does Wexford and Limerick while Kilkenny has jacked in football altogether. Even in Cork, which had a great football tradition, it is hard not to feel sometimes that hurling people run the county board and wilfully disrespect the big-ball game. There is a tinge of hurling snobbery about this attitude and it means that footballers rarely get a fair shake in those counties. What makes this maddening for the players involved is that the football areas are usually distinct from the hurling areas. In West Cork, South Limerick, South Tipperary and West Waterford, football is the number one game, but the GAA people from those areas are doomed to forever hear outsiders tell them they come from a hurling county.

There were other withdrawals from the team. Niall Geary, an outstanding defender, had decided to throw in his lot with Cork. And Niall Curran, the Player of the Year for the previous two seasons, had opted to drop to junior level. Gary Hurney's enthusiasm notwithstanding, it looked as though the 15-year losing run was beginning to drive players away from the team. Even Gary admitted that the losses were having a further detrimental effect that threatened to perpetuate the run.

'When the other teams are playing against Waterford, they have great confidence because they look down on us. They feel good about themselves from the start and if they go ahead they can relax completely.'

I headed back to my garage and watched Tyrone grind out a 0–17 to 1–5 victory against Derry in what was probably the most bad-tempered game of the entire championship. There would be games that would attract more opprobrium but none that would give off that marvellous sense of personal animosity that the Tyrone–Derry matches are so rich in. Perhaps, as the cliché goes, the players from either side are the best of friends off the pitch, let bygones be bygones and get together for a few chummy pints. It's just that, if they are, a marvellous job is done of camouflaging it. That evening in Casement Park it looked as though every player felt about his opposite number the same way Martin Keown feels about Ruud van Nistelrooy. It would have been enough to make a man feel mildly discouraged had Ger Canning not appeared on my screen to conduct his usual magnificent post-match interview, the highlight of which came when he informed the Tyrone manager, Mickey Harte.

'There's another Mickey Harte in action tonight.'

The real Mickey Harte looked puzzled for a second before

twigging what he was supposed to say and mumbling a brief message of good luck to the Irish contestant in that night's *Eurovision Song Contest*. It seemed important to Ger and the Tyrone manager was too nice of a guy to let him down.

'Another Mickey Harte in action.' I knew immediately what Ger was on about because I felt like that other MH had been stalking me all week. There wasn't a media outlet that hadn't given Mickey *Joe* Harte the kind of saturation coverage not seen since 9/11. He'd won RTÉ's *You're a Star* and now he was about to win the *Eurovision* and, if you were allergic to him, well, you'd have to emigrate because he was everywhere.

I'd hoped for some relief in *The Irish Times* but no. Inside the magazine, he was answering that most difficult of questions, 'What's in your fridge Mickey Joe?'

'A human head taken from one of my female victims. I've stripped the skin off with a hunting knife and will be making it into a table lamp later on this evening.'

Except Mickey Joe didn't say that because he is a compendium of every kind of lovely-young-fella quality imaginable. Plaster saints have more obvious faults than this Donegal man who seems to have been created by a computer fed with a program entitled 'How to win reality-television show votes'.

Never mind the man, what about the song. For weeks it had been following me. 'We've got the World Tonight (Dass ryat)'.

It seemed as though I was the only person who didn't love the song and the only one who noticed that the backing singers sounded exactly like one of the codgers in *D'Unbelievables*.

'Dass ryat.'

But really it wasn't Mickey Joe who was irritating me as I lay in the Dungarvan garage, it was Ger and his yoking together of the *Eurovision Song Contest* and the All-Ireland championship as if they were being contested by figures of equal talent and import. In reality, *You're a Star* and everything that surrounded it bespoke all that was worst in contemporary Ireland, the primacy of bottom-line merchants like Louis Walsh, the frenzied hyping of something that wasn't in the least interesting to begin with, the presumption that winning the vote in a reality-television programme indicated real substance. There didn't seem to be a local festival that wasn't headlined by someone whose sole claim to fame was having appeared on *You're a Star*. Singers of real talent and experience appeared down the bill. It appeared that if the media said you were a star, you were one.

So it goes. But one of the most refreshing attributes of the championship is that it cannot be falsified. Players can be hyped all right, but that won't make them able to catch a single extra ball, score any more points, win any more games. It doesn't matter who the papers and the public want to win the All-Ireland, the best team will win in the end. And I think that's one reason why public affection for sportsmen is currently at an all-time high. In a world where achievement can be faked, GAA stars might soon be the only Irish people famous for being genuinely good at something.

Hence the totally unfair set I took on Mickey Joe Harte back in May. He might be a genuinely lovely young fella but he didn't belong in the same breath as Mickey Harte. And when 'We've got the World Tonight' dawdled home in 12th place out in Riga, I presumed that would be the last I'd hear of the singer and the song. Presumption is a dangerous thing.

Leaving Dungarvan on Sunday morning, I noticed that admission to the Communion Disco in Davitts Bar was by ticket only and wondered if this would cut much ice with the young lad in the bar.

'Have you got your ticket there, son?'

'Ticket? Fuck the ticket.'

The sound of sporting anticipation is both a strange and a comforting one. There's no fan whose step and pulse don't quicken when they hear in the distance the buzz of thousands of voices wondering exactly what's going to transpire over the next couple of hours. Even a visitor from another planet would know that something special was going on when they heard that pregnant murmur behind the high walls of a Gaelic ground. There's excitement in it and speculation and prediction, but above all there is tension. The sound you hear at championship time is one you don't hear during the National League.

And it was totally absent from Walsh Park. The home fans seemed resigned rather than worried. Other supporters had delusions of grandeur; the Waterford football supporters had delusions of adequacy. They'd be pleased if the team won but, after 14 straight first-round defeats, they weren't going to indulge in anything as foolish as expectation.

Another fact I'd picked up that morning underlined the enormity of Waterford's task. When they'd won their last championship game, one Eddie Rockett had been playing in their defence. (I checked but there had been no R. McDonald or A. Kebabara among his team-mates.) Today, his son Edmund was lining out for the team. It was reminiscent of some horror-movie family curse that passes down through the generations.

And then they arrived at Walsh Park with the unmistakable air of big-time county players, laughing nervously, chewing gum, looking out at the pitch with grim determination. They were team-mates, they were completely focused on the task in hand – they were a bunch of 11- and 12-year-old girls. The National Schools teams from Waterford and Tipperary had arrived to play the curtain-raiser to the senior match.

Flann O'Brien used to include in his list of Great Bores the man who would always say, 'It could only happen in Ireland', no matter what trivial incident befell him. It's easy to fall into this trap when writing about the GAA. All kinds of commonplace occurrences are frequently adduced as being unique to the association when, in fact, they've got many equivalents in the world of sport. But presenting schoolkids with the chance to share the big championship stage is something that isn't repeated in many other sports. There are things about the GAA that would drive anyone but the most partisan central-council delegate mad. But there are far more things that are wonderful whatever way you look at them. And the National Schools games are one of them. The fact that some of today's inter-county stars have played in those games is interesting but irrelevant. What matters is giving kids the opportunity to be part of the big days in their county's calendar. One look at the seriousness with which the girls of Tipperary and Waterford warmed up and checked their boots told you how much it was appreciated.

As Waterford set about taking control of the girls game, I fell into conversation with a woman from Solohead in Tipperary whose daughter, Rebecca, wasn't playing badly at all. Annette Cummins was the epitome of motherly pride.

'It's her second year in the National Schools game. There's a lot of training and travel to the sessions, then I wait around for an hour till she's finished. There's no team in Solohead so they play with Cappawhite. Her sister plays Under-12 too. We have four girls and they're mad for football.'

'Do their brothers play?'

'Oh, they don't have any brothers. They got into the football themselves, they never stop kicking around between themselves.'

'They're playing the full length of the pitch.'

'They're well able for it. Come on Rebecca, mark your woman.'

Solohead, of course, was the site of the ambush by Dan Breen and his cohorts widely regarded as beginning the War of Independence. You could extrapolate a moral from this, to do with the vigorous state of distinctively Irish games in the Republic that eventually resulted. But then you'd have to think about the attitude of the State's founding fathers towards women – barely consenting to let them out of the kitchen, never mind having them play football in front of a large crowd.

Despite the best urgings of Cummins *mère* and the best efforts of Cummins *fille*, the young Waterford women won well. This would be no surprise to anyone aware of the balance of power in Waterford football. There is a bitter irony in the fact that, while Waterford's male footballers were bottom of the heap, their women won several All-Irelands in the 1990s and players, such as Áine Wall, Geraldine O'Ryan and Mary O'Donnell were far bigger names than anyone playing for the supposedly stronger sex. I didn't know the effect of such success on the Waterford men but, at times, it must have been a bitter pill to swallow. Judging by the performance of their schoolgirls, the ladies production line wasn't exhausted yet. A young woman called Lenny Kirwan of Fews National School gave an exhibition of the basics – catching, kicking, scoring, soloing – that would have shamed many of the senior men I was to see later in the championship.

Meanwhile, the Waterford men's hopes of victory took a ferocious blow even before the game started. Declan Browne managed to complete the warm-up without incurring an injury. That seemed to be that.

Hang on a minute. Waterford win the ball from the throw-in and it is played down to Gary Hurney who wins it brilliantly. He shakes off his man and finds John Hennessy piling through the middle. Tipp goalkeeper Philly Ryan brings Hennessy crashing to the ground and the referee signals a penalty, which is converted by Connie Power with Brazilian panache. A couple of scores later and Waterford are five points clear inside half-a-dozen minutes. It couldn't happen, could it?

For the first quarter, the unthinkable continued to look on the cards – Waterford having pulled a crafty one by withdrawing John Hearne from their full-forward line and placing him in front of Declan Browne. Now Browne didn't just have a marker behind him to contend with, he'd got someone intercepting his supply as well. It was a good stroke by Waterford manager Denis Walsh.

Cork people are constantly going on about how unlucky Denis Walsh was in 1990. He won an All-Ireland senior hurling medal that year and just missed out on a place on the All-Ireland winning Cork football team, which would have made him one of only two players in history to win hurling and football medals in the same year. I suppose it counts as a variety of bad luck, but you couldn't imagine Walsh getting much sympathy from his Waterford players if he brought it up.

As the half wears on, it becomes clear that even two markers are not going to stop Browne exerting a profound influence on the game. From frees and play, he's always one of the top scorers in the game and, true to form, he'd end the 2003 championship as the player with the best scoring average. All of which is praise-worthy enough in itself but unrivalled when you take Browne's circumstances into account. Tyrone, Kerry and Galway forwards have class players supplying them with good-quality ball but Browne lives largely off scraps, making something from balls hit too high, too long or way out on the wing. And forwards from the bigger counties have team-mates to share the load, whereas opposition defences know Browne is the only major threat on the Tipperary side and can give him their almost exclusive attention.

It never seems to make any difference. By half-time, Browne had kicked one incredible point while facing away from goal and had been fouled for a series of frees that he points himself. That didn't seem to satisfy him and, at the beginning of the second half, he decided to give a good impression of an adult thrown into an U-12 match. Twenty seconds after the restart, he charged right through the middle of the Waterford defence and sent a shot inches over the bar, next he spun away from a couple of desperate tackles and scored another point before squirming through an impossibly small gap, motoring in along the end-line and fisting the ball over the bar. By the eighth minute, Tipp were five points clear and looked set to give Waterford their annual trouncing.

But it didn't quite work out like that. Waterford hung in there. Gary Hurney won every ball that came his way and, with nine minutes left, his side were level again. The buzz in the crowd was different now. Could they? Ah no, never, but who knows? It's not bad, is it? With a minute left, Waterford were still just a point behind and were attacking with purpose. Yet, and perhaps the length of the jinx had something to do with it, composure suddenly deserted them. Like Devon Loch, their legs gave way with the post in sight. Tipperary regrouped and, right at the end, Browne won a free and kicked it over the bar. *Plus ça change*.

If the noise of the crowd before the game had been one indicator of how far Waterford footballers were from the big time, the scene around the dressing rooms after the final whistle was similarly eloquent. The post-match crush outside the dressing room is one of the great features of the GAA, with players pushing their way through milling hordes and officious county-board men at the door trying to prevent an invasion, while dozens of supporters insist that they've got a legitimate reason to be inside. At Walsh Park, the dressing-room doors were wide open and there was hardly a soul waiting outside. The players just hoisted their bags over their shoulders and walked unmolested to their cars in an atmosphere of eerie quiet.

Even Declan Browne passed unnoticed. His summer would be the usual story of extraordinary excellence in a losing cause. He almost single-handedly destroyed the Kerry defence in his next game, forcing them into a hasty realignment that would haunt them for the rest of the season. And when Tipperary drew Donegal in the second round of the back-door series, they were rewarded with a trip to Croke Park. Browne finally got the chance to show what he was made of on the biggest stage of all. The press coverage that week treated him like some legendary bluesman who'd been invited up from the Mississipi Delta to play in Carnegie Hall. When the eyes of the wider world were upon him, would he live up to his legend? He did, scoring five points from play and winning the Man of the Match award even though Tipperary suffered the expected hammering.

I travelled back from Waterford to Dungarvan with local journalist Johnny Murphy and Seamus O'Brien, who, at 83 years of age, is the longest-serving central-council delegate in the country. The cliché about central-council delegates is that they are the *ne plus ultra* of conservatism, backwoodsmen totally bewildered by the modern GAA. Seamus O'Brien was intelligent, witty and courteous, informing us of the weekend's encounter between the world of sport and the world of crime.

'There was a match this morning in Knockanore and this man turns up and says to the lads at the gate, "I was training here during the week with the county team and I think I left my tracksuit inside in the dressing rooms." They tell him to go on ahead and when the teams come back to the dressing rooms after the match, your man has all their valuables looted.'

'You wouldn't expect that in Knockanore,' said Johnny Murphy.

The list of places where you wouldn't expect this seems, however, to be getting shorter all the time. Seamus and Johnny had taken great encouragement from Waterford's better-than-expected performance and even dared to suggest that the end of the 15-year losing run might be in sight. They could draw London or Carlow or Wicklow in the first round of the back-door and the job would be Oxo.

They drew the All-Ireland champions Armagh who trimmed them 2–21 to 0–8. Gary Hurney managed to take four points from play off the country's meanest defence but that performance was hidden by the starkly one-sided scoreline. It must have been a very disappointing end to a season that he'd been so genuinely hopeful about when I'd spoken to him on Communion Day in Dungarvan.

Fuck it, I was disappointed. I'd felt genuinely upset when Waterford failed to end the most miserable run in Gaelic games. In fact, I felt a *grá* for Waterford I was to feel for few other teams in the championship.

Why was this? Perhaps it had something to do with my personal circumstances. I've written a couple of novels, which have been moderately well received and sell a reasonable few copies, but already I'm beginning to realise that I'm not one of literature's big hitters. The Saul Bellows, the Salman Rushdies, the Toni Morrisons occupy a sphere I'm never going to approach. And every year new writers with far more talent than me come along and push me a few rungs further down the ladder. So perhaps the question I put to Gary Hurney should be turned back on me.

Why do it? Why put in all that effort when you're never going to win the Nobel, the Booker or any other one of writing's equivalents to the Sam Maguire and Liam McCarthy cups?

Why? Because I'm still part of the minority who have managed to get a novel published and can console myself by thinking that, even if I'm not in the same league as Saul, Salman and Toni, I'm in the same game. Perhaps that's what keeps the Waterford footballers going. Maybe they'll never win the All-Ireland but, when they watch the final on television, they can be proud of having competed in the championship, of the link between themselves and the top of the tree. Maybe this explains why so many of us have such a love of the underdog, why you'll often see a pub full of people rooting frantically for a small team that appears to be on the verge of overturning the natural order. Because most of us aren't champions, most of us don't live remarkable lives in the spotlight, we're just happy to give life our best shot. Most of us have more in common with Waterford footballers than with their Kerry counterparts. And, after all, without the Waterfords of this world, there wouldn't be a championship. Somebody has to make the giants look big.

There was an unexpected and wonderful postscript to the Waterford footballers season. The county U-21 team shocked everyone by defeating Cork in the Munster championship and then won their first ever provincial title with a victory over a

Kerry team that included several senior inter-county players. Their All-Ireland semi-final defeat against Dublin didn't detract from perhaps the most remarkable GAA success story of the season. The U-21 team proved Gary Hurney's contention (at the time I'd thought it was wild wishful thinking) that the county's young footballers was as good as anyone given a chance.

Starring at centre half-back was Edmund Rockett and it now looks very unlikely that the senior losing run will be passed on to a third generation of the Rockett family. The future has never looked brighter for Waterford football. Now, where did I put that Nobel Prize acceptance speech?

2

Hill 16, La La La

1 June: Leinster Senior Football Championship
Quarter-finals, Croke Park
Dublin 1–19, Louth 0-9; Meath 2–13, Westmeath 2–13

Hill 16 is different. It never seems to conform to the norms of the GAA. Whereas the association prides itself on the fact that fans from opposing counties can be interspersed with each other on match days, Hill 16 is almost exclusively the preserve of Dublin fans when their team is playing. GAA crowds are generally reserved and quiet, producing remarkably little noise for their great numbers. Hill 16 is raucous, boisterous and impossible to ignore. The new Croke Park is streamlined, all-seater, covered over, corporate friendly. The Hill 16 terrace was the last remaining uncovered section of Croke Park. Like any interesting phenomenon the Hill engenders wildly different responses. The attitude of Dublin fans is relatively simple: Hill 16 is a national monument and the best place anyone could watch a match. There are two separate views of the place down the country. One is that Hill 16 is an unrivalled venue for 'banter' and 'Dublin wit'. The latter phrase always makes me think of being trapped on a long train journey with Brendan Grace and Maureen Potter and scarcely counts as a recommendation. People who think that the various pet-names placed by Dubs on the capital's various hideous lumps of public sculpture are hilarious forms of demotic humour may feel differently.

The anti-Hill camp are just as extreme and affect to believe that any unfortunate culchie who happens to stray up there and cheer for his team will be scalped by a terrifying bunch of tattooed, skinheaded, hard-man Dubs reminiscent of the lads who hung out with Charlo Spencer in the TV series *Family*.

The Hill does have a whiff of sulphur about it, but this probably has more to do with the ingestion of vast quantities of porter rather than any connection with the demonic. Nevertheless, on the days when the Dubs aren't playing, nothing pleases country fans more than to strut their stuff on the Hill. It's almost as though they hope either the banter or the hardness will rub off on them. You see, no other county can boast anything remotely like the Hill, a piece of territory that undisputedly belongs to the home fans. Like the Stretford End at Old Trafford, the North Bank at Highbury or The Kop at Anfield, Hill 16 is far more than just a piece of terracing.

The unspoken rule that Dublin always warm up in front of the Hill has been challenged just once when Tyrone got on to the field before the Dubs for the 1984 All-Ireland semi-final and proceeded to the sacred end. When Dublin arrived on the field, they went down in front of the Hill as usual and spectators were treated to the sight of two teams warming up at the one end, risking injury as they collided in the small space. There were suggestions that the home team should have given in and gone down to the Canal End. But most people saw the incident as a prime piece of acting the flute by Tyrone, a gesture so crass it would never be repeated.

There is no doubt that Dublin have a huge advantage in playing all their important games in Croke Park (though the association ludicrously claims that Croker is a neutral venue and that Parnell Park is the actual native heath of the Dubs) and the Hill often seems to be worth a couple of points to them. John

Cleary, an excellent Cork forward who scored two goals against Dublin in the 1989 All-Ireland semi-final, once told me about making his debut in Croke Park against the Dubs while still in his teens. 'You'd look up there and when the Dubs scored it was like the whole terrace was shaking, the crowd all moving at the same time.'

So there was only one place to watch Dublin's first championship match of the season. Given everything that was to transpire subsequently, it's funny to think of the enormous unquestioning enthusiasm that surrounded the team at the start of the campaign. Their Leinster championship win the previous year, and the fact that they'd lost the All-Ireland semi-final by a point to eventual champions Armagh, meant they were many people's favourites for the 2003 All-Ireland. Ray Cosgrove, Alan Brogan and Ciarán Whelan were on the verge of becoming folk heroes, Croke Park had been opened up back in March so that 30,000 (10 times the usual attendance) could watch the team play their opening National League match and Tommy Lyons – their chirpy, media-friendly manager – was incredibly popular. The eventual decline and near fall of Lyons would tell a salutary tale about the fickleness of supporters, the demands of the media and the almost unbearable expectations that pressed down on the managers of the bigger counties.

Yet it seemed impossible that the season would be anything but successful when the Dubs' fans made their way towards the Hill for the opening game against Louth, the kind of county whose teams weren't bad but who could be relied on to roll over when facing Dublin in all their pomp. Such was the interest in the game that the man who'd got me a ticket during the week had it stolen from his desk at work. (The thief lost his job shortly afterwards as, unfortunately, did many others when the *Dublin Daily* went for an early bath. Its star columnist was Tommy Lyons. Who jinxed who is hard to say.)

Fans spilled out of Gaffney's, the Fairview Inn, Meaghers,

pubs synonymous with big match days at Croke Park and noisy, boozy pre-match pinting by men in blue jerseys stamped with the Arnotts logo. The chatter was less about Louth (who didn't merit much more than a cursory dismissal) than about the deadly enemies of the Dubs – Meath. Mee-yad.

'There was these three guys on the road and a car drove straight through them. It was a Mee-yad number plate.'

'I saw the Mee-yad fans in town. The big, well-fed, thick fucking heads on them.'

'Don't give the Louth people any stick. They hate Mee-yad almost as much as we do.'

No one doubted that all the other games in the Leinster championship would just be preparatory skirmishes before the inevitable final between Dublin and Meath when a full house would see Dublin confirming that the era of Seán Boylan had been supplanted by the time of Tommy Lyons.

Your first impression of Hill 16 is of how homely it is, of how it suggests a general meeting of a club whose members are all acquaintances at least, if not friends. There's plenty of chanting all right but it has nothing of the aggression or fanaticism you'd find at a Premiership soccer ground. There's a considerable amount of irony and self-deprecation (Dublin qualities far more quintessential and attractive than the much advertised wit) and an impressive amount of knowledge about the game. If you want people to listen to you on the Hill, you have to do a bit better than just express blind love of your team. In front of me, a guy was telling everyone round him about his experiences at the recent UEFA Cup final between FC Porto and Celtic, 'You think this is hot. In Seville at ten o'clock at night it was twice as warm as this. It was like watching the game in a fucking oven.'

'You're some Irishman. Going to Spain to watch a Scottish team playing an English game.'

'Ah come on, lads. Celtic are Sinn Féin FC.'

There are chuckles from the man's friends. He's obviously one of those guys doomed to be wound up good naturedly by his buddies while they elbow the people beside them and roll their eyes in theatrical amusement.

'Tell them about Malaga. Go on.'

'Malaga. Don't get me started about fucking Malaga. Three hours on a fucking bus going to the game and no bleeding air conditioning.'

There is laughter from three rows back; the Celtic fan has won himself an audience. On the field, it's obvious almost immediately that Louth haven't got the stuff to prevent Dublin from scoring the expected easy victory. There's only two minutes gone when the hero of the year before, Ray Cosgrove, a man with a better eye for goal than almost any other forward in the game, turns his man and cuts through with only the keeper to beat. In an act of quixotic unselfishness, he flicks the ball across for Alan Brogan to apply the finishing touch. Our man from Seville rages, 'You fucking eejit Cosgrove, you bollocks, you clowen.'

'What has your friend got against Ray Cosgrove?'

'He had five hundred on him to score the first goal.'

By half-time, Dublin are almost out of sight and Louth are merely going through the motions. The Wee County are piss poor. But the second half is worth watching because of the way Ciarán Whelan is playing at midfield for Dublin. There's a particular trick that Whelan loves to essay and Louth fall for it every time. He slows down, hops the ball on his toe and, as his opponent comes in to make the tackle, surges away like a sports car moving from 0 to 100 in the blink of an eye. When he plays like this, it's hard to see how anyone could possibly mark him. In the previous year's All-Ireland quarter-final replay against Donegal, he hit seven points (something no other midfielder is going to do in the next decade, I'll bet anything on that) and in the semi-final he scored the goal of the year against Armagh, powering through the middle of the defence and unleashing a rocket of a shot that flew past the goalkeeper from 25 yards. He is big, strong, brave, quick and has mastered all the skills of Gaelic football. There's another move he frequently pulls, racing out to the right wing and hoisting a huge high shot over the bar from near the sideline, which no other inter-county player can manage.

But even the Hill 16 fans find it hard to give Whelan the unmitigated admiration you might think he deserves. Because the mystery of the Raheny man is that some days he will be completely anonymous, others he will put in an astounding 15 minutes and then mysteriously disappear from the game, making no impact at all. These misfires and absences don't seem to be connected with tight marking or rough tactics by the opposition. They just happen. And, given the supreme athleticism of the player bedevilled by them, it stands to reason that there is a mental aspect to these fade-outs. Yet Whelan comes across as a decent, uncomplicated young man, not highly strung in the same way as Graham Geraghty, his rival in talent and inconsistency. No one can explain why he moves from the sublime to the ridiculous with such frequency. And that worries the Hill because, despite the presence of several other highly talented players on the team, if Whelan goes missing in a tight game, Dublin may well be sunk. It's deeply worrying.

Today, though, he is supreme with three points already to his name when he embarks on another awesome run through the middle and thumps past the keeper a shot moving at such speed that, when it rebounds from the crossbar, it travels a full 30 yards out the field. As Whelan cocked the trigger, someone shouted, 'Go yourself, Ciarán.'

'Go yourself, Ciarán? Like he ever does anything else.'

Much laughter greeted this voicing of an undeniable truth by the Celtic fan who seems to be enjoying the game despite more torture being inflicted on him by Ray Cosgrove. At the start of the second half, the full-forward had once more rounded his man and looked certain to find the net. Instead, he laid the ball off to Senan Connell who fumbled badly.

'Jesus Christ, Ray. Jesus Christ, man.'

'What's wrong with him now?'

'He had Cosgrove to score the first goal of the second half as well.'

There is no goal in the second half but everything else has gone according to plan for the Dubs, and then some. Brian Cullen, in his first year out of minor, sprays the ball around from centre half-forward with extraordinary facility, the young wing-back, David Henry, ploughs upfield with intent and lands a great point, the Dubs bring on a giant wing-forward, Tom Mulligan, and he is excellent, then they bring on a pint-sized corner-forward, David O'Callaghan, who looks even better. Old favourites Dessie Farrell and Jason Sherlock (both rumoured to be out of favour with Lyons) don't make an appearance. Louth's veteran midfielder Seamus O'Hanlon, charged with marking Whelan, gets fed up of chasing him round Croke Park and kicks him in the leg right in front of the referee. He almost appears relieved by the sending off that follows. By the final whistle, the Dubs' fans are working out just who their biggest threat for All-Ireland honours will be.

Who can stop the Dubs? Who dares to imagine they can stop the Dubs? Perhaps Meath, those perpetual rivals whose fans begin to slope on to the Hill in advance of the second half of the day's double bill, their meeting with Westmeath.

Here is a remarkable thing about the Hill. Since I got there, hardly a minute had passed without a comment being made about the awfulness, ignorance and arrogance of the entire population of the county of Meath. An outsider would imagine that any Meathman daring to walk up here would be hung, drawn and quartered. Yet a good number of Meath supporters wearing county jerseys come on to the Hill and not a cross word is said to them. It's not that no one notices them. Being Meathmen, they feel compelled to roar and shout and generally declare their presence. The only response to them is mild amusement.

This is a defining quality of the GAA. Maybe it is the most unique feature of all, the total lack of aggression between fans. Not only does no one challenge the Meath supporters but it is unthinkable that anyone would. There is a sense in which Hill 16 polices itself and all its habitues know the appropriate way to behave on the historic terrace. The Meathmen are left alone not because of any moral qualms but because this is the way things are done in the GAA. Attacking the opposition would be wrong but, worse than that, it would be stupid. It would show that you weren't a real fan of the game at all. So fans from both sides mix freely and not a punch is thrown even when the matches themselves get unbearably heated.

Think for a second of how extraordinary this is. There are plenty of guys in Gaelic football and hurling crowds who'd take your head off if you spilt their pint or looked at their girlfriend in the wrong way. It's hardly as if we live in a country where violence is unknown. And the crowd is full of young men with a lot of drink on them, something that, in other circumstances, would almost guarantee trouble. But it doesn't spill over on to the GAA terraces because of some powerful innate prohibition. Compare this to the frequent trouble involving fans of Bohemians and Shamrock Rovers. There's no way opposition fans would watch a game from the territory staked out by the hard-core fans of those and half a dozen other soccer clubs at least. Yet the crowds are so much smaller than GAA crowds and should be more manageable. Maybe a cult of hooliganism will develop at big GAA matches, but it seems unlikely. There have been some nasty incidents at club matches but, when it comes to the big championship matches, you can take your grandfather, your wife, your baby daughter to any part of the ground without fearing for their safety. If that was the only achievement of the GAA, it would be a proud one indeed, but we're all so used to it that the good behaviour is taken for granted. It shouldn't be.

It's strange how expectations of a team change so frequently and so hugely during the course of a championship. By the end of their campaign, Meath would be regarded as a busted flush and Seán Boylan as a manager under pressure. But there were still moments when they resembled the merciless machine that had run right over teams in 1999 and most of 2001. When those moments occurred, people used the word 'ominous' a lot. Because Meath at their best possessed an inexorable quality not apparent in other teams, though Armagh are gradually building something like the same legend.

They might have eventually sputtered out completely but, in their first half against Westmeath, first 20 minutes against Kildare and first half against Monaghan, Meath played well enough to make us suspect that they had located top form and were about to kick on and make life miserable for the other counties. That was how you felt watching them play rings around Westmeath, scoring a goal after 48 seconds, almost scoring another a minute later, building up a five-point half-time lead that didn't flatter them at all. Boylan seemed to have done it again, unknown youngsters called Regan, Crimmins and McKeigue slotted in and played as though they'd been winning championship matches for years.

Making this all the more impressive was the status of Westmeath as everyone's idea of a coming team. They had underage success, a bright, popular manager in Luke Dempsey and a forward, Dessie Dolan, who wasn't far behind Declan Browne in the talent stakes and had better players around him to bring out that talent. Their main problem was that they had never, ever beaten Meath and kept bumping into them at moments that might otherwise have been propitious for a breakthrough. And, at half-time, it looked as though Meath, who are regarded as a team who take great delight in doing this kind of thing, were mercilessly slapping them down, like an older brother letting a feisty sibling know who is the boss.

This apparent romp didn't bring out the best in the Meath fans on the Hill. There weren't many of them there, but they were a right royal pain in the arse. All the unpleasant qualities that sceptical countrymen are prone to attribute to the Dubs – aggression, ignorance, rubbing the nose of the opposition in the dirt – were being displayed in spades by the men from Meath. A couple of youngsters from Westmeath who'd had the temerity to cheer one of their side's rare scores were told to 'shut the fuck up'.

Then a Meath wit added, in reference to the Westmeath colours, 'Red and white, the colour of shite.'

Maybe the man had piles. I don't know.

The Hill regulars treated this exhibition of bad manners with bemused amusement, the way you'd react when the Beverly Hillbillies started washing their car in the swimming pool. There were sniggers when the second half got underway and things started to go badly for Meath. The Westmeath midfielders Rory O'Connell and Martin Flanagan owned the ball and started finding Dessie Dolan with regularity. Dolan picked off the points, and Westmeath clawed back the lead. They would have drawn level much more quickly had corner-forward J.P. Casey not been having almost as bad a game as it's possible to have in Croke Park.

Time and time again young Casey would beat a couple of defenders, set his sights, take aim and root the ball yards wide. The wides were made all the more disheartening by the utter confidence with which he struck them.

It was, I think, Johnny Giles or Eamon Dunphy who introduced the phrase 'moral courage' into the sporting lexicon where it was eagerly seized on by sports journalists keen to use phrases redolent of depth and seriousness. 'Moral courage' had Hemingwayesque undertones and soon it was being bandied about with glee, as though the decision to make a short pass or play a one-two on the soccer field was akin to going out into no-man's land to rescue a wounded comrade. The favourite application of the 'MC' phrase in Gaelic games was when a player hit a string of wides in a game but continued to shoot. As in, 'He could have passed that to a team-mate but he had the moral courage to go for it himself.'

You could have said that J.P. Casey was showing plenty of moral courage as he refused to be diverted from shooting every time he got the ball. Or you could have pointed out that a man in a hole should stop digging.

Not that this seemed to matter because the Meath goalkeeper, Cormac Sullivan, was having an even worse day. A harmless ball floated it into his hands, he let it pop up and Dolan fisted the ball into the net. For his second trick, he let a feeble shot from Shane Colleary trickle through his legs and just about make it over the line. Sullivan looked for all the world like a benign uncle encouraging his four-year-old nephew out in the garden by deliberately letting in shots. His travails meant that Westmeath were five points clear with 15 minutes left to play. The Meathmen had gone very silent but the Dubs were back in high spirits.

'Sorry bud, you couldn't tell me the score, could you?'

'Jaysus lads, ye must be very embarrassed at the moment.'

But, because Meath are like the horror-movie monster that keeps coming back to life even after it's been bludgeoned, blowtorched and buried, their supporters weren't unhappy for long. With four minutes to go, Graham Geraghty scored a goal that put them a point ahead. The boys in front of me did a jig of joy, then turned around and shook their fists under the noses of the people nearby. 'Come on ye fuckers. Now ye fuckers. See that ye fuckers.'

If there was going to be trouble it would have happened at that moment, but the Dubs just continued to chortle. The Beverly Hillbillies had finished the car and were now trying to tuck their prize cow into a four-poster bed. Behind it all, the Dublin supporters held a grudging affection for Meath, the kind that Michael Caine feels for his opposition in *Zulu*.

Anyway, there was no time to pursue grudges because the crack hadn't stopped on the field. Dessie Dolan (what a player, outstanding for Leinster in the Railway Cup, Ireland in the Compromise Rules series, frequently struggling with injury but always there when Westmeath needed him) took a sideline ball and incredibly drifted it over the bar. And anyone who might have suggested that this was a lucky shot would have to discount the evidence of him doing exactly the same thing two years before against Mayo when Westmeath were in a similarly tight spot. Meath were rattled now and down to 14 men, Donal Curtis having gone for headbutting Martin Flanagan. Incidents of Meath violence on the field are like incidents of Fianna Fáil corruption – you feel you should take a balanced view and point out that they aren't the only offenders, and yet they almost always seemed to be involved. Which made it deeply ironic when ex-players from the county led the late-season chorus denouncing Tyrone as barbarian invaders who played football in a mean-spirited way never witnessed below the border.

Then, with only seconds remaining, Westmeath were awarded a free, 30 yards out from the Meath goal. The decision so incensed the Meath defenders they engaged in levels of protest that would have made Joe Higgins TD proud. Their reward was to have the ball moved forward 10 yards. The free had been transformed from easy to unmissable and Dessie Dolan would be the man to execute the *coup de grâce*.

It was the easiest of frees but it wasn't a simple one. In over a hundred years, Westmeath had never beaten their neighbours in the championship – for most of the time, they hadn't even been able to give them a game. Since the arrival of the talented young players who'd won minor and U-21 All-Irelands, they'd been threatening to win a first Leinster title ever. But Meath kept getting in their way. Four times in the three years Westmeath had been given the opportunity to finish that hoodoo but they'd come up short each time. Now that bogeyman was about to be laid to rest. The Meathmen on the Hill shrugged their shoulders and walked towards the exit, their postures eloquent with hurt. It was a tap over, a gimme, as easy a chance as you'd ever have to make history.

The crowd on Hill 16 looked on in puzzlement after Dolan had taken the free. The umpire was signalling it wide. What was wrong with the eejit? It was a point. It must have been a point. The excitement of the moment must have made him get his signals mixed up. The Meathmen looked back over their shoulders and a horrible reality began to dawn on the rest of us. One of the best forwards in the country had just driven an unmissable free wide. Westmeath had been one simple kick away from the greatest victory in their history and their finest footballer had botched it. The final whistle blew and Westmeath people stood around in shock, as if they were waiting for a recount, as if they'd just been the victims of some terrible practical joke and Jeremy Beadle would doff his umpire's disguise and tell Dessie Dolan, 'I really had you going there for a minute son, didn't I? You really did think you'd missed that free.'

'Jesus, Jeremy,' Dessie Dolan would say. 'You're a terrible man. I mean I knew that I couldn't miss a free from there but, when I saw you signalling it, I couldn't be sure.'

There was no such reprieve and, as the Dubs made their way to the exits, they wondered aloud about the possibility of there having been a worse miss in the history of Gaelic football and decided against it. Dolan's miss reminded me of the British Open when Doug Sanders, a relative unknown, had a putt of around 18 inches to win by a stroke over the great Jack Nicklaus. Sanders twitched, the putt rolled to the side, and he was hardly heard of again.

Tragedy is a word so promiscuously used in reference to sporting failure as to have become meaningless. Yet it seemed to fit the dejected figure of Westmeath's star player. You could have blindfolded him and he would have kicked the free from there, you could have made him kick in his street clothes and good shoes, made him kick a basketball rather than a football, moved the ball 10 yards further out the field, made him use his wrong foot. The ball would still have gone between the posts. He could have been left out there for a few hours and taken that free 500 times and, more than likely, he wouldn't have missed once.

The miss was bad enough, but it became worse. That one kick illustrated better than anything else the teleological fallacy by which All-Irelands and provincial titles are presumed to be decided by plans hatched long in advance.

'I knew we'd win the All-Ireland when we slogged our way through to win that league match in March,' a manager will lie.

'We'd worked out what went wrong in Croke Park last year and there was no way the lads were going to lose this year,' a team captain will claim.

In reality, teams are at the mercy of events. Luck, refereeing decisions, individual moments of madness can destroy the best-laid plans. The fate of Westmeath shows this clearly.

Let's direct that free between the posts, allow the logical thing to happen. Dessie Dolan taps over without a second thought. West-meath have ended their losing run, overcome their greatest psychological obstacle by proving they have what it takes to beat Meath. They have fought back from a huge deficit in the first half and, from a point down with four minutes to go. This is the victory Luke Dempsey has been waiting for. Their supporters celebrate long and hard, the confidence of the players is massively boosted. Meath are out of the way and soon Dublin will be too. The traditional objects of Westmeath fear have been removed. They become favourites for the Leinster title. Perhaps they would have the year that Laois end up having. We'll never know, but it wasn't an impossibility.

Instead they are obviously demoralised by having the victory elude them so capriciously. Another cruel trick awaits them in the replay. They are awarded a penalty at a crucial stage in the game. Dolan (Courageously? Foolishly?) steps up to take it. But that missed free has broken something in him for the moment. His spot kick is a gentle tap into the goalkeeper's arms. Meath break down the field and score a match-clinching goal. How were a team going to come back from that? Westmeath slide to ignominious defeat and soon after are despatched from the championship by Monaghan. There are only so many blows the self-belief of a team on the verge can take.

Everything changed for Westmeath football the minute the ball set off on its unexpected trajectory from Dolan's boot. By the end of the season, Luke Dempsey had resigned as boss having previously been a hero, the man who had guided the county to unbelievable underage successes, an unprecedented eminence at senior level. Bright, articulate, purposeful, he was one of the half-dozen most respected managers in the country. You would have imagined that the job would have been his as long as he wanted it, but the Westmeath county board asked him to reapply and suffer the humiliation of going before an interview panel and explaining to them why he was the best man to run the county team. If that one simple free had gone over, Dempsey would have been chaired off the pitch as the officials congratulated themselves on their perspicacity in appointing such a man. But he is gone and the super-talented Westmeath team he'd largely brought through from underage level departed the 2003 championship without winning a game. All because of one misplaced kick. If that's not a tragedy, then it deserves some other word expressive of great sadness.

And if I could have one wish for the next few football championships to come, it is that Dessie Dolan plays so well and wins so much that he will be able to laugh off that last second disaster. Better still, let him stand over a close range free to win that first Leinster title for Westmeath, savour the moment and make no mistake this time. Let the reporters wonder afterwards if that was a nervous few seconds for him because of, you know, how can I put this Dessie, you know what happened back in 2003.

'No, not at all. It never entered my mind.'

He'll be entitled to the lie.

The Dubs, like fans from 31 other counties, were sorry for Dessie Dolan, but mainly they were hugely happy with their own team's performance as they trooped back down towards Meaghers, the Fairview Inn and Gaffney's, singing, 'Hill 16, la la la, Hill 16, la la la.'

They weren't even bothered by the news that the Hill would be closed for their next game against Laois because of preparations for the Special Olympics. There'd be plenty more happy days on Hill 16 after Laois went the same way as Louth.

3

Too Smart to Lie Down Anymore

7–8 June: Munster Senior Hurling Championship
Semi-Finals; Semple Stadium, Thurles
Waterford 1–12, Limerick 0–13; Cork 1–18, Clare 0–10

One of my favourite speeches by an All-Ireland winning captain is the one delivered by Cork's Mark Landers after the 1999 hurling final. It was barely comprehensible, just a series of huge emotional roars, which meant that the sense of the words remained obscure while the emotion was clear. The Landers' speech seemed more appropriate to the occasion than many of the carefully wrought speeches that you just know the victorious skipper has been prac- tising in front of the mirror for the past fortnight. Its inarticulacy was truthful. What the winners of an All-Ireland final want to do is roar with joy and that was precisely what Landers did.

When I met him four days before Cork were due to play Clare in the Munster semi-final, Mark Landers was in full corporate mode. He works as a financial adviser with Permanent TSB, 'A senior consultant, a qualified financial adviser', and he'd come straight from the office. The suit was immaculate, the shirt sharp, the speech still prone to lapse into nostrums culled from the world of financial advice. Yet the man who'd given that famous speech four years previously wasn't too far hidden beneath these accoutrements. Landers is a passionate man and, when he spoke, about what he saw as the injustice perpetrated against the Cork players, he fairly seethed. At the same time, you could see why customers trusted him to do the best by their money. He's someone who burns with self-belief and who can persuade people that, in his own words, 'I won't let anyone down if the shit starts flying.' By his own admission he wasn't a particularly skilful player but he was a born leader. A neighbour of his in Killeagh had told me a story about him playing in an U-12 final. The referee awarded a penalty to the opposition while Landers was still out around midfield. The young captain immediately started shouting at the referee, disputing the decision with him, distracting the official, who didn't allow the penalty to be taken till the kid was back on the goal line. Landers saved the shot and pucked the ball out the field. Killeagh won by two points.

These qualities of leadership and the ability to argue his point had been crucial when Landers became one of the leading figures in the most memorable controversy to hit the association in a long time.

The Cork hurlers' strike had been a complete surprise to almost everyone the previous December. On first glance, there was almost something comical about the dispute. Comedian Colm Murphy's jibe at the players on *X-it Poll* might have been unfair, but it was funny and had a grain of truth in it. I paraphrase from memory.

'Look at them, the whole suede-headed bunch of them. Who do they remind you of? Roy Keane. Hasn't anyone told them that you can't go on strike when you're not being paid? Mind you, they've made history. They're the first Cork people ever to say that something about Cork is crap.'

It was odd to see amateur players claiming to be on strike. Yet the image of inter-county stars sitting at a table and explaining that relations with their county board had broken down to such an extent that they weren't going to play again till the situation was resolved was a very powerful one. For over a hundred years, the relationship between players and officialdom had been the same as that that had pertained in soccer up till the mid-sixties. The players took the knocks, kept their mouths shut and were told what to do while the officials were the adults in the relationship. Years ago, I'd seen a county-board official in Roscommon comment that the GAA could get on fine without the players. It might have sounded outlandish but it pretty much summed up the attitude of some officials towards the stars of the game. An inter-county career was short, while a spot at the top table could be maintained for decades. It was like the Chinese Communist Party apparatchik who, when asked if the French Revolution had been a good or a bad thing, answered, 'It's far too early to tell.'

The officials had time on their side. Sit tight and today's thorn in the side would be tomorrow's forgotten star.

No one conformed to this popular picture of the county-board official as inscrutable *éminence grise* more than Frank Murphy, Cork's county secretary. Consider Bruce Arnold's comment that he'd only believe Charlie Haughey was dead when he saw him buried at a crossroads with a stake through his heart and garlic around his neck, well the legend of Frank's invincibility was of the same order. Time and again he had outwitted the opposition by his mastery of the GAA rule book. Diarmuid O'Sullivan should have been suspended for striking an opponent in the 2000 Munster championship against Limerick. Frank's machinations, allegedly, made sure he was not. Cork should have lost the 2002 Munster football final replay on a technicality, but Frank skilfully invoked the letter of the law to make sure they kept their title. Other counties were envious of his power in the committee room.

As Haughey had found out, cunning is not universally viewed as a praiseworthy quality. Frank had his detractors who saw him as a relic of an age when deals were done behind doors and official decisions went unquestioned. His grip on Cork GAA was undeniably tight and he was an obdurate conservative. When the vote had been taken in 2001 on whether or not to open Croke

Park to other sports, Frank had made an impassioned plea to maintain the status quo, employing the argument that not to do so would be ungrateful to a Fianna Fáil government, which wanted to build a national stadium. The *nos* came out on top. The *nos* usually came out on top. Frank usually came out on top.

The legend of Frank the omniscient and all-powerful meant that, when the rumours began about the Cork hurlers being deeply unhappy about the way they were being treated, no one thought their tristesse would have any concrete results. They were dealing with Frank and men like Frank, who might have lacked the boss-man's intelligence but shared his obduracy. They included the man who when informed that Prince, shortly to give a concert in Páirc Uí Chaoimh, was given to lascivious display on stage had commented, 'That's not good enough. Prince will have to come to the next county-board meeting and explain himself.'

After all, what could players do when they weren't happy? True, the GPA had been formed and occasionally indulged in sabre-rattling but no one thought they had sufficient power to force a deviation in policy in the association. County boards would only pass heed if the players refused to play, and they were never going to do that.

Except Cork had. They had announced their strike and presented a list of demands to the county board. It was a shocker for the officials. The normal way of dealing with criticism of the association was to accuse the complainants of being anti-GAA. Only this wasn't an option when you looked at the players who'd attended the press conference to announce the strike – Joe Deane, Alan Browne, Donal Óg Cusack, Seán Óg Ó hAilpín. They were GAA through and through, model hurlers, local heroes. There were a few half-hearted attempts to suggest that the players had been led astray by sinister elements in the GPA or the media, but these fizzled out. Cork hurlers had snookered their county board and the demands had to be met. The invincible Frank, singled out between the lines by the players, had been defeated. He even had to forego a place as selector on the county team that would, in the normal course of things, have been his. The first incidence of player power in the history of the GAA had been a huge success.

But that victory could easily be rendered meaningless. For the past two years, the team's performances in the championship had been abject. The precipitous drop in form was widely ascribed to the friction between the players, the county board and the two managers – Tom Cashman and Bertie Óg Murphy – who'd both got caught in the crossfire and eventually resigned. The players had nothing left to complain about now. If they produced a third disappointing year in a row, the Cork public would be quick to regard the strike as an attempt by underachievers to find excuses for their failure as players. The last laugh could yet be with the humiliated officials.

The situation when I met Mark Landers was that Cork had to beat Clare in the Munster semi-final. The pressure was nearly greater than it would have been before an All-Ireland. The question of who had been right during the strike would, in the minds of supporters, finally be answered by Sunday's result. Landers knew this but he hadn't one ounce of regret about the action the players had taken.

'Players have moved on in terms of expectation and county boards haven't. They're too long telling players what to do instead of working on a relationship with them. Frank is not the problem, the problem is the power the delegates from the clubs allow him. That comes from years of clubs not standing up for their rights and just accepting what Frank says.'

A lot of disagreements had needed to pile up before the strike was eventually called, but Landers pinpointed one particular weekend as the beginning of the end for normal relations between the two sides.

'GPA membership forms being handed out in training happened to coincide by pure fluke with the same night we were told the arrangements for the Derry National League game on the

Saturday. It was half-nine on a Tuesday night and we were told that we were leaving at one o'clock on Friday afternoon for Derry. Everyone went back to the dressing room and said there was no way they were going to go in to their boss on a Wednesday and asking for fucking Friday off. And we were going by bus, 300 miles by bus to play a game the next day, back in the bus after the game and 300 miles back, getting into Cork in the early hours of Sunday morning. We decided to meet to ask if we could fly up like we had in 1999. Otherwise guys wanted €200 compensation for taking the day off work.

'Then we were having a chat about the GPA, handing out membership forms, having a chat about joining as a sign of support for our fellow players around the country. The dressing room was locked and the manager couldn't get in, we didn't know this. We only found out when we went to for dinner and he wasn't there. We rang him but his nose was out of joint, he felt there was a coup on and that was where the trouble started.'

Cork's trip to Derry became a nightmare when Niall Mc-Carthy, one of the youngest players on the team, received a facial injury that needed several stitches. Senior players suggested that he be flown home but McCarthy was forced to travel on the bus in some distress and visit the hospital in Cork to get extra stitches. The bad feeling engendered eventually led to the strike and to the resignation of Murphy as manager and his replacement by Donal O'Grady, a circumstance Landers profoundly regretted.

'He took everything as a go at him but he was wrong. We would have gone to the grave for him but he didn't know that, he was badly advised. The players weren't against him but they were against the selectors. And then Bertie Óg resigned but the rest of the selectors fucking stayed there. It showed they didn't have the interests of Cork hurling at heart. A blind man could see that their attitude was there was no way a bunch of players were going to fucking shaft them.'

Landers had been dropped from the Cork panel, a combination of work commitments and injuries having curtailed his effectiveness. This gave him the freedom to be totally frank but, chances are, he wouldn't have held back anyway. There had always been an appealing, unbuttoned quality about him, a dislike for pussyfooting around an issue that must have made him an inspiration to players not quite sure how to go about taking on the county board. As a piped muzak version of *Yesterday* rang round the antiseptic confines of the Midleton Park Hotel, he gave no signs of forgiving his former adversaries.

'The day of the strike was one of the worst days of my life but the county board caused the dispute with their arrogance and their unwillingness to give us anything. An article appeared in the paper by a member of the county board saying we were only young fellas with no brains. Jim Cronin wanted to know how we could expect the board to pay for our gym membership, well six months later every player had their gym membership paid for. And the summer before the strike, when I was involved with the GPA, a selector told me to take a good look at Páirc Uí Chaoimh because I wouldn't be seeing it again. My regret is that I didn't challenge him on the night and hit him into the mouth, which is what he fucking deserved. He said it was a joke, it was far from a fucking joke.'

Cork players had got gym membership, more match tickets, better meals, greater flexibility about travel arrangements and several other concessions that seemed so commonsensical and minor that it beggared belief to imagine that officials had pro-voked a strike over them. Landers reckoned that Cork's action had probably caused other county boards to address the grievances of their players before a similar impasse was reached. Yet he knew too that there were people who disagreed with the action he and his team-mates had taken. Even some of his club mates had let him know that they thought he was wrong. For players to act like this cut across hallowed traditions, failed to recognise the special status of the GAA.

I knew this argument. For a start, I've had it twice with Tom

McGurk on *The Sunday Show*. Recently, when he was host, and a few years ago when Ryan Tubridy was in the chair. The players getting paid, or even compensated, struck Tom as a denigration of the essential spirit of the GAA.

'But they make such money for the association and they get next to nothing in return,' I pleaded.

'They get All-Ireland medals,' replied Tom in that emphatic I-won't-hear-another-word-about-it kind of way.

There are plenty of people, not all of them veteran GAA officials, who feel that the game is somehow improved by players being left out of pocket. It's an ancient commonplace that the association looks after players by fixing them up with good jobs. And there are those who think that the demand of players for expenses is just a ruse to put untaxed money into their pockets and is indicative of a Celtic-Tiger mentality whereby monetary reward is the highest of all values and no one does anything for free anymore (though it seems a bit rough on GAA players that they have to bear the burden of displaying ancient-Irish virtues while the rest of us rake it in). I put all these arguments to Landers.

'I've got a boss to answer to, I've got clients. The GAA have to realise what it means for me to get injured and have to take time off work. We have professional people on the team but we also have guys who aren't in good jobs and guys who've been out of work for a while. The GAA won't give them a job, the GAA don't get any inter-county player a job, that's a misconception. If Mark Landers doesn't have the figures for the boss then it's like a match, Mark Landers will get called ashore. There's no point telling the boss I was training four nights a week. If you tell an employer you're an inter-county player, it actually tells against you. In a 50–50 situation, they'll give a job to the non-player because they'll get the extra couple of hours out of him on a Tuesday or Thursday night. The inter-county player, takes three or four days to recover physically and mentally after a big match.

I gave up work opportunities when I was younger to play inter-county and I know other players who gave up the chance of promotion because the commitment was too great. No one will ever be able to prove it, but I think most players would have higher salaries and better perks if they hadn't played for their county. But we're too smart to lie down anymore. When I was dropped off the panel, they were upset that I was late for a couple of training sessions. But I was working on SSIAs and I was holding 10 staff members behind till eight o'clock, how could I leave them when I'd asked them to work late? Guys have work commitments but the whole fucking crux is that the public want you to play and act like a professional when you're still an amateur.'

And that, I submit, is as good an argument in favour of inter-county players being looked after properly as you're going to get. Perhaps the GAA did get jobs for players once, but they were largely sales-rep positions that held little prospect of long-term advancement and stability and might disappear if the player lost his place on a county team. People were grateful for those kinds of jobs when the economy was the basket case of Europe, but the country is different now and expectations are different too.

The giveaway was how Mark Landers spoke about himself in the third person and the relish with which he employed the lingo of the corporate world. Many members of his generation loved talking about targets and bonuses and clients and managers, words that, not too long ago, would have sounded alien in a countryman's mouth, wouldn't have been uttered without a trace of self-consciousness. I remember reading an English magazine review of a Christy Moore concert back in the eighties that, in passing, stated condescendingly that there was no such thing as an Irish yuppie. Contentions like that belonged to another age. These days we'd yuppie the English off the field.

'I deal with pensions, lump-sum investments, that sort of thing. Someone might come in to me to find out how they could best protect their family in the event of their death. Or they might have a £100,000 lump sum they want to invest. Ninety-five per cent of people buy because they believe in me rather than the products. It's like going to a dentist, you don't know what he's doing but you know he'll ease the pain.'

I was only sorry I didn't have a few spare grand lying around on which Landers could have worked his wiles. The opportunity for a consultation was there and I didn't take it.

And, by the way, I'm not using yuppie as a term of abuse. It's easy to take the piss out of corporate speak, corporate behaviour, corporate ambition. That's why *The Office* is everyone's favourite comedy. But this world is one which people, by and large, enjoy being part of. It's as much a part of Ireland as all day breakfasts and drink driving. As I write this I'm looking at an ad in the *Irish Examiner* for:

NO GUTS NO GAIN
What's Holding You Back?
Have you ever felt as if invisible forces prevented you from
enjoying a more productive
– and rewarding – career and personal life?
ENROL NOW FOR THIS INTERNATIONALLY
ACCLAIMED SEMINAR

For just €495, you could participate. A workbook, six audio CDs, a CD Rom, lunch and refreshments were included in the price. And, in the case you're wondering what this had to do with the GAA, who was the guest speaker? D.J. Carey.

Yes, the same D.J. Carey who some romantics regarded as a symbol of a traditional Ireland unsullied by commercialism and motivational hype. D.J. Carey, chosen to make the speech solely on the basis of what he had achieved on the hurling field. Proper order too. Like Mark Landers and probably most of the other young men who play inter-county GAA, D.J. was plugged into the spirit of the age. He'd embraced the *Zeitgeist* so fully that, at times, it was hard to tell which was the *Zeitgeist* and which was D.J.

Bien-pensant moans about the loss of our spirituality, our hospitality, our Celtic Soul (cue wafty Enya music) might fill the letters pages of the newspapers but the undeniable fact was that the majority of people loved the Tiger era. Opinion polls showed that the Irish were the most contented folk in Europe.

The GAA is so all embracing that its players will always reflect the national mood. Christy Ring and the players of his generation attended mass on the morning of a game, offered up prayers for success, were honoured to kiss the ring of the bishop before the throw-in because that's how most people felt in those days. And many of their heirs subscribe to the work-hard, play-hard, getting-down-your-golf-handicap, breakfast-briefing, I'll-tell-you-one-man-I-admire-and-that's-Michael-O'Leary contemporary ethos. The GAA would never define itself as being against the current mood or pay more than lip service to values the majority didn't subscribe to. The day it did that, it could join traditional Irish music in the ghetto.

Snobby bastards like me could whinge about the Midleton Park Hotel's suburban aesthetic but people like to stay in these places. The old country hotels they replaced might have been full of authentic character but they were also prone to itchy blankets, moth-eaten curtains, malfunctioning sockets and grimy cutlery. People wanted a bit of comfort now, they'd been making do for long enough.

So it was with the Tiger. Mark Landers was proud of having worked his way up without the benefit of third-level education and only a madman would suggest that Ireland was a better place when the only option for country lads like himself was hod-carrying in Boston or London. There were opportunities now and the people who took them didn't give a stuff about the loss of the Celtic Soul. Leave that to the academics.

The Cork players' strike had been bound up with this huge

cultural change. A large proportion of the panel were white-collar workers who'd been schooled in the professional imperatives of the new economy. They'd been taught to behave in a businesslike manner, get to appointments on time, bring people for a decent lunch, treat customers with respect. Then they arrived at Páirc Uí Chaoimh and found that the same old nod-and-wink culture applied. The food was lousy, they weren't equals but subordinates, corners were cut, it was all back in the sure-it'll-do bad old days. This wasn't deliberate, it was just the way the county board had always acted. But the contrast between what the players knew from their working lives and what was offered to them in their second career was too great. The Cork county board had run smack into Irish corporate culture and there was only going to be one winner. I bade farewell to Mark Landers and walked away from the Midleton Park Hotel.

'Hey, where's your car?'

'I don't have one.'

'Jesus, you're a terrible man.'

He shook his head as though I'd just confessed to a murder. The cultural chasm between someone scraping a living from writing and Landers was as great as the one between him and Frank. Mind you, he did give me a lift into Midleton.

History and economics might have been on the side of the Cork players, but they'd still be in the wrong if they lost to Clare, which, on the face of it, was the most likely result. Tipperary had been hot favourites for the Munster title but, three weeks previously, Clare had demolished them in Páirc Uí Chaoimh, getting on their case from the start, demoralising them so comprehensively that you wouldn't have been surprised if one of the Tipp players seized a white flag from an umpire and waved it in surrender midway through the second half. A repeat of that form would probably be enough to account for Cork.

Except the general consensus was that Clare wouldn't repeat that form because they had no axe to grind with Cork. The frenzy of their play against Tipperary was explained by the dredging up of perceived insults from the past, recent narrow defeats and a newspaper interview in which Tipp manager Michael Doyle had neglected to mention Clare as contenders for the Munster title. There being no such history with Cork, the theory went, the Banner wouldn't be able to motivate themselves to the same extent and would be there for the taking.

On the face of it, this seemed bizarre. Was defiance and spite really such an integral part of the Clare make-up that they wouldn't be able to function without it? Surely there were more subtle factors that brought them to perfect competitive pitch.

Perhaps not. Most GAA teams affected great offence at something or other during the championship season (newspaper headlines, television predictions, refereeing decisions, an unfair choice of venue or date, alleged arrogance by the opposition) and claimed that these insults spurred them on to far greater efforts. Yet Clare seemed uniquely driven by slights. Even their great years in the mid-nineties had apparently been sparked by a brief laugh from Nicky English in the 1993 Munster final. Given that the Banner subsequently beat Tipp in a Munster and an All-Ireland decider, it had to be the most expensive moment of mirth in the history of the GAA.

In their heyday, Clare's antennae had been permanently on alert for disparagement. They were like the hard man who struts around a disco in the hope that someone will tell him to fuck off and provide the opportunity for a row.

This was Clare's way, always hitting back at an invisible 'they' who wanted to run the Banner into the ground. But maintaining a persecution complex is hard work and counter-productive. It had lost them an All-Ireland in 1998 when they were so much stronger than all the other counties that there was no need to carry on with all that old malarkey. They weren't able to resist.

The feeling this time was that Clare had poured so much of themselves into the game against Tipperary that they wouldn't be anything like the same force against Cork. Unless Donal O'Grady slipped up by suggesting that the entire county of Clare should be concreted over and its people exiled to a remote Pacific archipelago. And he was too cute for that. Clare's problems were compounded by the fact that Seán McMahon, one of the truly great hurlers of the modern age, had become embroiled in a pointless scrap when the game against Tipperary had already been won and clipped Conor Gleeson across the head with his hurl. McMahon had been sent off and would miss the Cork match through suspension. Sometimes it seemed as if Clare might have been better off cutting back a bit on the motivation.

Cork and Clare wasn't the only Munster hurling semi-final that weekend. Limerick and Waterford would play in Thurles on the Saturday night, having drawn their first match 4–13 each. It had, apparently, been a classic but only the people who'd been in Semple Stadium would know for sure. Television coverage had been cancelled because the local council had refused to give a fire-safety certificate to the camera area. It might as well have been a legendary 19th-century game for all that the general population saw of it.

To anyone familiar with the GAA's traditional attitude towards press facilities, there was a certain rough justice about the fire-officer's decision. At the smaller country grounds in particular, press facilities had been low on the list of priorities and the result was that journalists often ended up in seats the authorities would hardly have dared issue to a paying customer. Visibility would be poor, there would be nothing like enough seating and the press box would be a cold and grimy place to carry out your afternoon's work. The nadir, I think, came at Hyde Park in Roscommon. For the 2001 National League semi-final, press accommodation consisted of a few planks laid out on scaffolding. You needed a ladder to climb up to the platform and the roof leaked constantly, and heavily. It would have comfortably held four people rather than the dozen who were crammed in there. Leaving the box wasn't an option because rain was pelting down. Climbing the ladder and trying to pull yourself up on the slippy scaffolding made the experience dangerous as well. No one bollocked the local officials because there were renovations going on and the press reasoned that everyone could have a bad day. Nearly a year later, I visited Hyde Park for a league match between Roscommon and Donegal and the same ramshackle edifice was still *in situ*. Jesus wept.

The problem for well-meaning officials was that, given that attacks on the media were one of the great traditions of the association, it would take a brave man to stand up at a county-board meeting and suggest that more money should be spent on coddling the press. Older delegates might wonder why reporters were allowed into the grounds at all. This attitude has changed somewhat, the facility in Croke Park is as impressive as you'll see anywhere. But one look at the Páirc Uí Chaoimh press box – where, on a big-match day, reporters stand up and lean over one another's shoulders to try and see what's happening on the wings – suggests not everyone in the organisation worries about media comfort. The drawbacks of such an attitude appeared to have been demonstrated the previous weekend in Thurles.

Rooms in Thurles being impossible to find, I booked myself into the Templemore Arms Hotel for the weekend and, before setting off for the Saturday-night match, watched Brian Kerr's Ireland struggle to a 2–1 win over Albania. In Semple Stadium, someone asked a steward if he'd seen the soccer match. They were asking the wrong man.

'I did. If they picked a few Irishmen on that team they might be some good.'

There are still a few GAA people who hope fervently for the triumph of the opposition every time the Irish soccer team play, just as there are soccer people who pray for Croke Park to propel the association into bankruptcy. Personally, I think they should act like grown-ups, settle their differences, embrace a spirit of liberal tolerance, and gang up on rugby.

Given that full television coverage had been restored to Thurles, it was obvious what would happen. The unseen Limerick–Waterford game had been a thriller, the one broadcast to the public was a stinker. Waterford eventually won 1–12 to 0–13 but the only highlight of the game was the display of Paul Flynn. He'd swooped onto a loose ball in the first half and buried a shot in the far corner of the net from a position where most players would have been content with a point. In the second half, he was under pressure from three defenders and off-balance out on the right sideline and managed not only to get a shot off but to steer it between the posts. He was in the kind of form that would have been impressive on any occasion but which was made to look all the more wonderful by the mediocrity that surrounded him. It was as though the *Mona Lisa* had turned up at an exhibition in the local arts centre. Monday's *Irish Examiner* rewarded the Man of the Match with the deathless headline: 'Ballygunner star displayed flashes of Ring, claims McCarthy.'

If it wasn't as good as the classic *Examiner* headline that had appeared to mark the exit of a certain German golfer from the Irish open – 'Langer out in day of shocks' – it wasn't far off.

We all have players from other counties who command not just our admiration but our affection, lads you want to do well for their own sake. Paul Flynn is one of mine because I feel the man has been severely undervalued. Here's a guy who's not far behind D.J. Carey in the skill category and, despite having been doomed to play on the outside courts for most of his career, has frequently been spectacular, ever since he was helping Waterford to win an All-Ireland U-21 final when he was still a minor. Even on his quiet days, he does one or two things that can elicit a shiver of aesthetic bliss. And those quiet days are not as frequent as you'd be led to believe by some Waterford fans. Flynn has arguably had just as many fine games for his county as Tony Browne or Fergal Hartley, has contributed far more than team-mates whose dedication to the cause is never questioned. Yet the words enigma and inconsistent are usually lurking close by when the corner-forward is described. It would be a pity if he retired and the blame showered on him rivalled, or even outweighed, the praise. I mean, one journalist even criticised him for hitting his frees too high over the bar because there was a danger they'd leave the ground and get lost, thus costing the GAA money.

Flynn is mistrusted by a sizeable proportion of fans because he's a ballplayer, a skill merchant, a Flash Harry. This distrust isn't specific to the GAA, the same mentality pertains in English soccer. But I think it's peculiar to this corner of the globe with its rain-lashed Northern-European privileging of graft over guile, sweat over skill. Corner-backs and wing-backs of merely reasonable ability win the affection of supporters with comparative ease. The ball is coming at them, they can make a charge at it, block the opponent, give off an impression of bravery and effort. It's different for a corner-forward. He has to win the ball, think about what he's going to do with it, devise some method of extracting maximum advantage from the possession he's won. No one criticises the full-back who catches a high ball and then roots it out over the sideline. But let a forward send the ball wide and he's a demon, no matter how hard he had to battle to get in that shot.

It's a law of nature, which begins at underage level, when referees allow young mullockers of corner-backs considerable latitude in trying to curb talented forwards. You can see it in ref's eyes, 'What do you expect him to do? It serves you right for being skilful.'

Corner-forwards learn that, if the team is going badly, they can be taken off after 20 minutes even though the ball has never come near them. Even though they eventually become the glamour players of the game, still they never seem to be fully trusted by the management or the fans. It's as if someone possessing all that flashy ability has to be a bit flaky, a bit suspect. This happens to the greatest of them. D.J. Carey might be God now but remember all those doubts about whether he fancied it in the really big games. He has had to get used to unfair criticism. So has Paul Flynn, which is why his *tour de force* in Thurles did me good.

What position did I occupy in my playing days? What do you think?

There was a curiously bereft atmosphere about Thurles. A weekend of hurling in the home of hurling, two Munster semi-finals and Tipperary not playing. I got a taxi back to Templemore and for some reason we got talking about the cancellation of the revived Lisdoonvarna Festival, which would eventually be re-routed to the RDS.

'I remember when we had the Trip To Tipp around here. It was brilliant, everyone round here did well out of it, shops, pubs, taxis. I used to spend the whole weekend carrying people over and back to Thurles. They were sound kids the lot of them, you'd take pity on them by the end they were so tired and dirty looking. But it gave great life to the place.'

'Why did it stop?'

'I don't know, but it won't start up again. Look at that Lisdoonvarna, that could have done a lot for the town but they had to go and object to it. There's always the few these days that'll put a stop to anything and the judges have to pass heed on them. It would be the same in Thurles now. That's the way things are gone. If people don't want those festivals, couldn't they go away for the weekend? But there's no give now, everything gets taken too serious.'

It's not often I find myself agreeing with a taxi driver, but the man from Templemore had a point.

There's not much wrong with the Templemore Arms. They're friendly, they give you a good feed in the morning and the rooms are grand. The only problem is that the aforementioned rooms are a bit too close to the bar where a local group was giving it loads that Saturday as I tried to bed down for the night. Still, a bit of music in the background can be soothing as well and I was drifting away when a few shouts for an encore and some applause indicated that the band were going to play their *pièce de résistance*. Grand. 'Wonderful Tonight' or 'American Pie' or 'If Tomorrow Never Comes' would do the job.

Jesus, that was loud. They seemed to have upped the volume for their final turn. What was that song? It sounded kind of familiar. Dah dah dah moonlight dah dah dah dah hair. Very familiar. Horribly familiar. And now everyone join in the chorus. The band and customers combined to blast me from my slumber as though they'd crept into the room and were serenading me to sleep, 'We've got the world tonight, dass ryat, da da da *forever*.'

The song seemed to have a dozen verses and the cheerful singalong downstairs told me that I was the only person in Ireland who didn't like it. Defeat in Latvia had not withered him or staled his infinite variety, Mickey Joe Harte was having the last laugh on me. Or the second-last laugh as it turned out. My sleep was fitful and tormented by dreams of MJH in a Cork jersey lashing goal after goal past Davy Fitzgerald who kept screaming, 'I care too much about the *Eurovision* to let anyone put down the song contest that I love.'

Sometimes you think you'll never see the morning.

After about 10 minutes, the result of the Cork–Clare match was pretty obvious. It's not often that you see a team refusing to countenance defeat though, theoretically, that's the frame of mind in which they should always take the field. But Cork were driven that day in Thurles to an unprecedented extent. The provocations that had led to the strike, the awful displays of the past couple of years, the pressures imposed by the strike, the palpable feeling of goodwill the fans bore towards the players, all seemed to combine and bring Cork to a rare level of determination and achievement. Even Kilkenny, I reckon, wouldn't have beaten Cork that day. Clare certainly seemed to throw their hat in early on.

The new boys, Tom Kenny and Ronan Curran, in the half-back line were managing that old Cork trick of looking like they'd been playing championship hurling for years within minutes of making their debut and, in the 13th minute, came one of the best goals of the year, although it took a few seconds to work out what was going on. Ben O'Connor tore down the middle and flicked the ball to Joe Deane, Deane pulled first-time and the ball came crashing back into play. Clare were busy trying to clear it when the umpire informed the referee that the shot had hit the stanchion inside the net rather than the crossbar and, although Davy Fitz looked even unhappier than usual, the goal was given.

Clare launched a bit of a comeback at the start of the second half but Cork regained control and the closing stages would have been an unremarkable procession had it not been for a couple of telling incidents.

I'd seen Setanta Ó hAilpín when he was an U-16 playing a City League final for Na Piarsaigh against Blackrock. His brother Seán Óg was already an inter-county star and there was a bit of a buzz about Setanta but he was disappointing that evening, just a few days before the elder Ó hAilpín played in the 1999 All-Ireland senior final. He was effective all right, but that seemed largely because he was a 15-year-old who was almost six-and-a-half feet tall. There was an awkward gangling quality about Setanta that suggested he'd be caught out when he moved up the grades and his size wasn't such a factor anymore. His career at minor level wasn't bad but, once more, there seemed to be other youngsters more likely to make it.

No one had really thought about Setanta as a possible championship starter at the start of the season. Then he was thrown on in a league game against Tipperary that Cork were losing comprehensively and scored two goals to give his team an unlikely win. One good performance against Kilkenny later and Ó hAilpín uimhir a dó was being fast-tracked onto the championship fifteen. The word was that he'd grown into his tall frame and developed a new subtlety while playing with Waterford IT in the Fitzgibbon Cup.

Going on the evidence of what I'd seen a couple of weeks earlier, Setanta looked a good bet to make a big impression in the championship. He'd been playing football rather than hurling for his club against Skibbereen in Clonakilty in the Cork senior championship but had dominated the game to such an extent that people left talking about nobody else. There'd been a 60-yard run early in the game, a couple of great points, a 20-yard drive, which whistled into the net past Kevin O'Dwyer one of the best goalkeepers in the game and, right at the end, a fetch of the ball under his own crossbar to preserve a one-point lead and a solo out to the middle of the field. It's dangerous to extrapolate anything about football from hurling (and vice versa) but the power, the confidence, the maturity of that display suggested that the coltish youth had been replaced by a fully rounded athlete.

All the same, you could have excused him if his debut had been less than earth-shattering. He was marking Frank Lohan, the epitome of a sticky corner-back. Frank's brother, Brian, might have been the folk hero and the headline gatherer, but Frank was just as effective, he was quick, resourceful, mean and far from the ideal opponent for a youngster making his debut. Nobody had ever got anything easy from Frank Lohan but, in the first half, Setanta whipped the ball away from him as he was about to clear and sent it over the bar.

Lohan had done pretty well in the second half before the players began to jostle each other and a dig of the hurl into the stomach left Setanta stretched on the ground. If he'd wanted to mind himself for the rest of the game, he wouldn't have been blamed. The game was won and he was a young lad up against a very tough man. But, when the next ball came in less than a minute later, the young lad soared above the very tough man, skinned him for pace and scored a brilliant point. At that moment, most people could see that Setanta was going to be one of the stars of the summer, a hurling equivalent to Jason Sherlock, who'd been such a crowd darling eight years previously. Like Jayo,

Setanta was an exotic presence in the world's most exclusively Caucasian games. He played with the same kind of brio and also preferred going for goals rather than taking his points. The Del Piero pencil-thin beard indicated a liking for attention that would help as well. By getting up off the ground and making Frank Lohan's attempt at intimidation backfire, Setanta showed he wasn't going to be distracted from his destiny. From the teenager he'd been, when it looked like a heavy challenge would have snapped him in two like a breadstick, it now seemed as if Setanta Nua required something a bit more substantial to stop him, like perhaps a truck.

The other significant move in the endgame was the red mist descending on Colin Lynch. This was hardly a novel experience for Lynch, but normally the midfielder played with a controlled fury. Clare had been nothing like their old selves in 2002 but had still reached the All-Ireland final, largely because of Lynch's superb performances. No one got up and down the field as effectively as Lynch, no midfielder picked off points with such alacrity, no player in Gaelic games was as reminiscent of Roy Keane in terms of competitive spirit, accomplishment and a tendency to dice with the dark side.

But in Thurles that day, he'd been frustratingly unable to find his form and had been harried at every turn by Mickey O'Connell, a player with far less ability making his first start for Cork in three years. With the match almost over, Lynch lamped O'Connell across the head and got sent off. It was a piece of silliness that would cost Clare dear. They were drawn to play Galway just six days later and lost by a point. The suspended Lynch missed the match and would have probably made the difference. Had Clare got their second wind, they might well have had the same kind of back-door run as the previous year. But another fit of temper meant that, after the heroic win over Tipperary, they'd be the first major team out of the championship.

Cork, on the other hand, celebrated as though they'd won the All-Ireland and now knew that they'd put the memory of the strike behind them. No matter what happened, no one could upcast that to them now.

4

All the Culchies Are Delighted

15 June: Leinster Senior Football Championship
Semi-Final; Croke Park
Laois 0–16, Dublin 0–14

The reaction when I told people I was going to meet David Hickey surprised me. I didn't even get as far as the explanatory 'he's the former Dublin footballer who's involved in giving medical aid to Cuba'. Just David Hickey was enough.

'He's a cool guy.'

'That's going to be very interesting.'

'Tell me what he was like when you come back.'

'Fair play to him.'

Put part of this down to the power of the GAA. Because David Hickey irreversibly linked himself in the Irish mind with the Cuban struggle when he revealed a T-shirt with a message decrying the American blockade while being honoured as a member of the great Dublin team of the seventies in Croke Park at half-time during the 1999 All-Ireland final.

Those anniversary celebrations are prosaic enough affairs. No doubt they're tremendously gratifying for the players of the past, but it doesn't seem as if the crowd pay much attention and the ceremony isn't jazzed up in any way that might rectify that. But no one who saw it, either live or on television, will forget David

Hickey's gesture. Mention Cuba now and he's the Irish name that comes to mind.

So the affection with which Hickey is regarded isn't solely to do with his previous life as a flying-machine wing-forward. The plight of Cuba, overshadowed and bullied for so long by a bigger neighbour, still strikes a chord with Irish people. There is almost a schizophrenia at work in this country. On the one hand, we are proud of the Tiger economy and reluctant to say one word that might offend the United States. On the other hand, we like to identify with the downtrodden nations of the world and pay lip service at least to the notion that those countries should decide their own destinies rather than be dictated to by multinational corporations. It wasn't long since the line, 'Ireland is a Third-World country', had been guaranteed to earn you the hushed assent of a bar-room audience. The perceptive academic and cultural commentator Luke Gibbons has said that Ireland was 'a First-World country with a Third-World memory', which seems pretty near the mark. The fact that Luke Gibbons' father Hugh, a Fianna Fáil TD, won an All-Ireland senior medal with Roscommon at right corner-forward in 1944 is yet another confirmation that there's no getting away from the GAA.

So people are fond of David Hickey and what he stands for, while, at the same time, believing in the ultimate benignity of the USA. I met him when debates about the Shannon Stopover were still going on and when the war in Iraq was pretty much the number one topic of conversation.

Hickey works as a transplant surgeon in Beaumont Hospital, which was also in the headlines around that time with tales of patients spending days on trolleys and the health service falling apart.

He greeted me wearing a surgical mask, gown and gloves, explaining that he'd be late before nipping back to theatre to continue operating. The sense of uselessness that most of us feel in the company of doctors immediately came upon me – that what-do-any-of-us-do-to-improve-the-human-condition-in-comparison-to-the-medical-profession feeling. Someone ushered me into an ante-room where doctors came and went, eating sandwiches, talking about their plans for the weekend. It reminded me of a mini-cab office. There was the same hot and airless feel to the place, the same atmosphere of irregular hours being worked and people waiting around to be called on the next job. The difference was that these men and women would leave the room and save someone's life. A porter asked me what I was doing there.

'Dave Hickey? He's a great guy. Nothing stuck about him like some doctors. His whole team call him Dave, everyone likes him.'

At this stage I'd been assured by so many people that meeting David Hickey would be a rewarding experience, it would almost have been a relief if he'd turned out to be a complete gobdaw. No such luck.

'Why did I do it? Because of the injustice of the actual situation in Cuba. I'd known Cuban doctors for a long time and been impressed with their commitment. And I was aware of the sanctions against them and that the last seven votes of the UN have decried this as a humanitarian crime. I felt there wasn't enough knowledge in this country about it. We have a very similar history to Cuba with colonialism and freedom fighters dying every 50 years but we've never done anything to show solidarity with the Cuban people. Here was an unbelievable opportunity in front of an audience of 50 or 60 million people, a lot of them in the United States. I couldn't believe that no one had done anything like it before.'

Thus he became David Hickey the doctor who wanted a fair deal for Cuba as well as David Hickey who'd been a star of the great Dub team, arguably the most charismatic outfit ever to play the game of Gaelic football. Kerry won more titles and were unarguably a far better team, but Dublin's flair and panache still stick in the mind. Hickey had played in six All-Ireland finals in a row, from 1974 to 1979, winning All-Stars in 1974 and 1976 before Pat Spillane moved out to left half-forward and won five awards in a row. And with six minutes to go in the greatest game of all-time, the 1977 All-Ireland semi-final between Dublin and Kerry, he scored the goal that turned the game. He felt that this GAA experience informed his current activities.

'The other guys from the team were very supportive and the ones who didn't know about Cuba were shocked when they heard what was happening there. I think it fitted in with the GAA because the ethos of the association is one of individual rights, national sovereignty and cultural identity and these are exactly the things the Cubans are fighting for. The GAA is an anti-imperialist organisation.'

The more you talk to Hickey, the greater the sense that he's passionate about his cause to the point of obsession. This is disquieting at first because, nowadays, we're not used to complete sincerity. Irony walks tall this weather and people who insist that something must be changed make us uneasy. That kind of conviction seems to belong in sixties newsreels of Martin Luther King and protests against the Vietnam War. Hickey doesn't believe in soft-pedalling his message. There's no point in hitting him with, 'Get a life.'

He has seen what he has seen and it is not to be taken lightly. The issues are too important.

It's the medical man in Hickey who is most outraged by the American blockade. One of the experiences that marked him was seeing children with cancer becoming violently ill because the Cubans had not been able to import anti-nausea medicines – now he organises the sending of medical supplies unwanted by Irish hospitals to Cuba.

'The hospital here is very good about letting me send stuff. The stuff thrown out in hospitals here staggers the imagination. You can't use a pair of crutches more than once, right. So there are aluminium crutches with rubber tips, a guy comes in with a sprained ankle and goes home with them. He comes back in the next day and gives them back to the hospital and they go in the garbage. Those crutches cost €50 or €60 a pair and they won't be used a second time because some insurance company said they wouldn't be safe. This applies right across the board, there are drugs with arbitrary expiry dates and the only reason those dates are on them is a cynical move by the drugs companies so that we'll have to restock.'

The Hickey world-view is Chomskyan and indeed he's given to quoting the good professor. The rich nations of the world are actively engaged in the oppression of the weak ones, and American imperialism is the greatest danger to us all. Other wrongs pale into insignificance in comparison with the ones perpetrated by the USA. At times I found him tunnel-visioned. His comment that dissidents jailed by Castro are 'not dissidents but traitors', is a hard one to stomach. Vaclav Havel, a man who knows from experience that the Left sometimes nods at political repression from its own side, has called for those dissidents to be freed. Yet Hickey cannot see anything wrong with Cuba. It is his ideal state, superior to an Ireland that he believes has joined the ranks of the colonisers.

'We've developed a colonising mindset. We go to countries where doctors are as scarce as hen's teeth and have been trained at enormous expense. And we steal those people, we bring them over here for jobs which deny their own countries of their services. The Third World, you know, contributes $1 billion in medical education to the First World.'

It would be easy to lumber Hickey with the familiar right-wing terms of abuse.

'Fellow traveller.'

'Anti-American.'

'Useful idiot.'

And it would also be nonsensical because, on balance, he's in the right. He's not a dour individual, he's immensely charming and good natured, but Cuba's plight is something he can't be light-hearted about. When the talk switches to football, it's a different story. Hickey loved being a Dub and he still loves the GAA.

'I love it even more now than I did when I was playing. They do such a fantastic job in preserving what little native culture we've got left. Hill 16? Hill 16 is a great place whose fearsomeness is much exaggerated. It's full of people who know about football. One of my great memories is of the noise they made when we played Cork in the 1974 semi-final and the boost that gave us. The noise, the colour, it's very impressive.'

Just as I take my leave of Hickey, who's got another operation to do, I mention the fact that several members of the Dublin team have become very prosperous since retiring from the game. It's almost a defining characteristic of the side. Robbie Kelleher is chief economist with Davy Stockbrokers, Paddy Cullen has done very well in the pub trade, Kevin Moran followed professional soccer fame by setting up a high-powered PR agency, others have achieved considerable success as well. And then there's Hickey the transplant surgeon. It's hardly the normal profile of an inter-county GAA team, or is it?

'I don't think there's any typical GAA team. The great thing about the GAA is that it covers all stratas of society. The GAA embraces working-class people and professional people and people who have no job, even writers.'

It would make a fine motto and is a succinct explanation of what gives the GAA its edge over other sports in this country. David Hickey, the urban surgeon and socialist, probably hasn't a single political point of view in common with Mark Landers, the rural financial adviser. Yet both of them felt at home in the GAA. Hickey's idea of an anti-imperialist organisation and Landers of one that would have to take cognisance of new financial realities were both, in a way, true. The GAA can be anything you want it to be, once you play the game. That is its huge strength.

But David Hickey was grievously wrong about one thing. He was sure that Dublin were going to beat Laois and probably win the Sam Maguire.

No one gave Laois a chance that day against Dublin. Given that I'm writing this book when the season is over, I could chance my arm and say that I had a sneaking fancy for an upset, but that would be a lie. The Dubs were looking very good at this stage and Laois didn't look to have the stuff to bother them. Maybe next year, when they'd chalked this one down to experience.

Mick O'Dwyer was newly in charge of Laois and you could advance the theory that Micko knew how to win games against Dublin. You could also say that it had taken him years at Kildare before he'd been able to get past the Dubs. There was a case to be made for Laois based on their run to the National-League final, but the humiliating defeat they'd suffered there against Tyrone also suggested that they were a few steps below top class. And then there were the two exciting games against Offaly that Laois had come through. Sure, they'd do the team good but, if they were really going to compete against Dublin, shouldn't they have nailed their neighbours in one?

There'd been an interesting face in the crowd during the first game against Offaly, the Brazilian soccer legend Jairzinho casting an eye over the game while preparing to launch the Samba Soccer Schools, which seemed to be claiming the allegiance of half of Ireland's kids.

What about Laois's record with underage prodigies? People had been proclaiming the future greatness of Beano McDonald, Ian Fitzgerald and their cohorts since before they'd been legally entitled to drink a pint. When you looked at this though, it seemed more of a disadvantage than an advantage. The country's miracle workers at minor level often didn't come through as they'd been expected to, especially when they came from counties who hadn't much going on at senior level. Aged 18 or 19, they were expected to suddenly transform the fortunes of a county team. When they understandably didn't, judgement could be cruel. McDonald and Fitzgerald were just reaching their mid-twenties, yet they seemed to have been written off as has-beens several times already. There were dark murmurings about the attitude of the young Laois players who'd been heroes in their county just five years back. It was scarcely fair but All-Ireland minor success sometimes seemed to be a prime example of making a rod for your own back.

There appeared to be too many strikes against Laois and the most telling statistic of all was that Dublin didn't lose games in Leinster when they were favourites. Take Meath and Kildare out of the equation and the last time they'd lost in the province was when Offaly had beaten them in the 1982 final. Good teams, some of them from Laois who'd looked to have a reasonable chance against the Dubs, crumbled when the heat came on in Croke Park. There was a strut about Dublin when they took on the lesser counties, a certainty that seemed to demoralise the opposition and often led to big scores being run up quickly. Look how Louth had jacked it in after only a few minutes.

These theories of Dublin superiority weren't immediately disproved. The favourites cut lanes through the Laois defence in the first 10 minutes, looking the much stronger and quicker team, knocking the ball around with considerable bravado, disdaining point opportunities as they bade to bury the outsiders in jig time. And that, as Hercule Poirot might put it, was their first mistake. Dublin's normal elan transmuted into hubris. They had, for example, neglected to pick a reliable freetaker. John McNally had been left off, Tomás Quinn was languishing on the bench and so Tom Mulligan and Ray Cosgrove were put up and missed chances to hurt Laois and make the most of this early advantage.

The problem with hubris is this: if things go right, then it's a great help to a team to be relaxed and confident but, if things go wrong, it's tough to get footballers out of strolling mode. Laois buckled and bent but they didn't break. Instead, they sniped away on the counterattack and edged into a lead. Still, Dublin didn't look worried.

Perhaps they should have noticed what was happening between Pauric Clancy and Ciarán Whelan. Clancy is nothing like the athlete or classical footballer that Whelan is. At first sight, he looks like one of those beanpole midfielders who play at every club ground in the country. You walk into a game and the big fella makes a tremendous catch way over his head and you say to the guy beside you, 'How come that fella never got a run for the county?'

Just as the beanpole touches the ground and roots the ball 30 yards past his corner-forward.

'That's how come.'

Clancy had a bit of that about him. He was a fine fielder but he didn't look filled out in the same way as Whelan or Darragh Ó Sé or Paul McGrane. He could look a bit statuesque when in possession and his deliberate and awkward solo runs suggested things didn't come to him as easily as they did to some midfielders, yet, as the half wore on, it was Clancy who was winning the ball at midfield and Whelan who started to have one of those days the Dublin spectators dread. The home hero tore through twice and ballooned shots massively and monstrously wide. His ginger-haired opponent looked to be enjoying the game more and more.

It wasn't as if Dublin didn't have chances to score the goal that might have restored the natural order, persuaded Laois that there was real substance behind the strut which was beginning to look slightly false. The Laois keeper Fergal Byron made a great save from Liam Óg Ó hÉinneacháin and then saw Alan Brogan stick the rebound wide. Right on half-time, Tom Mulligan was put through but Byron stopped his shot too. You could sense the Laois folk beginning to imagine all sorts of unthinkable things.

At half-time, Laois were 0–6 to 0–4 ahead and as the teams were going off there was an almighty row in the tunnel. The television viewers had the best view of it but both Clancy and

Whelan seemed to be involved and the word was that Dublin had started the fracas but Laois had finished it, responding to a thump on one of their players by piling in mob-handed with extreme prejudice.

Did the scrap have any effect on the game? The Hemingway school of analysis, which sees all sporting competition as an effort by two sets of men (always men) to get a psychological edge over each other by dint of mental or physical intimidation, would reckon it was a deciding factor. Never mind the goals and the points, the dig was the real match winner. This was probably fallacious. There were very few cowards at inter-county level so intimidation was probably a waste of time.

Yet Laois seemed a different team in the second half, suddenly confident where Dublin looked tentative and fearful. Perhaps the fight had given them an adrenalin rush at just the right time, given them something else to talk and think about instead of reflecting that they were two points ahead of the Dubs. Outsiders often led at half-time and you saw them emerge for the second period and wait for the favourites to come back to them, as if their sudden good fortune was too great to be borne, as though they were Wile E Coyote going over the cliff, in no danger till he realised that he was standing on thin air. The realisation was what always got Wile E and sent him crashing to the valley floor. So it was with weaker counties who couldn't bear the enormity of what they were about to achieve and handed the initiative back to the oligarchs of the game.

Not so with Laois. They were as dominant at the start of the second half as Dublin had been at the start of the first. Ross Munnelly scored a great point and they were five points ahead with 20 minutes left. The spirit of this Laois team could be summed up by Ross Munnelly. He hadn't been an underage prodigy, in fact he was still a youngster and no one outside Laois had heard of him until Micko took over. But what a delight he was to watch. He held the ball kind of loose and was distinguished by ferocious optimism. Laois gave the ball to Ross and he just ran past defenders as if he didn't know these were experienced inter-county men who deserved a bit more respect. He shot for points that looked unlikely till the umpire was waving the white flag and, later on, he'd go for a goal that the wise and cautious attacker wouldn't have dreamed of. And he had a hell of a time. Like a 16-year-old playing his first game for the club junior team, Ross Munnelly got out there and enjoyed himself, seemed surprised sometimes at how easy it was. You waited for some crabby veteran to clobber him and let him know it wasn't that simple and you waited for his honeymoon to end. Except it didn't. He was a joy to watch and will remain my abiding memory of a Laois team who played without fear and who, though this certainly can't have been the case, gave the impression of constant improvisation.

An outraged Dublin scored three points in a row but Laois had points from Mick Lawlor and Damien Delaney, their two veterans who'd suffered plenty at the hands of the Dubs in the past. With the Hill out of commission, it seemed more difficult for the Dublin fans to lift their team. There was a chance of a goal for Ray Cosgrove, not an easy opportunity but the kind he'd scored every time the previous year. He missed it.

In 2001, Cosgrove was an unknown and, in 2002, he deserved to win Footballer of the Year because, every time he came within 20 yards of goal, he went for it and succeeded. Then, with his very last kick of the championship, he had missed an easy free to give Dublin a draw against Armagh. Since then, nothing had gone right for him, though he looked to be working as hard as ever, hadn't slowed down and was still getting a good supply. Football had decided to be cruel to him again.

Three minutes left now, Laois three points ahead. Dublin were putting on serious pressure but Pauric Clancy had one of those moments that make the opposition realise they have no business trying to win the match. There he was, rising to cleanly fetch a kick-out and, from 50 yards out bisect the posts – Laois weren't going to be caught now. It was probably the point of the year and

Clancy had done a Dessie Dolan in reverse in that he could shoot from the same position under the same kind of pressure a hundred times and never get the same result. When the umpire raised the white flag for that one, the Laois fans looked beatific as lottery winners.

After all the hype, all the expectation, all the talk of how the game would be well served by a Dublin All-Ireland victory, a pin had been stuck into the balloon and Dublin would never recapture their shine. Not in 2003 anyway, though the back-door was still open for them. Armagh would grind their teeth after defeat and regroup but Dublin couldn't because confidence was so important to them. Robbed of their swagger, they didn't look half the team. Tommy Lyons didn't look the same either. Nothing but good had happened to him since he'd taken over as manager, even the defeat against Armagh had been so narrow and so subsequently validated by the Ulster team as to just give more hope for the future. He was a chirpy man who revelled in success, but defeat by Laois was a bad thing that offered no consolations. The Dubs would struggle on, but they were like a young wife who'd just discovered her husband's first adultery. They could patch things up and give it a go but things weren't going to get back to the way they had been. It would just be a case of waiting for the next letdown.

Laois hadn't even dared to think of the weekend's other shock and what it implied. The night before, Kildare had beaten Meath. Meath had held an Indian sign over Laois for some time and, even more than Dublin, revelled in the chastising of upstarts. Kildare, on the other hand, were eminently beatable. Not pushovers, but not as forbidding as Meath would have been. Laois youngsters checked a date with their elders. 1946? Yes, 1946. That long ago. No Leinster title since then. Imagine, just imagine.

Anyone with a bit of romance in their soul had to be happy for Laois, or so I thought when the cab driver who was taking me to Heuston asked me what I'd thought of the match.

'It was a great win for Laois. I'm delighted for them.'

Now, I don't know if this is just me, but I've met some bizarre characters driving taxis in Dublin.

A guy stoned out of his brain who kept rolling down his window and squirting passers by with a water pistol. A man who burst into tears because his girlfriend had gone back to her previous fella even though the ex had recently cooked her cat in a microwave oven. Another man who told me he was cheating on his wife with a young one from the country and then produced a wallet snapshot of the young one with very few clothes on. A guy who thought Hitler was unfairly criticised because the Germans had taken a lot of annoyance from the Jews. But there's always room for one more.

'You're delighted for Laois. You're delighted for Laois. Well, if Laois had beaten whatever shithole you fucking come from do you think I'd be delighted? I wouldn't, or I wouldn't tell you if I was. But you're delighted for Laois. All the culchies are fucking delighted when Dublin get beaten. Can you explain that to me, bud? How come yiz are all so happy when Dublin get beaten? Is it jealousy or what?'

We were only at Aston Quay yet. Make conversation, some kind of conversation.

'I should just about make my train.'

'Oh yeah, back to whatever kip you come from where they'll be all be fucking delighted that Dublin lost too. Back home, home to your mother. Cause that's what yiz all do down the country, live with your mothers till yiz are 50 years old. Farming, lying back and collecting the money from the taxpayer and the EU. And then yiz come up here and are delighted that Dublin get beaten.'

Merchant's Quay. God.

I only said I was delighted Laois won for fuck's sake.

'Jesus chum lighten up. Where's your sense of humour?'

Waiting in the station bar with its weird light and shell-shocked clientele, I got talking to some Laois fans. They were definitely Laois fans. I checked first. They were all wearing Laois jerseys but

I made sure just in case they were disguised Dublin fans eager to expose the perfidy of the culchies. The funny thing was that I hadn't been half as delighted about Laois winning as I was since I'd met the taxi driver.

The Laois lads confessed to being hurling rather than football fans. They were from Borris-in-Ossory but had already despaired of the county hurling team ever doing anything in their lifetime. I told them about my idea for the book and they seemed to approve. Then a lightbulb went off over one guy's head.

'I knew I seen you somewhere. You're on the telly sometimes with your man John Kelly talking about films.'

'Sometimes. Not in a while.'

'I don't watch it. I just catch it sometimes when I'm flicking through the channels. But you seem to be the whole time giving out. Will you be giving out in this book too?'

No. Not at all.

5

I Left My Heart in Mayobridge

22 June: Ulster Senior Football Championship
Semi-Final; St Tighearnach's Park, Clones
Down 2–10, Fermanagh 0–11

Midway through the second half of the Ulster semi-final in Clones, Fermanagh looked embarrassingly superior to Down. After a poor start, which had left them four points down at half-time, Fermanagh had scored five points in a row and almost had a couple of goals too. Down had been reduced to 14 men and, though only a point behind, looked in trouble all over the field.

Then Michael Walsh surged forward from midfield and found former Fermanagh player Shane King, who let go of the ball just as he got clobbered by a couple of backs. James McCartan did the rest by planting a shot in the corner of the net and the game was as good as over. There shouldn't have been anything final about that breakaway goal, Fermanagh were only two points behind with an extra man, but there was. Confidence restored, Down pulled away to win comfortably and proved that, when their tails are up, they take a lot of stopping.

The recent heroics of Armagh and Tyrone notwithstanding, Down remain the Kerry of the North. They were the first team to bring the Sam Maguire across the border in 1960, and the side that broke a 23-year provincial famine by winning it again in 1991, beginning the current golden age of Ulster football. There has always been a glamour about them. Down are the famous red-and-black jerseys, Sean O'Neill twisting his body like a contortionist to score the incredible opening goal against Kerry in the 1968 final, Paddy Doherty returning from professional soccer in England to inspire the team of the early sixties, Mickey Linden swerving past defenders to pick off another point. If Kerry are the Real Madrid of Gaelic football, undisputed kingpins, then Down are Manchester United, a team synonymous with flair who intrigue even when they're in the doldrums. Given that they were up against all that, it's not surprising Fermanagh folded.

Down, or more precisely Daaan, were also Chelsea Mick's team from his old man's manor. And they've always been one of my favourite teams too. Like Wexford hurlers, the glory of their past seems to promise present-day fireworks even when the form book suggests they've sunk to a quotidian level. This was one trip I was really looking forward to.

The road from Dundalk to Newry is now the only one that still gives you a sense of crossing the border. The crossing between Blacklion and Belcoo was one I knew well as a youngster when it was hard not to feel a chill at the hugely fortified barracks and the British soldiers pacing nervously at the barrier, sometimes breaking into a run, which did little for my teenage nerves. Now you don't even notice it. Ditto with the road from Emyvale to Aughnacloy. But, while there's nothing to indicate the actual passage from Louth to Down, there's a strange few miles on this side of the border that still marks the area as a twilight zone – ramshackle buildings functioning as currency exchanges, exhortations to buy the last fuel before the border, businesses that must be some of the last thriving from that anachronistic boundary that caused so much trouble and cost so many lives. That few miles reminds you that you're passing into another jurisdiction.

Mayobridge had won two Down senior titles in a row, three of the last four, and had done this without anything like the population of some of their rivals. It's a toss up as to whether you'd call it a village or just a collection of houses on the side of the road a few miles outside Newry. The GAA pitch totally dominates the place (its only other claim to fame is as the birthplace of Tommy Sands and Kieran Goss, there's obviously a sensitive acoustic thing going on here).

I had a feeling I'd like the people here if the club PRO James Gallagher was anything to go by. James Gallagher was one of those characters who can never do enough for you. He'd responded when I'd emailed the club web page to express an interest in coming up. Since then, there'd been several phone calls to make sure I was happy with all the arrangements. Two days before, there'd been one to give me the name of the best place to stay in Newry. The day after that, he'd rung to tell me he'd booked me into Mayobridge's only B & B, so I could enjoy the night without worrying about getting back to Newry. When I landed at the ground, he was mortified that I hadn't rung him to arrange a lift out of Newry. But he quickly atoned by arranging for the landlord of my B & B to pick up my bags while I watched Mayobridge take on Loughinisland in a Down senior football league match. He was the kind of guy you dream about having on your side when you visit a strange place. Before the referee had thrown the ball in, I'd been introduced to nearly everyone at the match.

Small clubs don't win senior titles unless they're seriously well organised, and the Mayobridge setup was highly impressive. They had even produced a programme for this routine, Friday-evening league match, one packed with enough advertisements to make county teams jealous. It was an striking testament to the amount of commercial activity generated these days by formerly isolated rural communities that, a couple of generations back, would have done most of their business with about three people. If Western civilisation is ever destroyed, the Mayobridge GFC programme will be a fair guide to what's needed in order to rebuild it.

There was McEvoy's Self-Service Drapery 'where everyone

gets dressed better for less'. Natacha McMahon and Caroline McNeill's Mobile Beauty-Therapy Service, which provided tea-tree skin care, St Tropez tans and aromatherapy oils. Keenans Bar with 'multimedia screen and projection facilities'. Friar Tucks 'the home of the cheeseburger'. Fegan Plaster Mouldings, Executive Wood Products, The Kitchen Workshop, A.J. Plumbing Supplies, Trufit Tyre and Exhaust Centre, D.E.F. Plastering Contractors. And Mac's Bathrooms and Tiles, 67 Newry Road, Mayobridge, County Down, BT34 2EU. 'Support our advertisers,' said the programme, 'they supported us.' They had, in spades.

Weekday evening matches are a relaxed affair, the province of the diehard fan and someone who fancies looking at an hour of football where the pressure attending county and club championship games is absent. They're the matinees of the GAA world if you like, although the opening few minutes of the match were given a bit of spice by that venerable GAA institution, the serial slagger of referees. These lads, usually middle aged or a bit beyond that, operate at most grounds. There's usually just one of them, a kind of updated version of the ancient town crier. Instead of 'midnight and all's well', their war cry is, 'Two minutes gone and the referee is an *amadán*.'

Abuse of referees is, of course, no laughing matter – if you're a ref. No, actually, it's a blot on the game and we'll be coming to it later. But the serial slagger isn't connected to the people who lose their heads in tight championship matches and subject refs to vile personal and, occasionally, physical abuse. There's an element of ritual about what the serial slagger does. It doesn't matter whether the game is important or not, whether the score is close or not, it doesn't even matter whether the referee is good or bad, this boyo has to go through his performance. The comments are aimed as much at his fellow spectators as the referee. They'd feel uneasy if they turned up at the park and the air wasn't being rent with imprecations by their old favourite. Like the playing of the national anthem and the wearing of white coats by umpires, this form of abuse is part of the package. So within a couple of minutes of the throw-in, we got, 'Home to Bryansford with you, ref.'

'Take it in 30 yards, why don't you? I've glasses here, do you want a lend of them?'

'Ref, you're biological.'

The last of which drew both chuckles and enquiries as to whether he might have meant diabolical.

Yet for all the light-heartedness, both teams were deadly serious about the game. Mayobridge were leading the Down league while Loughinisland were near the bottom and fighting against relegation. Even though they'd played in the gruelling tie against Fermanagh five days earlier, the youngsters – Michael Walsh, Benny Coulter and Ronan Sexton – started for the Bridge with the other county players – Brendan Grant and Mickey Linden – held in reserve. The caution didn't seem to be necessary, they'd put 17 points on Loughinisland a few months back and no one seriously countenanced defeat.

The main Mayobridge worry was Benny Coulter, the slight, red-headed forward who'd been the best player when Down had won the 1999 All-Ireland minor final. He'd been outstanding too when the Bridge started winning county titles, a boy doing a man's job. They raved about the football he'd played when Mayobridge won Páidí Ó'Sé's football tournament down in West Kerry. Yet that kind of form had been missing when Down had beaten Monaghan and Fermanagh, he'd looked like just another promising young corner-forward, a few steps off the pace at senior level. The fans wondered if he was short of confidence because they knew he was one of the best young players in Ireland. They had, they said, seen him do things few other footballers his age would even attempt.

The first quarter of this low-key league match didn't do much to assuage their fears. Coulter, in the right corner, was slow to the ball and snatched badly at a couple of point opportunities. Even worse, Loughinisland were making a game of it because Dan Gordon monopolised midfield.

Gordon was a youngster who had been impressive against Monaghan and Fermanagh. He'd arguably been more impressive than anyone else against Fermanagh. Stationed at full-forward, he won ball after ball off Barry Owens, who Fermanagh people thought of as their best player, and would have had a goal if the referee had not blown for a penalty just before his shot crossed the line. Gregory McCartan had slotted the penalty for Down anyway, but it was a pity Gordon hadn't been credited with the goal. What he'd done – outfielded the full-back, turned him and gone straight for goal – was something you didn't see very often from a Number 14 these days.

Big Dan was a throwback to an older model of full-forward, the *ne plus ultra* of which had been Kerry's Bomber Liston. Men with a few inches to spare over the six-foot mark on the wall, they waited at the edge of the square for high ball to be bombed in and caused havoc once it was. Liston had been unstoppable, there'd been Joe McNally of Dublin, Paul Earley of Roscommon and Ray Cummins during his football career for Cork.

Now (like their soccer counterparts, the old-fashioned good-in-the-air Niall Quinn-make of centre-forward) they'd gone out of fashion quicker than mullet haircuts. Managers had hit on the idea of the two-man full-forward line with pacey corner-forwards isolated inside to make hay from quick low ball. The lighthouse model of attacker had been remaindered, which was why it had been so good to see Gordon in action at Clones. He was like The Strokes, a new version of something from the past too good to just let die.

On that Friday night, though, Gordon wasn't playing full-forward, he was at midfield and dominating before someone had the bright idea of switching Coulter out to mark him, even though the Mayobridge boy was giving away four inches in height and a couple of stones in weight too. It might have been the decision that turned Coulter's year around because, from the first ball, you could see him relishing the challenge of taking on his county team-mate. Within a few minutes, he looked liberated, and much more interesting than the game, was the contest within it between these two prodigies. Coulter started by breaking the ball away from Gordon but soon he was producing prodigious leaps to rise above the six-foot three man's head and come away with the ball. The Mayobridge men turned to me as if to say look, do you see what we mean about Benny, that's what he can do when he's himself.

Coulter was winning enough ball for Mayobridge's attackers to begin the predicted demolition of the Loughinisland defence, but Gordon never dropped his head. As they say, he gave Benny plenty of it. First one of them would come out on top, then the next. The game was routine but this was enthralling, proof that the most unpromising of matches could yield great rewards. The only ingredient required was a couple of inter-county players.

A complete stranger could have strolled into the Mayobridge ground and picked out Coulter and Gordon as inter-county players immediately. When you saw duels like this, you realised how good county stars really were and how much they constituted an elite corps within the game. There were very many good club players with a wide range of skills who worked hard and were fit beyond the call of duty, but a real inter-county player, someone who could compete in the big games in front of the big crowds, had something special about him, a bit of oomph, a *je ne sais quoi*. He'd been showing these qualities often since he was an U-12. Even if he'd been a late bloomer, once a member of the elect, the inter-county player couldn't avoid showing his class every time he played. Clubs won All-Ireland championships with two or three county players on the team and, even against good club players, these guys starred. Kieran McDonald in the 2000 club final, Colin Corkery in 2002, Oisín McConville in 1997, they could look like overage players in a juvenile match. It was never any harm to be reminded of this, of the accomplishment and application it took to play in the big games of the summer, of how special the inter-county footballers and hurlers are. See them against their peers and you might focus on their weaknesses but see them in their original environment and you saw why they'd become the chosen ones.

Bernard Mulhern was the best footballer I ever played with. In secondary school, he played centre half-forward. I was in the full-forward line and bore the same relation to him as a parish-notes correspondent in a local newspaper bears to Shakespeare. There were other guys in the school who played underage football for Roscommon and Sligo but they were only trotting after Mulhern. By the time he was 15, he was the best player in the whole school. He'd score five or six goals in a school-league game, then produce the same form in a colleges match. By the time he was senior, other schools double and triple marked him in the knowledge that they had much less to fear from the rest of us unmarked than they had from Mulhern marked by just one defender. He could solo run quicker than most lads could sprint, kick points from 50 and 60 yards, was the best fielder, blocker of kicks and thrower of dummies on the team. He didn't drink or smoke and wasn't fazed by the worst of tackles, though he carried a back injury that would have caused most lads to beg off football altogether. When he was still an U-16, I saw him mark a player who'd been the star of the Roscommon minor team a year previously and eat him alive, scoring two goals that required 50-yard slalom runs through defenders unrestrained by strictures against GBH. I could not imagine how anyone could be better at football than Bernard Mulhern. He was playing a different game.

Mulhern went on to enjoy a respectable inter-county career. Sligo were, as usual, struggling for most of his playing days, yet he showed enough at wing half-back to make Railway Cup teams. A respectable career but not a glittering one. Yet he was, by any standards, an outstanding sportsman.

So what must the guys on the echelon above him, the players

who grew up to star in All-Ireland finals, have been like? What must it have been like to play beside them in school or with the club? How excited must the managers of the underage teams have been when they saw these lads playing for the first time?

What I'm getting at, I suppose, is the huge natural ability possessed by the guys who make it big at inter-county level. One of the strengths of the GAA is that these are ordinary people who remain part of their local community. Yet that shouldn't make us forget that many of them are also extraordinarily gifted. An analogy, I suppose, could be made with traditional musicians. I grew up in south Sligo, in one of the heartlands of Irish music. It produced Michael Coleman, arguably the greatest fiddler of all-time, and an array of other hugely talented players, Fred Finn, Peter Horan, Seamus Tansey, Jim Donoghue among them. Foreign television crews came to film them, enthusiasts from abroad came to record them, they played on television, at festivals, in concert halls. They were artists of the highest calibre. Yet, to the local people, they were also just men from over the road. People took great pride in them and knew they were talented but perhaps underestimated just how massive their achievement was because they were used to seeing them every day. So it is with the best footballers and hurlers. They are just like you and me, except in one crucial regard. Put them on a pitch and they're geniuses.

You could see that in the second half when Benny Coulter raced out the field and looked for a short pass from a 45. He chipped the ball into his hand, then threw two outrageous dummies that nobody saw coming and, despite being off-balance, drove a 20-yard shot into the bottom corner of the net. That was the county touch, the moment they'd be talking about in the bar afterwards. Mayobridge romped in for an easy win, but Coulter's victory over Gordon had been both narrower and more exciting.

If I'd suspected before that Mayobridge were the kind of club who do everything right, the social facilities confirmed my suspicion. The club bar was both pristine and huge, a cross between a sports hall and the bar of a multi-starred hotel. And the trophy room was something else altogether, a huge act of memory that was a tribute to everyone who'd been involved in the club. Some clubs aren't much into commemoration and make do with a few photos stuck up in the bar or in the local pub. But if they saw what Mayobridge had done, they'd realise how much inspiration can be drawn from remembrance of times past. There was nothing boastful about the room, it just made an eloquent statement about tradition. The dozens of team photographs, the framed newspaper cuttings of club and county successes and the medals and trophies themselves sitting in the space set tidily aside for them spoke of an immense and benign local pride. The star of the show was the Down senior championship trophy, which I was privileged to hold as one of the members explained, 'That was donated by a Mayobridge businessman in 1905.'

'It took a hell of a long time to come home,' said another.

'Eighty years.'

For 80 years Mayobridge had been also-rans, a position made all the more painful by the flourishing of their near neighbours and deadly rivals, The Burren, who'd even won two All-Ireland club titles. But, in 1999, they'd won their first championship in 80 years, largely because of a player who came in at the same time as a man bearing a tray of sandwiches that would have been sufficient to feed the two teams who'd played that evening.

'They're all yours, Eamonn.'

The player who'd just come in had caused a major stir at Clones, even though he'd only come on in the last few minutes and the ball had only gone in his direction twice. He won the first ball with ease and set up a score. Two defenders got the jump on him when the second ball was played in and were a couple of yards in front. The sub threw himself past them, caught the ball, somersaulted, and played it off to a team-mate. That elicited the biggest cheer of the day because this was no ordinary replacement.

For a start, he was 39 years old, easily the oldest player to line out in the championship. And, secondly, he had once been in an exalted position experienced by only a handful of players in every decade. In 1994, Mickey Linden was, indisputably, the finest player in Ireland.

Years like that, when a player was his side's Man of the Match in every game and simply could not be neutralised, were few and far between. Maurice Fitzgerald had enjoyed one in 1997, Seamus Moynihan's 2000 was similar. Peter Canavan's 1995 had been of the same order, though terribly spoiled by the fact that Tyrone didn't win the All-Ireland that year. But only Fitzgerald's eternally unmatchable year surpassed what Linden had done in 1994. He started off by scoring six points from play against a notoriously parsimonious Derry defence in one of the finest games of football ever. He then tore Tyrone and Cork apart before facing a tough Dublin back-line on a wet and windy day in Croke Park, the kind of day that could have been designed to neutralise speedy corner-forwards who liked to carry the ball.

The game was low scoring, tight and tense. Linden rose above all that and kicked four points from play as well as laying on the only goal for James McCartan, setting it up so exquisitely that McCartan was left with the easiest scoring chance in the history of All-Ireland finals. Linden's 1994 was a kind of Platonic ideal of corner-forward play. Yet, nine years later, when most of his peers had taken to the golf course or the pub, there he was tumbling between two defenders to win a ball in a game Down already had sewn up. Why?

'You don't think of the medals you've won when you're going for the ball in any game. If you have the desire to play football then you do what you can do at the moment. Lots of players call it a day in their early thirties when they have three or four good years left in them. It's like the papers on Monday calling James McCartan and Gregory McCartan veterans. They're only 32, they're young men. Instead of believing the press, players should say that if they work hard enough and stay fit enough they'll be able to carry on. Plenty of players could have carried on as long as I've done.'

Except that they haven't. Linden is the picture of physical fitness. His clubmates said he has a gym in his home and trains every day. He is the epitome of the old phrase 'there isn't a pick on him'. And he's also got that driven quality you notice in many top footballers and hurlers. Almost a week later, he was still bulling about the behaviour of the Fermanagh defence.

'You always have to deal with rough play but some of the antics of the Fermanagh players were just disgraceful, there's no place for it in the game. In all my career, I never got any verbal abuse but Benny Coulter got terrible abuse the whole game. They were constantly chipping away at him, it seemed to be a tactic.'

Linden seemed understandably protective of Coulter and Walsh – who'd been only 10 years old when Linden won his first All-Ireland medal with Down in 1991 and barely walking when he'd first played for the county. He knew they'd play for the county from when they were U-12s. It was a good time to be embarking on an attacking career.

'It's become a much better game, an awful lot better for forwards to play. The big change was taking the frees and sidelines from the hand. It totally changed the game, made it an awful lot quicker, made it more difficult for the backs because they had no rest. There's more protection now too. Back in the eighties, the corner-back would hammer you before the game even started.'

Sometimes he thought about quitting, maybe for as long as a month, but something always made him come back. He kept testing himself against the other players on the Down panel, checking that the speed was still there, and he was in the top five when the team did sprints. As far as he was concerned, there was nothing anomalous about his longevity.

It's a feature of Irish life that when someone leaves a room, the door will hardly be closed before someone gives their true opinion of them. There was a couple of seconds hush after Linden bade a courteous farewell and then everyone seemed to speak at once.

'That man has no airs or graces, you know, not like some county players.'

'He never changed at all.'

'He'd be down here coaching the Under-8s and the Under-10s, kids that weren't even alive when he was at his best.'

'A wee girl asked me at a match one day to go up and get Mickey Linden's autograph for her. I said why won't you get it yourself and she said she was afraid to speak to him. Mickey couldn't understand why that was when he's just an ordinary fella.'

I could see where she was coming from. This isn't a terribly cool confession, but I get a huge kick out of meeting players I admire. I've been lucky enough to meet quite a few footballers and hurlers who were heroes of mine in my younger days and the experience always knocks me out. In one respect, Mickey Linden is an ordinary fella. His job, a driving-test examiner, is the kind employed by sitcom writers to indicate diffidence and ineffectuality. But in another respect he is, well, he's Mickey Linden. The wee girl was merely showing the requisite amount of awe.

The man who told the story about the wee girl knew what Mickey Linden had experienced better than anyone else in the bar. If a greatest Down team of all-time were picked then Tom O'Hare would join Linden on the 15. He'd been left corner-back on the 1968 All-Ireland side and is regarded as one of the finest players to ever fill a Number 4 shirt. He was a big friendly bear of a man with more than a hint of devilment about him but he'd turned wistful when Linden had spoken about playing in his late thirties.

'You're right, Mickey. You'll be a long time retired.'

Something in his voice spoke about the way life might sometimes seem like an anti-climax when you'd scaled peaks in your twenties. He agreed that Down had brought a new tactical awareness to the game but, in the next breath, admitted that he hated tactics. Michael Walsh wandered in and insisted Down wouldn't get the hammering everyone was predicting Tyrone would administer in the Ulster final.

'We came within a point of them the year they won the Under-21 All-Ireland.'

'But they didn't have Peter Canavan on that Under-21 team,' said O'Hare but he waited till Walsh had left the room before he said it.

It was a long night and a good night until probably the most accommodating B & B host in Ireland, Pat Brennan of Hillview House, showed up to give me a lift home at two in the morning. Before I left, they presented me with a club top and baseball cap, which I proudly wore to several games later in the summer. The father of Ronan Sexton, another Bridge player on the Down team, insisted that there was nothing at all strenuous about my journey from West Cork to Down in one day.

'He's a long-distance lorry driver,' someone explained.

There were stories about games from the early days of the association. The one where a team had protested by uprooting the goalposts and running off with them, the local derby where a man had gone among the visiting supporters to take a sideline kick and wasn't seen again for two days, the team who'd puncture the ball with a knife if they were losing. And, inevitably, the talk turned to the days when the county we were sitting in had been part of a war zone.

To GAA people, Ulster might mean Jim McKeever and Kevin Armstrong, Frank McGuigan and Paddy Moriarty, Peter McGinnity and Sean O'Neill, but to the rest of the world it had meant car bombings, sectarian shootings, booby traps, plastic bullets and hunger strikes – apparently endless cycles of violence. The period in which the Sam Maguire hadn't crossed the border stretched from 1968 to 1991, a spell largely coterminous with the Troubles, or at least the worst of them. Yet, even in the most appalling of years, the GAA had continued to thrive. Every year produced county champions and club champions. Even in 1972 when 467 people died, there'd been an Ulster final. It had been a remarkable achievement to keep the games going in the circumstances.

'People say the Troubles had a detrimental effect on the GAA but I think it made people draw closer together. People became more aware of their Irish culture,' said James Gallagher.

'I'd retired before the worst of it started but you'd hear from lads about being stopped going to games and getting harassed,' said Tom O'Hare.

'We were lucky. This area wasn't really affected, it didn't impinge on us much here,' said Gerry Quinn an immensely likeable raconteur who'd once been chairman of the club but who, these days, had to miss matches because of heart trouble.

It didn't impinge on us much here. Think about that and then ponder the extreme resilience of the ordinary GAA people from the six counties. Strictly speaking Mayobridge had been almost untouched by the Troubles. A Catholic man had been abducted and killed by the UVF in the early seventies and there were allegations of collusion by the RUC. And, in 1989, three British soldiers had been killed by a bomb hidden in a derelict house in the area. But you're only talking about a small rural area here. Newry, just six miles away and town for people in Mayobridge, had an extremely bloody Troubles while few of the county's villages hadn't witnessed some carnage.

It was the same all over the North yet, when you talked to people from outside the exact black spots of the Troubles, they said the conflict hadn't really touched them, the worst things had happened a few miles over the road, they were happy to have been spared so they could get on with their lives.

I don't think I'd realised how noteworthy this attitude was till the aftermath of the September 11th atrocity when, for months afterwards, people rang television programmes, talked to news-papers, accosted you in pubs to explain how personally upset they were by what had happened in New York. They'd lost all faith in humanity, they couldn't go about their work, they were depressed and fearful that we were all going to kick the bucket before Christmas. A lot of people felt sorry for themselves. Yet, for 30 years, people in the North had to deal with bombings and shootings happening in the next parish over. And they got up to go to work the next day, raised their families, played football at the weekends. This wasn't happening on television and for them the chances of straying into the crossfire were considerably greater than those of Osama Bin Laden despatching anthrax to businesses in Waterford, Mayo and Sligo (as, and it's deeply embarrassing to remember this, some of us were convinced he had). People in the North got on with their lives against a hugely dispiriting backdrop and got very little credit from people down here. In fact, some people wondered why those Northerners were always going on about the Troubles. What was the big deal? Why couldn't they be stoic and accepting of their lot?

Loughinisland, the club beaten by Mayobridge that evening, are probably best known in GAA terms for being the home club of Mickey Linden's old county team-mate the excellent wing-forward Gary Mason. Yet that's not why the name of the place will forever ring a bell with people. On 18 June 1994, members of the UVF murdered six people in a bar there. The dead had just watched Ireland defeat Italy in the World Cup. Unpunished Catholic jubilation was obviously too painful to imagine for the gunmen. The mood turned sombre when I mentioned that night. Tom O'Hare broke the silence.

'I remember it well. We were watching the match in the bar here, delighted with the result, and then the news came on and showed what had happened in Loughinisland.'

He shook his head. That was something else I couldn't imagine, knowing that someone could come in the door of your pub or your GAA club and spray the place with gunfire because you kicked the ball with a different foot to them. Those decisions were random. It had been Loughinisland but it could have been any other Catholic village.

The people of Loughinisland might have been excused if they had sunk irretrievably into hatred and bitterness. Yet they didn't, and were one of the clubs that sponsored the Down motion to have Rule 21 (which excluded members of the security forces from joining the association) removed. Mayobridge were another of those clubs and when the rule finally bit the dust, after the RUC had been abolished and replaced by the PSNI, Down were the one Northern county that supported the removal. In doing so, they got the GAA out of a hole, as they'd hardly have been able to push through the motion without the support of at least one county board from across the border. And if they hadn't, the GAA would have been on the other side of the fence from the major political parties down here and the SDLP, all of whom supported the new police force. The association would have been corralled with Sinn Féin, away from the middle ground so important to its continued appeal.

The forgiveness and forbearance shown by Loughinisland is humbling and points the way towards better times on this island. That spirit of compromise and bridge-building is typical of the Catholic population of Down, which remains the greatest stronghold of the SDLP. The SDLP and the GAA have always been intertwined in Down. Maurice Hayes, credited as secretary of the county board with paving the way for Down's breakthrough in the sixties, was one of the senior figures behind John Hume's party for years. It's become kind of fashionable to dismiss the SDLP now that the war seems to be over and the party may well be doomed to a Fine Gael-style decline into sclerotic irrelevance. The muscular certainties of Sinn Féin can be afforded now that the guns are silent. Whether the guns would ever have fallen silent without the oustretched hand symbolised by the Loughinisland gesture is another matter.

The talk turned back to football and, when Pat Brennan dropped me in to Newry the next morning, the landmarks he showed me were sporting rather than political. There was James McCartan's house, a huge ranch of a place, D.J. Kane's bar, Ross Carr's estate agents. Mind you, I did meet a man in pub near the bus station who revealed to me exclusively how Armagh had won the All-Ireland the year before.

'You see, it was all politics. The Southern government were very keen to get the Armagh boys onside for the peace process. So your man, Dr Martin Mansergh, went down to the dressing room and asked Colm Cooper and Mike Frank Russell outside for a second. He tells them that they'll have to lose the game for the sake of the peace process and that's why the Kerry boys kicked all those wides in the second half. A lot of people don't know that, you know.'

Well, a few more of them do now. And you thought that there'd be no exclusive revelations in this book.

Benny Coulter seemed to be a different player after that evening in Mayobridge. In the Ulster final against Tyrone, he tore down the left wing and cut in along the end-line. The defence seemed to have him covered, but I remembered the outrageous dummies he'd thrown against Loughinisland and knew he wouldn't be able to resist trying one. It worked, he got through and scored a goal. Early in the second half, he spread-eagled the Tyrone defence and laid on another goal. Dan Gordon, the man he'd battled so hard against in the league match, got two goals in the same match. At the end of the season, young Benny was chosen on the Ireland team to play the Compromise Rules series against Australia. Dan Gordon just missed out.

As Michael Walsh had predicted, Down didn't receive the expected hammering from Tyrone in the Ulster final. They got a draw in what was probably the best football game of the year and might have won but for some slipshod refereeing. The hammering arrived in the replay when the extent of Down's humiliation hid the fact that it hadn't been a bad year for them. Their young players had finally started to look the part at senior level, the wins over

Monaghan and Fermanagh looked good in the light of subsequent performances by those two teams and there might be more big red-and-black days in Croke Park before this decade is out.

Mickey Linden retired from inter-county football at the end of the season. But he'll hardly be bored, there are those U-8 and U-10 teams to train, and there's a young Linden playing with them.

That Mickey will be down at the Mayobridge club training those teams in the first place shows another unique feature of the GAA. There are devoted people giving up time to train youngsters in other sports, but they're not often major stars. Michael Owen is unlikely to give up a couple of evenings a week to coach the kids from his home patch, Ronaldo doesn't alternate matches for Brazil with games for the barrio where he was reared. In the GAA, there is an everlasting connection between a player and his club, whose orbit he doesn't escape no matter how high he rises. This self-lessness and community spirit ensures that there will always be another generation of footballers and hurlers coming through.

Community spirit is something that is easy to invoke rhetorically, but hundreds of former inter-county players give it practical expression every week. After the heights they've scaled and the work they've put in, it would be easy to throw the boots and shorts into a cupboard and take to the golf course, the couch or the pub. Yet they go back to the most basic level of the game, the youngsters who have to be taught from scratch how to kick and catch and solo run. You could hardly be further from the Croke-Park limelight but the Mickey Lindens of this world carry out their new tasks with the fastidious excellence they brought to their former careers. And it bears fruit. Last time I heard, Mayobridge had won the county U-12, U-14 and U-16 titles. Their bid for a third Down championship in a row failed when they lost by a point to Bryansford in the county final. But they'll hardly have to wait another 80 years for their next title.

I know I'll be watching for their results from now on and, if you ever want to reassure yourself of the wonder of the GAA, then take the road out from Newry on a Friday night during the summer, watch for the signs to Mayobridge and if there isn't a game on have a pint in the bar and indulge in the pleasure of talking football with people who love it.

And the best part of it is that there are plenty of other places where you can do the same thing.

6

Train I Ride, Several Hundred Corkmen Strong

29 June: Munster Senior Hurling Final
Semple Stadium, Thurles; Cork 3–16, Waterford 3–12

A Munster hurling final in Thurles is one of the few Great Irish Experiences that lives up to its advance publicity. The Galway Races is a long traffic jam, drunken businessmen, second-class horses and corporate hospitality in the company of Charlie McCreevy. Traditional music sessions in West Clare pubs can involve four guitarists, three bodhrán players, two mandolins, two bouzoukis, a lad with a set of bongos and a solitary inaudible fiddler. And, if you've still got a shirt on your back and two eyes in your head as you leave Killarney after the weekend, you're one of the lucky minority.

But the Munster hurling final is special. It even imparts a bit of atmosphere to Páirc Uí Chaoimh, that unfortunate tribute to the architectural taste of Nicolae Ceausescu. In Thurles, it's irresistible.

It can also be a bit irritating. Neither Cork nor Tipperary people are noted for their reticence and most GAA fans have been informed several thousand times that there's nothing to match a Munster hurling final. There are memorable historical occurrences that illustrate this fact. Take the Cork centurion on duty at the grave when Jesus was raised from the dead.

'Truly this man was the Son of God, boy, but this is nothing compared to a Munster hurling final.'

Or the censored statement by the Tipperary astronaut who was the real first man on the moon.

'One small step for man, one giant step for mankind, but I'd prefer to be at the match in Thurles to be honest with you.'

Unfortunately, this insistence on the primacy of the Munster hurling final is well founded. While it hardly outshines the All-Ireland finals, it is far and away the most impressive provincial decider and arguably the only indispensable one. Many an argument in favour of an open draw has foundered on the rock of, 'Ah, yeah, but what about the Munster hurling final?'

Laois footballers would go on to make an even better argument in favour of leaving the provincial system as it is, but there's no tampering with the Munster hurling final. Easier to suggest lighting a fire with pages from *The Book of Kells*. All that tradition cannot be gainsaid. Mick Mackey playing with a bandage on his uninjured leg to fool Tipperary and scoring 5–3, people sleeping overnight in Liberty Square the night before the Great Bicycle Final of 1944, Christy Ring being chaired off the field with blood running down his face after preventing a Tipperary four in a row in 1953, Richie Bennis scoring a 70 with the last puck of the game to give Limerick their first Munster championship in 33 years, Richard Stakelum's 'the famine is over' speech. There is a magical and visceral quality about the legends of the Munster final that does not adhere to those from any other provincial shooting match.

A Munster hurling final is bliss indeed, but one in Thurles is very heaven because there is no better place in Ireland to watch a match.

Five reasons to be cheerful about Thurles

1. Many GAA fans are hopelessly nostalgic and secretly feel that big matches were probably more authentic and atmospheric back in the day. So they love the fact that Thurles is irresistibly antediluvian. The narrow streets, poky pubs, three-card tricksters, eating houses and general old-fashioned air of the place makes you feel like you've cycled a hundred miles to the game on your High Nelly, gone to mass that morning and will celebrate scores by throwing your hat into the air.

2. Thurles is small enough to be completely dominated by a big match. There isn't a nook or cranny in the place where you can be ignorant of what's going on in the town. Dublin and Cork are big enough for normal life to continue on the day of a final, Thurles gets completely taken over by one.

3. The pitch is actually in the town. I know this sounds like an obvious statement but think of Páirc Uí Chaoimh and the long, cheerless journey past warehouses, silos and industrial estates it entails. Or the Gaelic Grounds in Limerick, a couple of miles out a road that, on match days, is like a gridlock theme park. Markievicz Park, Pearse Stadium and quite a few others guarantee you a soaking when the day is wet, whereas you can leave down your pint in Thurles and be in the stadium five minutes later.

4. Liberty Square is a fantastic focal point. Just stand there and the big-match atmosphere comes straight at you.

5. Most of the crowd head back into town the one way, which enables conversations to be struck up about how great the match was, even if it really wasn't.

Croke Park might be the best stadium in the country but Thurles, town and ground, remains the best venue. It also had an ace propagandist for years in the late Raymond Smith, whose hurling books were largely a plea for the supremacy of Munster hurling and had, I believe, a character-moulding effect on a whole generation of youngsters who grew up to be GAA writers.

Smith was a Tipperary man himself and one of the old-style GAA hacks whose likes are rarely found anymore. His books aren't the slickest of reads and it's easy enough to take the piss out of them. For example – and this drawback is shared by the few surviving members of his generation still plying their trade in the country's press boxes – managers and players he interviewed would come out with quotations suspiciously long and journalistic. They go a bit like this.

'Well, we got off to a fine start and, during the first quarter, our greater experience at this level certainly told as we built up a 0–7 to 0–2 lead. However, our opponents were always going to enjoy a period of domination and they stormed back before half-time with stylish wing-back Ned Fitzpatrick lofting over two spectacular points. Nevertheless, we resumed command in the second half with powerful full-forward Jimmy Larkin scoring his fourth goal in three games, despite a couple of fine saves from acrobatic net-minder Tom Stack and, eventually, we managed to run out winners by seven points after a fluent exhibition of attacking hurling, Raymond.'

It's easy to sneer when you've got a dictaphone to help you with interviews of course. But when I was 10 years old, my favourite book in the world was *The Players' Number Six Book of Hurling* which was where I learned everything about Ring, Mackey and various other legends, including Martin Kennedy the Tipperary full-forward who would apparently stick a feather in the ground around the 21-yard line. When the ball came in, he would wait till it was near the feather, pull on it while facing away from goals and know it had found the net. Where else would you have got information like that? So I always think of Raymond Smith when I'm at a match in Thurles because, in his own way, he contributed as much to the legend of the place as many players.

There are other incidental pleasures to Thurles. Hayes Hotel might be an unlovely enough spot but anyone with a sense of history has to experience a *frisson* when they have a drink in the very premises where the GAA was founded. The town is not without its share of eccentrics so I wasn't surprised on the Saturday night to walk into a pub and find a grey-haired oul' lad beating a hurl off a table and roaring, 'Jimmy Doyle, Jimmy Doyle would beat the lot of them.'

Then there's the new joy of hearing the country's famous comic catchphrase said in the proper accent. There is nothing fundamentally idiotic about the Tipperary accent, it just so happens that when Pat Short of *D'Unbelievables* decided to award his characters a catchphrase, he drew from his home town – which is Thurles. A few years back, people used Cavan accents to denote bucolic imbecility, having picked this up from Niall Toibin. But that accent is being superseded as everyone's favourite funny voice by the Tipperary twang that features in so many *D'Unbelievables* sketches. (*D'Unbelievables*, incidentally, must know their GAA well because the skit with the fanatical underage coach is the funniest thing ever performed about the association.) Which means you can have hours of enjoyment luring the inhabitants of Thurles into unwittingly quoting Pat Short.

'John Doyle's from Tipperary, isn't he?'

'Dass ryat.'

'Cork and Waterford are playing in the final tomorrow, aren't they?'

'Dass ryat.'

'We've got the world tonight.'

'Dass ryat.'

A notable feature of the night before the final was the number of Cork people who'd opted to make a weekend of it in Thurles as well. Everywhere you looked, they were there in their red jerseys with a couple of bars of 'The Banks' primed behind their lips. They made it impossible to get a room next nor near the town itself so, once more, I repaired to the Templemore Arms where the only room left was the Bridal Suite. What could I do but take it? This time around Mickey Joe Harte didn't disturb my sleep. It looked as though I was in the clear.

In the morning, the hotel was swarming with Cork people whose progress to Thurles was in the nature of a triumphal

. procession. Waterford might have been Munster champions, and they might have beaten Cork the year before, but those were merely piffling details. There didn't seem to be a single Corkman who gave the champions a chance of making anything like a decent game of it. This must have driven Justin McCarthy, the former Cork star who'd done such a brilliant job with Waterford the year before, demented. But, in hurling especially, tradition always seems to trump recent achievement. The Waterford win was regarded as an aberration, fair play to them and all that but Cork and Tipp had taken their eye off the ball for once. A Cork win would be regarded as an inevitability, a restoration of the natural order.

There were more than a few mentions in the Thurles pubs of Bertie Ahern getting booed the day before when he travelled to watch Dublin scrape an unconvincing victory over Derry in Celtic Park. The general consensus seemed to be that if Bertie was going to keep presenting himself for the delectation of the fans, in the end they were just going to get fed up of it and realise they were being used as props to bolster the Taoiseach's man-of-the-people image. For the past year, he'd used sport the way the American president used war and these trips to Croke Park and Lansdowne Road looked increasingly like Dubbya's uniformed landing on an aircraft carrier. He couldn't step inside Croke Park without a remark being made by a commentator on how much the Taoiseach loved sport. The fawning tone that accompanied the comment was reminiscent of the way BBC commentators at Wimbledon greeted a sighting of the Queen Mother.

Back in the real world, Cork took over Semple Stadium and had once more managed to excavate enormous numbers of Confederate flags. I sometimes wonder if members of survivalist militias in Mississippi and Alabama stray into Irish-American bars and feel stirred by this inadvertent tribute to the memory of General Robert E. Lee and his boys – before noticing the Japanese flags and becoming totally confused.

After the huge tension in the build-up to the semi-final, Cork fans were considerably more relaxed this time out. Back in 1982, the Rebels had beaten Waterford by a record 31 points and some of their supporters seemed geared to witness a drubbing of the same order. When Setanta strolled in between Tom Feeney and Stephen Brenner, who had hesitated like two courtiers unsure of who had precedence, and calmly rolled the ball into the net from an awkward angle with most of the fans still settling themselves into comfortable viewing positions, that didn't seem to be an unlikely prospect.

Then, just a couple of minutes later, the Cork full-back line, who'd gone into the game with a huge reputation for unflappable impermeability and would be henceforth regarded as an Achilles heel, went into a complete panic under a routine high ball and gifted possession to Waterford corner-forward John Mullane, who struck a shot into the net with some glee as his team proceeded to show Cork that they weren't Munster champions for nothing.

Cork couldn't seem to get hand nor hurl near the ball and the discomfort of their supporters was made much worse by an unthinkable occurrence. Diarmuid O'Sullivan was being destroyed by John Mullane who looked not just yards faster but stronger and more determined as well. This would have been bad enough if O'Sullivan had been a normal corner-back, get skinned in that position and you were likely to give away painful scores. But O'Sullivan was a hell of a lot more than a normal defender, he was the Cork folk hero. When he did something well, it got twice the reception that a telling intervention from any other Cork player did and had a proportionately disheartening effect on the opposition. And when he did something badly? Well, that wasn't common but the man from Cloyne was probably suffering the worst 20 minutes of his career.

It was strange how some players, rather than others, became folk heroes. The status wasn't naturally conferred on the best player on the team, take for example Liam McHale and Willie Joe

Padden of Mayo. McHale had been a better midfielder than Padden and had contributed far more to Mayo over the years, yet the public seemed to regard him with a faint suspicion and dwelt on small weaknesses rather than major achievements. In contrast, they loved Padden and mourned him when he was gone, turning a few outstanding matches into a career of unparalleled brilliance for Mayo. Mick Lyons of Meath had been a folk hero, so too John Leahy of Tipperary. Fearlessness had something to do with it and flamboyance and expansiveness of character. O'Sullivan had all three of these qualities. When he wound up to make one of his massive clearances from the full-back line, there was a definite theatrical quality to it. Supporters could frequently see him driving the team on with a fist wave and a roar. He was a leader who hadn't yet lost the faith of his constituency.

The Battle of Clontarf, I recall from the history books, began with both sides nominating a champion to take part in the first fight of the day. If the tradition had held, the people of Cork would have nominated Diarmuid O'Sullivan as their champion. Except today, John Mullane was doing the equivalent of cutting O'Sullivan's head off and parading it around the battlefield on a pike. The first quarter was barely over when the corner-back was taken off. No one had ever expected to see that.

After the match, the word was that O'Sullivan was suffering from flu, but he was equally disabled by the decision to play him in the corner rather than at full-back where he was one of the finest players in the country. Away from the centre, the imposing build and barnstorming physical style looked quite crude and cumbersome. It was evident that he would only be a shadow of himself if forced to continue in this new position. O'Sullivan would eventually solve this problem the way folk heroes do, by seizing the day with a mixture of bravery and hubris, putting himself first for the sake of the team.

Late in the first half, Cork had fallen behind 1–8 to 1–1 and their defence had been rattled into unusual narkiness. Even Wayne

Sherlock, normally possessed of fakiresque calm, got involved in a wrestling match and ended up throwing an opponent's helmet on the ground. But, just before half-time, Cork scored a couple of points to leave them just five behind. When the whistle blew, you could see the Cork fans beginning to believe again. There weren't many Waterford supporters in the vicinity, but the few that were looked nervous and apprehensive despite being in the lead.

'We're the kings of fucking it up,' one of them said to me.

They were to an extent but the crown was not held solely by Waterford. There was a multiple monarchy of the counties from outside the very top echelon. Everyone agreed that Cork, Kilkenny and Tipperary hurlers and Kerry footballers expected to win every time they took the field. The corollary of this was that, when other counties played the bigger teams, they seemed to be nagged by a suspicion that, no matter how well things were going, it was still possible to manufacture a heartbreaking defeat. Waterford had done it just two years previously when blowing a much bigger lead against Limerick, scarcely giants themselves.

I had long and painful experience of this myself, coming from Sligo. Sligo's championship record was one of almost uninterrupted failure yet, if they'd won even half of the games they had drawn or lost narrowly, the story would have been very different. In tight finishes, they came out worst; when bad luck was being apportioned, they came away with an unwanted job lot. So it was with many of the weaker counties. This was one of the things the people of the bigger counties were referring to when they spoke of tradition.

The Sligo GAA History, an excellent if tear-jerking volume, should have been renamed *Inexplicably*. Sligo were cruising to victory in the 1965 Connacht final against Galway when *inexplicably* rampant full-forward Mickey Durkin was switched to midfield. They were beating Roscommon in the 1962 Connacht semifinal when someone *inexplicably* miskicked a 50 and Roscommon broke up the field to score a winning goal in the last minute. To be a player from Sligo or Leitrim, Fermanagh or Wicklow was akin to being the heroine of a Thomas Hardy novel. The minute hope reared its head, fate would beat it back down. Waterford's history wasn't that miserable but they had nevertheless been mightily unsuccessful compared to the big two in Munster and their next-door neighbours, Kilkenny, whose huge success almost stood as a reproach to the bigger county.

Is there a psychological component to all these famous fade-outs and legendary last-minute losses? Or is it that quality tells over 70 minutes and Waterford's half-time lead was illusory, bound to last just as long as it took Cork to get into their stride. Whichever is the case, it took Cork just eight minutes to draw level in the second half. The most wounding of their five points came from Tom Kenny, little known outside the county before the championship had started but suddenly looking like Cork's best player. He won the ball deep in his own half and just surged past the challenge of two Waterford players as if he were a sports car moving from 0 to 100 inside a couple of seconds. He repeated the move a few minutes later, moving past an opponent who might as well have been standing still. It seemed to speak volumes about Cork's sudden effervescence and Waterford's latest surrender to history.

The second half would, most likely, have been a procession were it not for John Mullane. By the end, I was hoping, my Cork domicile notwithstanding, that Waterford would win. Part of this was underdog solidarity, but mainly it had to do with the quality of Mullane's performance. He collected a crafty short free from Paul Flynn and beat a crowd of defenders with a superb shot but that was only a warm-up act for his third goal of the game. There was perhaps only one spot where he could have put the ball in order to avoid simultaneously a block, beat Donal Óg Cusack in goal and find the net. No problem to Mullane. Bearing in mind that Waterford were getting hurled off the field and the supply of ball was rare, it was probably the finest individual display of the year. It was also one of the best Munster final performances in many a day but, if Waterford lost, who'd remember it that way? I suddenly wanted them to win, so the man didn't have the game of his life in a losing cause.

A lot Cork cared about my wishes. Niall McCarthy, whose previous claim to inter-county fame had been bleeding on the bus from Derry, ran the legs off the normally invincible Fergal Hartley, Ben O'Connor landed a series of breathtaking points from way out on the right wing (fans wondered if he'd ever hit an ordinary point, no one could remember one, he seemed to prefer being off-balance, leaning backwards, a couple of inches from the sideline) and Joe Deane got the goal that wrapped it up.

There was a great deal of sympathy among the Waterford fans for Brian Greene who'd marked Deane out of it for much of the game. Then he got under one ball and let the full-forward get the wrong side of him and score. Three years previously in Thurles, T.J. Ryan of Limerick had beaten Deane to almost every ball. Midway through the second half, Ryan had once more shaken off his man and emerged to strike a mighty clearance to the middle of the field. A moment later, the ball was flying back in over Ryan's head and Deane transferred it to the net with a sublime overhead pull. A second had been enough to negate most of Ryan's fine work. The same thing happened to Brian Greene. Deane seemed to operate on the principle outlined by the IRA in their message to Maggie Thatcher after the Brighton Bombing. 'We just have to be lucky once, you have to be lucky all the time.'

One moment's inattention sufficed. Marking Deane must be an inordinately nerve-wracking job because he was so economical. In contrast, Ken McGrath, who'd scored seven points in the previous year's final, had got enough space and time to equal that tally, but managed to pull all his shots wide – not by any great amount, but wide all the same. And Paul Flynn? He'd picked off a reasonable three points from play but looked extremely discommoded by a belt in the face sustained when the ball was

111

flying over the bar in those early panicky minutes for the Cork full-back line.

Like the French rugby team or Brazilian soccer team, Cork were a side whose confidence seemed to expand with every score. By the final whistle, it was hard to imagine that half-an-hour earlier, they'd looked listless, puzzled, defeated. There would be reports the following day that the Cork crowd had sung 'The Banks' in celebration. This was pushing it a bit because 99 per cent of Cork fans, or at least that percentage of those doing the singing, only seemed to know one line from the venerable song. 'Where we sported and played neath the green leafy shade on the banks of my own lovely Lee.'

Not once was another word of the song uttered by the supporters, though it was still hard not to be collared in pubs for the next month by Corkmen eager to explain the rush of county pride they'd experienced when they heard 'The Banks' being sung in Thurles.

It's not surprising that 'The Banks of My Own Lovely Lee' doesn't get much more than cursory treatment. Though it's a stirring old song, it's also a relic of a very different Ireland, one where people could gather around a piano in a parlour and sing in all seriousness about green mossy banks and wild flowers, my fond bosom's partner, the shell-girdled shore and sea-feathered eagle. It comes from a world of the contests of athletic youths, the sporting of comely maidens, the rosary at night and the bishop throwing in the ball. A world epitomised by Jack Lynch who you could imagine rattling out all the verses of 'The Banks' at the drop of a hat before being followed by someone giving a recitation of 'Dangerous Dan McGrew' or 'The Night they Cremated Sam McGee'.

'Flow on Lovely River' belongs to that milieu as do 'My Lovely Rose of Clare', 'The Offaly Rover' and the other county songs, which is why they don't get much of an airing at matches. The gentle balladeers of the past have been vanquished by the Wolfe

112

Tones and Pete St John as surely as Bing Crosby got ousted by Elvis. The most popular chant among the Cork fans is actually the rhythmic, 'Ooh to be a, ooh to be a, rebel.' With rebel coming out something like Gggrebilll.

That was what they were singing in the pub near the station in Thurles, which must make a fortune every match day. The pub has the atmosphere of a carnival marquee because most of the bar furniture has been taken out the better to cram in the punters. I never envy the bar staff. One evening I missed the train home and watched them wade through the spilt drink and fag butts as they began to clean the place up. The Gggrebillls armed themselves with cans and bottles for the journey home and at Thurles station, for perhaps the only time in the championship, I saw what it might be like to look at the fervour from outside and not particularly like it.

That weekend I'd read a column by a female journalist who complained about feeling harassed by supporters travelling to a game. My feeling was that she was probably looking for something to complain about. How could you feel threatened by GAA followers for God's sake? I tend to react the same way when I see someone from a residents' committee complaining about there being too many matches played in Croke Park. Being caught up in the excitement of the championship means you don't have much sympathy for those who've resisted the spell. But, just this once on the train from Thurles to Cork, I saw how there could be people who dread encountering the aftermath of a major final.

Drink was involved. Sometimes, coming up to a game from Cork, you saw young lads lacing into cans of lager and cider in the train station at eight in the morning and wondered what kind of state they'd be in later that day. Here was the answer. You'd like to know where these guys drank in case you ever strayed in there by accident.

'Ooh to be a, ooh to be a rebel.'

A couple of women with Waterford banners set up a faint

answering chant on the opposite platform and were answered first by a few cans being thrown at them and then by the universal song of the woman hater. 'Tits out for de lads, getcha tits out for de lads.'

More than a few people were glad when the train arrived the next minute. I found myself entering a carriage after a couple of the guys who'd done the singing and throwing. A young African man in a suit was sitting in the end seat. One of the boyos glared at him and walked on, shaking his head, building up gradually from a mutter to a shout. 'Did you see him there, that black cunt, that fucking black cunt. What's he doing on the train?'

By the time they got down to the end of the carriage, they were in an extreme state of outrage. If you'd looked in the window and not known what they were saying, you'd have concluded that they'd been subjected to a serious assault or cheated out of an inheritance.

'The black cunt. Can you believe him? Down there at the end of the carriage.'

The companions they'd joined shook their heads sympathetically. A few other people seemed to be cringing for the African passenger. They stopped but I'm not sure anyone, myself included, would have intervened if they'd continued. There was a sense of entitlement to their racism which meant that challenging it would have been viewed as offensive. It was an awful moment. I remember when I lived in London during the late eighties and early nineties the sudden silent dread that would infect a Tube carriage when soccer fans got on. I'd hate to think that any person would ever feel that way when they saw county colours approaching. Especially if it was because of their race or sex being held against them.

The trip down was boisterous but it was also tuneful because I ended up sitting across from a bunch of Cork supporters whose number included a man of exemplary vocal prowess. He was in his forties, red-faced, carrying a few extra pounds, was liberally sprinkled with tattoos and wouldn't have struck you as one of life's canaries. But he silenced the whole carriage by singing a perfect version of that mushy seventies slow-set favourite 'Hey there Lonely Girl' by Eddie Holman. OK, it's not the greatest song in the world, but the original is sung in a falsetto you wouldn't imagine a big burly lad from Cork would be able to approach. He matched it note for note. Perhaps I'm giving him too much credit, it could be that Eddie Holman has moved to the northside to Cork city and developed an interest in hurling.

Holman and his crew sang us out of Tipperary into North Cork and, for a hardy-looking bunch, they were unusually addicted to tender lyrics and melodies. 'Ain't No Sunshine When She's Gone'. 'Seasons in the Sun'. And 'Katie', which they all sang together. Seeing that unlikely gang intoning with great love Jimmy MacCarthy's sensitive lyrics about the genius of druids when the sunlight hits the tomb and stained-glass streaming lights and yellow-coloured lampshades, it struck me that here was a song which had become a ballad the same as 'The Banks' once had.

'We are red, we are white, we are fucking dynamite.'

The young Rebels had put up with enough sensitivity from their elders. When we got off the train, there was a fight in Kent Station between about a dozen youngsters, where one lad was pushed to the ground and kicked in the head. I wasn't surprised.

By some miracle, I get a taxi near the station that brings me as far as Bandon. In Bandon, they're jubilant about the Munster final too, so jubilant that a group of men have emerged from a pub on the bridge to play a game of bowls. Bowls, or road bowling, is probably the biggest sport in West Cork after Gaelic football with tens of thousands of euros being wagered on games every weekend. It doesn't have followers as much as devotees who travel to as many scores as they can to see who can get the small steel ball around the roads in the smallest number of shots. There's a whole subculture surrounding the sport, like those connected to the other old sports of trotting and coursing, and a lot of the same people tend to be involved.

There's almost a pre-modern air to the whole thing, an agrarian wildness you also see sometimes at the big race meetings when the all-night poker games are going on in the hotels and people are trying to beat the three-card tricksters and playing pitch and toss. They take their sports very seriously indeed. If the GAA hadn't been organised, perhaps these sports would be the most popular all over the country instead of the rural pockets in which they survive. They're worth a book of their own. The national coursing meeting at Clonmel, for example, has pulled 50,000 spectators over the three days, yet the only national media coverage it ever gets is the same photo every year of a hare being chased by a hound. Yet anyone who's been to one of those meetings knows it's attended by the same kind of people you meet at GAA matches, not the bloodthirsty savages of urban legend. The last time I was in Clonmel, the winning dog was owned by the current Clare hurling manager Anthony Daly, and Tony Considine, one of Ger Loughnane's great backroom team, got up to sing 'My Lovely Rose of Clare' at the presentation ceremony.

Anyway, the men of Bandon are playing bowls by the bridge at one in the morning. The score has everything – spectators, men charging up to take their shots, a lad showing where the bowl has landed – except bowls itself. The Italian director Antonioni got great praise back in the sixties for the closing sequence of his film *Blow-Up*, which showed a group of people miming the playing and watching of a tennis match. Apparently, this interrogated conventional notions of reality and perception. Well, the boys were interrogating them in Bandon as they played their imaginary game, their only guide an excitable dog who would run out to where the bowl might have landed and bark furiously. When one mighty throw was unleashed, the dog went a couple of hundred yards away and the man jumped with victorious joy. Just then his opponent pointed at me and said, 'He called it.'

The erstwhile victor suddenly became deflated and walked over to me.

'Why did you call it?'

'I didn't say anything.'

'Well,' he said pointing to my accuser, 'he hardly made it up.'

On Monday I went to Sheehy's Pub on The Square in Skibbereen, my preferred venue for the post-mortems that are almost as enjoyable a part of the championship as the games themselves. But my mind wasn't on the game. I had to clear something up with the landlord.

'Gerry, what does calling mean at a bowls match?'

'Who called who?'

'A man in Bandon said I did but...'

'Eamonn, you should never, ever call someone. It's the worst thing you can do at a score.'

And I still don't know what it is.

7

Home to the Dark Province

6 July: Connacht Senior Football Final
Pearse Stadium, Galway; Galway 1–14, Mayo 0–13

The man giving out the tickets at Cork bus station warned me to queue early for the bus to Galway.

'There's some big do in Knock this weekend. The buses are going to be wedged.'

And wedged they were. Half the old dears in Cork seemed to be making the pilgrimage to Monsignor Horan's old bailiwick. One of them was accompanied by a boy of around eight who, for 200 miles, told us all his secret.

'I'm blessed by God. He saved my life five times. One day I was on the road and a car came fast round the corner and, only for God, I would have been nearer to the corner and that was one time. Then Daddy was out feeding the cattle and the bull kicked him in the stomach and I would have been with him only for God. That was the second time.'

God continued to watch over the youngster. If there'd be anyone with a short fuse on the bus, they might have snapped. But there wasn't. And that was the sixth time.

As we neared Knock, the pilgrims began to break out cans of lager and sing, 'Can you hear the devil sing? No-oh, no-oh. Can you hear the devil sing? We can't hear a fucking thing.'

OK, they didn't, but it's thoughts like that which get you through the tortuous collection of bus journeys that brings you from West Cork to South Sligo. Going to Croke Park for the Leinster hurling final would have been handier, but I was bound for the Connacht final. We went back a long way.

All the way back to 1975 when my father, my mother, myself, my two brothers and my two-year-old sister travelled to Markievicz Park to watch Sligo play Mayo. It was a draw and we dutifully trooped off to the replay in Castlebar as well. I'd love to be able to say that the historical significance of Sligo's first provincial title in 47 years is etched upon my psyche. But, when you're seven, you're more bothered about not being tall enough to see over the other spectators, never mind the hawkers, then ubiquitous at all games. I knew that Mickey Kearins was the greatest footballer of all time and that was enough for me. (I still believe that, as does everyone else in Sligo.) But what exactly it meant for Sligo to have gone since 1928 without winning Connacht didn't have much impact on me. When you're seven, a year seems a long time and beyond five is prehistory. Now that 28 years have gone by without a repeat of that victory, I fully appreciate how much it must have meant. At this rate of progress, I'll be 54 when Sligo manage it again. My baby daughter, not yet two, will be 20.

I've been at a lot of Connacht finals. My mother would just say, 'Let's go to the Connacht final', and, a couple of hours later, we'd be in Hyde Park or Castlebar just in time for throw-in. There was no need to worry about tickets in the eighties, a crowd of more than 15,000 was considered a bumper house. The football seemed to be taking place at one remove from the All-Ireland because nobody ever named a Connacht side as a serious contender. A promising Galway team had threatened great things briefly at the start of the decade and then fizzled out, humiliated by the failure to beat a 12-man Dublin team in the 1983 final. The Croke-Park humiliations were legion. Mayo failing to get a single score in the second half in the 1981 semi-final against Kerry, Galway losing by double scores to Kerry the year after, Galway losing 0–18 to 1–4 to Cork in 1987, Mayo being completely outclassed by Meath in 1988, even if a couple of goals at the death took the bad look off it, Mayo losing by an incredible 23 points to Cork in 1994. As far as the outside world was concerned, Connacht football stunk worse than a cattle lorry running over a skunk in an alley full of dustbins behind a fertiliser factory.

Yet the Connacht final remained the biggest game of the year for me and many others. When I moved to England, I timed my summer holidays to coincide with it, and so did other lads I knew. It helped that my girlfriend of the time watched football as well (an uncle and a first cousin had played senior for Roscommon, her father had won county medals, there *is* no getting away from the GAA). Why the dedication to something so apparently substandard? To quote Shakespeare, specifically Touchstone in *As You Like It*, it was 'an ill-favoured thing, but mine own'. We knew that neutrals weren't going to travel in their droves as they did to the Munster hurling final, so the Connacht final remained an expression of defiant regional pride in a place that needed all the occasions of pride it could get.

The Sunday Game was what really stuck the knife in. Connacht finals looked slow and sloppy with loose defences and inaccurate attacks compared to the Leinster and Munster deciders. Part of this had to do with the television coverage itself, the camera placings and huge crowds can make the most quotidian of Leinster finals look thrilling, while RTÉ always seemed to send second-string equipment down to Castlebar or the Hyde. But it also reflected a genuine lack of quality in the play. We could cod ourselves all we liked, but none of the teams that won Connacht titles in the eighties (discounting the fine Roscommon team that had its last kick in 1980) were realistic contenders for the Sam Maguire.

One journalist even described Connacht as 'the dark province' a comment that, with its undertones of a footballing Third World, was resented. We were good at resentment in the West, All-Ireland winners in fact. The newspapers bristled with reactions to slights real and imagined. I remember the *Leitrim Observer* describing a harmless bit of joshing in the *Sunday World* as 'racist'. Racist! The people of Leitrim were a race suddenly. So at different times, app-arently, were the people of Sligo, Galway, Mayo and Roscommon. One thing we knew for sure was that 'they' had it in for us even if we weren't completely sure who 'they' were. The decrepit state of football in the West merely mirrored the parlous condition of the province as a whole. Around 1986, you could hardly pick up a paper without reading a prediction that, in 20 years, there wouldn't be anyone left in Connacht, everyone would have emigrated, villages would be completely deserted. I got my first job that time on the *Roscommon Herald* and I used to love poring through back copies of the paper from the unimaginably halcyon days of the early seventies. There were dancing carnivals every weekend of the summer, music in the pubs a few nights a week, people returning from England instead of going there. I had, I decided, been born too late. A prosperous West would never be seen again. The proof of that were the kids with English accents who arrived home aged seven or eight and 10 years later got their Leaving and went back to the land of their birth. There were a few of them in every school – Paddies in England, Brits when they came back here.

But here we were in 2003, myself and the mother going to an all-ticket, full-house Connacht final in a refurbished Pearse Stadium involving one of the All-Ireland favourites. Things had changed utterly and the managers of the two teams – John Maughan of Mayo and John O'Mahony of Galway – were the architects of that change, in the football world at least.

O'Mahony's 1989 Mayo team had come the closest to securing a Connacht victory in an All-Ireland final since the 1966 Galway win that hung like a millstone round the province's neck. But what he'd done with Leitrim in 1994 really shook up football in the West. Leitrim not only won the Connacht title for the first time in 67 years, but almost went the hardest possible route, defeating Roscommon and Galway away and beating Mayo in the final at Hyde Park. At this remove, it's an even more remarkable achievement. Leitrim had, with a couple of exceptions, an ordinary squad of players and a history of failure weighing down on them. Their victory had, I think, important repercussions. The major counties in the province realised that, if Leitrim could win a Connacht title, there was no excuse for the likes of Galway or Mayo especially. And people had been sheltering behind excuses for too long, blaming emigration for the state of the game in those counties though they still remained two of the most populous GAA units in the country.

John Maughan was the manager who made Connacht football a serious force again. When Mayo defeated Kerry in the 1996 All-Ireland semi-final, it was the first championship win by a Connacht team over Munster opposition in 30 years. When they beat Offaly at the same stage a year later, it was the first over a Leinster team in 26 years. Today, when Connacht teams compete on an equal footing with teams from those provinces, those statistics are incredible. But Maughan made the breakthrough and the fact that his team narrowly lost two finals shouldn't detract from the immensity of his achievements with Mayo. They weren't the most gifted team either and he got everything possible from them. He's perhaps the most underrated manager of modern times, doomed to be remembered more for his alluringly exhibitionist line in sideline wear than his contribution to the Connacht revival.

Maughan, it turned out, was fated to be John the Baptist to O'Mahony's Messiah. Galway, who had more skill and confidence than the dogged Mayo boys, won the 1998 All-Ireland. They'd lost the 2000 final in a replay and won the year after. That was why the stadium would be full, the television coverage would be live and contenders in other provinces would take serious note of what transpired in Salthill.

And if the dreary dogfights of the brass age – Galway 1–8, Roscommon 1–5 in 1986; Mayo 0–8, Galway 0–7 in 1987 – had reflected the wider culture at the time, the new improved Connacht final did as well. Like the footballers shocked into effort by Leitrim in 1994, the people of Connacht had tired of bemoaning their dire state and had done something about it. Admittedly, the upturn in the economy had helped but there was a plethora of community activity, a turning away from the idea that Connacht was headed towards oblivion. Some of these initiatives weren't much more than talking shops but they did at least get people thinking about change instead of silently accepting that it could never be.

All kinds of things contributed to a change in the province's self-image. John Waters' brilliant *Jiving at the Crossroads* for example challenged the idea that the West was a repository of backwardness and bigotry and that wisdom lay solely with the panjandrums of Dublin 4. His unabashedly contrarian position gave people an identity to work with. Dublin 4 might have been overrated as an enemy, but it was something to be united against and it stood for all the simplifications that had bedevilled life in the West. When Sean Doherty shafted Charlie Haughey in the Hell's Kitchen pub in Castlerea, there was proof that the peripheral tail could not just wag the metropolitan dog but have it put down as well. Even the success of a group of unlikely rock stars played a part. I arrived home one summer to find people who had, heretofore, consumed nothing but English indie rock gleefully listing the ways they could identify with the songs of the Sawdoctors – haymaking, Ford Cortinas and thumbing on roads bounded by stone walls. Not forgetting Galway not beating Mayo if they had Willie Joe, the Red and Green of Mayo and John Donnellan lifting the Sam Maguire. The Sawdoctors couldn't get away from the GAA either, but there was no sense that they wanted to. Perhaps the most poignant example of how the economic and the sporting renaissance dovetailed had been

Charlestown winning the Connacht club football title in 2001. Charlestown, the epitome of Western stagnation and decline, was described in *No One Shouted Stop* by local-boy-made-good John Healy. It is a great book and the great man who wrote it wasn't to blame for the fact that, for too long, people had thought that no one shouted stop because it wouldn't have made any difference if they had. It didn't matter. They'd shouted stop in the end and 10 miles over the road Knock airport was being used more for sun holidays than emigration. And when Charlestown won that Connacht title, their manager was Steven Healy, John's nephew.

We were at the first Connacht final in Pearse Stadium for many years and the fact of the final being played in Galway city also spoke of the new centrality of the GAA in Connacht. Galway had been playing their home games in Tuam for a decade and a half. Tuam was a ground with a great tradition and would command far more affection among hardcore football fans. But bringing the final to Galway was putting it in the shop window and would attract the more intermittently committed supporter, the kind of person responsible for the growth in attendances. It was easy to deride these people as the 'prawn-sandwich brigade' or to engage in cheap populist sneers at their peers who filled the corporate boxes in Croke Park (so easy in fact that I'd done it myself a few times). But they were the people who fuelled the GAA boom. The crowds at club matches weren't getting any bigger so, it followed, the new spectators were people who weren't fiercely committed to the association, they just enjoyed watching the big games. It had been easy to do the diehard act on it as well when Croke Park was being redeveloped, to say, 'Isn't the place grand as it is. Sure the real fans don't care about all this luxury, they just want to watch the game.'

Which was true up to a point. But the GAA would always have the real fans, the people who were involved in their local clubs and made a trip to some kind of match nearly every weekend of the year. It needed to attract the uncommitted, people who'd fallen in love with the championship on television or who wanted to experience the sporting thrill they'd first experienced when Jack's Army fever had erupted. By doing that, the GAA had made the championships the central communal experience of the nation, instead of just another sporting event.

The proof was in the figures. Provincial finals had never been all-ticket in the past and, in the seventies and eighties, attendances had dropped off dramatically everywhere. Cork had played Galway in an All-Ireland hurling semi-final in 1985 in front of 7,500 fans and the 1980, 1981 and 1982 All-Ireland football-final crowds had fallen several thousand short of capacity. It might look as though the Irish people were irrevocably committed to watching big championship games in big numbers but that wasn't the case. The floating fan couldn't be taken for granted and that was why the future was Pearse Stadium rather than Tuam, even though Galway city was remarkably barren in GAA terms and didn't have a single player on either the county football or hurling teams.

Hardcore or floating, the player most of the fans were looking forward to seeing was Michael Meehan, who was probably the first footballer to become a celebrity before he'd even kicked a ball at inter-county level. The attention given to Meehan was unprecedented and more like an American focus on some college football star and first-draft pick than anything the GAA had seen before. It had to do with a country increasingly comfortable with hype but also with Meehan's obvious status as a prodigy. The previous year, I'd seen him kick seven points from play when St Jarlath's, Tuam, drew 0–22 apiece with Coláiste na Sceilge, Caherciveen, in an All-Ireland colleges semi-final, which probably been the finest game of pure football I'd ever seen at any level.

The players on either team could do no wrong, phenomenal scores became an ordinary currency and, amid all this brilliance, Meehan still stood out. Jarlath's went on to win the final with Meehan again outstanding and he'd gone on to play a starring role in Galway's U-21 All-Ireland win over Dublin even though he was still a minor. Stories filtered through of astounding feats in club games. Even before the National League, Michael Meehan was Gaelic football's wunderkind, its very own Wayne Rooney. And, judging by the league, he'd taken well to senior football. If he hadn't completely lived up to his advance billing, he'd done enough to promise stupendous achievement on the hard grounds of summer.

So there was considerable disquiet among the Galway fans when it was announced over the PA that Meehan wouldn't be starting and that Michael Donnellan, his predecessor as young player with all the gifts, was missing from the starting line-up. Given that Galway were also worried that Derek Savage and Padraic Joyce, the two forwards who'd been consistently excellent for the team since making their debuts five years previously, didn't seem to really be at it this year, Mayo's cause didn't seem to be so completely hopeless all of a sudden. The outsiders confirmed this prognosis by tearing around the pitch in the first 20 minutes, after which they led by a point despite having played against the wind. Maughan's record against Galway was as good as any manager's and the chances of him working the oracle again were being discussed. Then Mayo got a penalty nine minutes before half-time.

You could tell Stephen Carolan did not fancy taking that penalty. He approached it in the manner of a man at a Christmas Day charity swim approaching the icy water. I was right behind the goals and, before the run-up even began, the Mayo followers were predicting a miss. Not even the most pessimistic of them could have forecast just how horrible a miss it would be. Carolan leaned back and put the ball way too high and miles wide. Just to round it off, he'd kicked the ball so weakly that, if it had been on target, the keeper wouldn't have had any problems. It was probably the worst penalty I'd ever seen and I felt extremely sorry for Carolan, one of those players who worked his way into championship contention by picking up a few points in league matches and then had an awful summer. I don't know if I'd ever seen him finish a championship match. Then again, he was a corner forward and his mistakes were forgiven far less readily than those of players in any other position on the field. He didn't finish this game either.

The extreme tension that accompanies the taking of a penalty in Gaelic football has to do with the fact that missing the kick doesn't just deny you three points. A penalty miss is quantified negatively. Sure the goal chance has been missed but the opposition has also received a massive unearned boost. A missed penalty can seem to cost a team six points. An especially good example of this is the one that Kevin McCabe put over the bar for Tyrone in the 1986 final against Kerry. Tyrone were six points clear at the time and, when I visited Ballygawley in the county's footballing heartland, it was a truth universally acknowledged that they would probably have won that match if they'd never been awarded a penalty. Instead, you could see them thinking for the next few minutes about how much easier their task would have been had McCabe put the ball in the net. And, while they were doing that thinking, Kerry were busy wiping out the lead and setting up an easy victory. A missed penalty is one of the best weapons devised to knock the stuffing out of a team, especially if the opposition rub it in by getting a score of their own soon after.

There was a sorry inevitability about it all a few minutes later when two Mayo defenders went to cut out a routine long ball, bumped into each other as if they were 66 per cent of the Three Stooges and left Matthew Clancy in the clear. Clancy, one of those odd players, like Eddie Brennan the Kilkenny hurler, who seems to score nearly as many goals as points, might have been giving a practical demonstration of the word insouciance as he strolled goalwards before sliding the ball into the bottom corner. Mayo had played well for most of the half, Galway had been poor. Galway were 1–5 to 0–4 ahead and that said plenty about the respective merits of both teams. I don't think even John Maughan had any doubts as to how the game was going to turn out once Carolan had muffed his golden moment and Clancy had embraced his.

You could see the difference between the old-school GAA supporters and those who dug the new breed at half-time. The wonderful Roscommon team of the late seventies were being presented to the crowd at half-time as sides usually are on the 25th anniversary of notable triumphs. Some people watched and applauded respectfully but the majority of the crowd did a Mexican Wave that rendered the on-field ceremony a bit ridiculous. The wave must have gone round the ground a dozen times and you wondered what hardy old campaigners like Pat Lindsay and Harry Keegan must have made of such goings on. Objecting to a Mexican Wave makes you look like a first cousin to Oscar the Grouch from *Sesame Street*, but it seemed a pity that the Roscommon players didn't get the tribute they deserved and which must have been planned for a while. I had a real mid-life crisis moment when I heard a father nearby explaining to his young son, 'You see that Dermot Earley. He's Dermot Earley, the Kildare footballer's father.'

Time was surely passing by when a new generation knew the Kildare Dermot rather than the Roscommon one. I suppose it must have been the same for my father when he had to explain that young Michael Doyle of Tipperary had a father named John who'd been one of the great hurlers of his day. Sons replace fathers on the field and the spectators count out their days by the succeeding generations.

By the start of the second half, Galway had brought on both Michael Meehan and Michael Donnellan and were moving with considerably more purpose. Mind you, neither Savage nor Joyce looked anything like themselves. Mayo were given faint and false hope by their corner-forward, Conor Mortimer, whose blond dye-job made him look as though he should be hanging around the poker machines in an O'Connell Street amusement arcade. But every time Mortimer restarted the game as a contest, Joe Bergin broke Mayo's hearts. There'd been a lot of talk about Mayo's James Gill's coming of age as a genuine inter-county midfielder. Gill would undoubtedly be a star soon, but he was giving away a couple of years' experience and a couple of inches in height to Bergin. And where Gill would be at tomorrow, Bergin had reached today. One point where the Galwayman fielded a sideline kick and calmly mapped out space for himself before shooting over the bar was a clear statement of primacy. I knew that John O'Mahony had enormous time for Bergin as both a player and a person and foresaw potential greatness there. This was the clearest confirmation yet that he might not be wrong.

It was all entertaining and bloodless, like watching a match on *The Sunday Game* when you already know the result. Young Meehan didn't fully live up to the hype (it would almost have been impossible to), but he did score two good points and might have had a goal but for a fine save by the keeper Fintan Ruddy. By the last couple of minutes, his brother Declan was soloing the ball first laterally and then backwards as Galway coasted in. The crowd behind the goal got some light relief when an umpire signalled a Matthew Clancy shot as a point though everyone else could see it had gone at least a couple of feet wide. You can't blame umpires because the archaic logic of the game has decreed that they must stand in the very worst place for seeing if a ball actually goes between the posts or not. The mistake didn't make any difference unless you'd had a spread bet on Mayo plus four points.

Besides, the umpire did have a legitimate excuse as, for the last five minutes of the game, his attention was probably drawn skywards as planes from the Salthill Air Show zoomed over the nearby seafront. We could see them as we walked from the pitch to the promenade and the spectacle was, by turns, heart-warming, impressive and disturbing. Heart-warming because the first thing we saw was a demonstration of Air-Sea Rescue by a coastguard helicopter. Impressive because the planes that followed it went supersonic. One second it was announced that they were over Barna and the next they flew into Salthill like the very dream of speed. And disturbing, above all disturbing, because among the planes were jet fighters, built for no other reason but to kill people. And with the Iraqi conflict barely having left our television screens, the American Air Force gave the organisers a treat by providing two F-16 fighters.

Ten days later, I met up with John O'Mahony in Ballagha-derreen. My bias about all kinds of things is probably evident in this book so I'll declare my position here. I think John O'Mahony (along with Brian Cody and Mick O'Dwyer) is the best manager in the game. And, knowing him better, I have a greater *grá* for O'Mahony who had nothing like the illustrious playing career of the other two.

I also think that he's undervalued at times. When Armagh reached the All-Ireland final for the second year in a row, there was an enormous hullaballoo about the feat of management this represented by Wily Joe Kernan. Much scratching of heads went on as people tried to remember the last time a football manager had achieved such a milestone. Yet O'Mahony brought Galway to the All-Ireland final in 2000 and 2001 and came tantalisingly close to steering them to two wins in a row. It took Kerry a replay to get rid of them the first year and Galway's win over Meath the second year was way more convincing than Armagh's victory over Kerry. They'd also won the 1998 final when O'Mahony became the first manager for many a year to bring a team from practically nowhere to win the Sam Maguire.

The side he took over had been well beaten by Mayo in two previous championships, included a number of debut boys and had no background of success in the National League to blood them. It's easy to say now that Padraic Joyce, Derek Savage, Michael Donnellan *et al* were a spectacularly talented bunch of youngsters, but there had been no minor or U-21 All-Ireland win for them. Galway had been blessed with brilliant college players for a couple of decades and done next to nothing with them till O'Mahony took charge.

I've already mentioned the miracle he wrought with Leitrim and he gave Connacht some pride back when the 1989 Mayo team confounded everyone by coming within a goal of beating Cork in the Connacht final. So I wasn't that surprised when a poll of players taken before last year's championship chose him as the most respected manager in football. Yet O'Mahony remains low profile in comparison to several other managers whose achievements are less than his. This is because self-effacement appears to be his chosen strategy to counter the pressures of the inter-county game. You don't read O'Mahony going on about the new scientific way he's worked out to play the game or the cunning psychological games he's devised to goad his players on. Emoting isn't his style, he prefers to stay in the background. Even on Pat Comer's superb video of the 1998 campaign, *A Summer of Sundays*, the man indulges in very little self-congratulation and never points out the many things he got right during the season.

Managers had been very much in focus on the weekend Galway had routinely put away Mayo. The Dubs had bit the dust the previous day, blowing a big half-time lead and getting overhauled by Armagh 0–15 to 0–11. The result was hugely significant and seemed to colour the way the rest of the football championship was viewed to an extraordinary degree. For a start, chirpy Tommy Lyons got the kind of media treatment that would have shook that former Dublin hurler Liam Lawlor. In a year that would produce several firsts in the way the championship was covered, Lyons became the first GAA manager to get a full-blooded, soccer-style, sack-the-boss number done on him.

I found The Chirpy One a bit hard to take myself but the doing he received seemed way too harsh. One of the pretexts for making it open season on Lyons was that he said, after the game, that the sending off of his goalkeeper Stephen Cluxton was the turning point of the game and that Cluxton had been silly to kick out at an opponent. Both of these points were basically true, yet Lyons got the kind of abuse that once greeted Renaissance astronomers who deigned to suggest the Earth might be round. He had let down his players by criticising one of them in public, he was trying to steer attention away from his own deficiencies, etc., etc. The hero of 2002 had become the villain of 2003 with astounding alacrity. For more than a week, papers fulminated against him and it seemed as though the pressure might drive him from the job. He held on and may yet be vindicated.

So why the brickbats? First, Lyons had made mistakes, Dublin looked ridiculously hubristic against Laois and he seemed to lack confidence in his selection policy after that, bringing back players (Jayo, Dessie, Senan Connell) he had previously jettisoned. But that hardly merited the scourging he had received, which could be traced to a situation not of his own making. This was the way his predecessor Tommy Carr had been shafted by the county board two years previously. Carr was an articulate operator possessed of considerable charm and good manners and this may have accounted for some of the outrage provoked when he got his P45.

On the other hand, Carr had failed to bring Dublin a Leinster title during five years in charge, the longest such drought for the county since Kevin Heffernan rejuvenated football in the capital back in 1974. It was said in defence of Carr that the talent just wasn't there in Dublin and that reaching the Leinster final was as much as could reasonably be expected of the team's manager. Another canard that did the rounds was that the sacking of Carr would prove ruinous to Dublin football. And then Lyons came in and won the Leinster championship in his first year in charge, proving those opinions pretty conclusively wrong. No one likes to be proved wrong, which was why the 2003 backlash was so vicious. The fact that Carr was doing very well at the helm in

Roscommon didn't help Lyons' case either. Still, he must have found it ironic that former players called for his resignation and compared his style of management unfavourably with the, apparently, more mature style employed by his predecessor. For all its maturity, it hadn't yielded much in terms of results.

So miserable a weekend had it been for the Dubs that they scarcely noticed their enemies from Meath suffering a far worse defeat – Fermanagh 1–12, Meath 0–9 in Clones was probably *the* shock result of the championship, one that no one could have countenanced. For all their pluck and grit, Fermanagh had been comprehensively beaten by Down a fortnight earlier while Meath had been attracting the old ominous tag when they recovered from defeat by Kildare to beat a very handy Monaghan team. Yet the one county whose players would usually be carried out on their shields rather than surrender had given up the ghost tamely, allowing Fermanagh to run rings round them in an unreal second half. It was probably the greatest win in Fermanagh football history, but the natural jubilation you'd feel when a little county humbled a giant was tempered slightly by a wrenching post-match interview with Seán Boylan.

Seán Boylan was one of those people who naturally elicited your sympathy. Hence the fact that it seemed *de rigeur* to describe him as the 'mild-mannered herbalist'. But he'd almost been ousted as manager of Meath before the start of the season (some far-sighted delegates realised that they'd been a whole year without appearing in the All-Ireland final). And, in the pictures from Clones, you could see that he thought the jig was up. His voice trembled, his face shook, there were tears in his eyes. You could see him thinking that, after all the big games in Croke Park, it would be some indignity to manage his final match in a half-empty Clones on a Saturday evening with his team playing their worst football ever. In the event he survived but these days no one seemed to be unassailable. Not even John O'Mahony with his two Sam Maguires and four Connacht titles in six years.

The weekend's happenings had also copper-fastened an idea of Armagh as some kind of irresistible force, a footballing equivalent of the dark riders from *The Lord of the Rings*. John O'Mahony and myself go back a while. I remember tramping out to the lovely converted clock house that is his home when I was in the first weeks of my first job as a trainee reporter from the *Roscommon Herald* that paid 50 quid a week. The duties included ringing up funeral directors to get local death details, ringing the marts to get some sample cattle and sheep prices, making sure that the wedding notices were all correct (right down to the song played as the happy couple marched up the aisle and the location of their honeymoon), painstakingly taking down the announcements of county councillors concerning recently approved group water schemes and collecting the local notes from the towns of Elphin and Ballaghaderreen, a process that generally involved calling on people whose name the editor had given me.

'Any news?'

'Not a bit.'

'Thanks.'

'Bye.'

O'Mahony was one of those contacts, but he generally had some bit of news to do with the local football club or with St Nathy's College where he taught. At the time, he had a minor local fame as the manager of the Mayo U-21 team, which had won the 1984 All-Ireland title, and one thing I had found out in those early days was that nothing makes a man more arrogant than minor local fame. Not so in O'Mahony's case, he treated the gauche teenager that I was very well, rarely let me go on my way without a cup of tea and a chat and gave me plenty to think about when we talked about football. When I left for England, he'd just got the job as Mayo senior-team manager. Our paths had diverged but, last summer, I was knocking on the door of that house out the Charlestown Road again and his wife, Geraldine, was answering as she had back in the summer of 1987.

Her husband is one of those men who make management sound like a job that merely requires the application of common sense and attention to detail. Brian Cody belongs to this camp, so do Seán Boylan and Brian McEniff. Then there's a messianic tradition to which the likes of Ger Loughnane, Liam Griffin and Mick O'Dwyer belong. These guys probably make for better copy because of the suggestion that they are the conduits for some unknown force that can turn losers into winners. In this reading, force of personality matters far more than calmness and rationality. A newer strain contains the technocrats who feel that success is the result of the precise calibration of technological and psychological variables. They talk about stats and science and their day is nigh. Joe Kernan is probably the brand leader.

One of O'Mahony's more endearing qualities (though one which bugs the hell out of some people) is his refusal to ever admit that Galway should be favourites in any game. Time and again they've played teams, for example Leitrim, who obviously don't have a snowball's chance in hell of causing an upset and O'Mahony has insisted that this is a difficult one for Galway, there's only a kick of the ball between them, it's 50–50. Because of this, myself and a friend had taken to calling him Comical Johnno as he's like the famous Iraqi PR man in reverse. Yet he was genuinely worried about his team's prospects the day I met him. The year before, a long break after an undemanding Connacht championship had left them ill-prepared for a quarter-final against a Kerry team that beat them by eight points. O'Mahony practically shuddered as he contemplated being in more or less the same position again.

'In my heart of hearts, I know the quarter-final will be the big game for us. I just feel that when we get into Croke Park I'll know how well we're going. A four-week gap before the Mayo game, a five-week gap after that. It's hard. But if we get through the quarter-final, I'd feel we have a real chance. A few things have to happen before you win an All-Ireland. First, we'll have to up our level from the Connacht championship and I feel we're capable of doing that. The other thing teams need is some player coming out of the woodwork and really, really taking on the mantle in the knockout stages like Michael Donnellan did in 1998 once we'd left Connacht. Or Alan Keane who wasn't even on the panel when we started the 2001 championship and ended up getting an All-Star nomination as goalkeeper. Looking round we have a fella like Paul Clancy coming to the peak of his powers, there's Matthew Clancy and Michael Meehan is an obvious candidate.'

Meehan. The wunderkind. An 18-year-old country lad who was expected to perform miracles by people who just knew him by reputation. A test for any player … and manager.

'The injury before the Connacht final didn't help him. There's a lot of pressure on him, I try to find out what he's comfortable with. Even if you don't allow the media access, they'll print a profile. Like one of the tabloids talked to Ollie Hughes who trained him in Jarlath's and shouted his praise from the rooftops. You look at that and wonder if it would have been better had Michael talked and kept things in perspective instead of Ollie Hughes saying "this is the best guy I ever trained". I try hard to get the balance right but, in Michael's case, he just doesn't want to do interviews.'

O'Mahony had always been one of the most open managers with the media. You could ring him at home and he'd answer the phone himself and tell you the truth. He allowed Pat Comer to film behind the scenes during a 1998 championship campaign, which might have ended badly and made everyone look foolish. He hadn't hesitated when I asked him for an interview. Yet I'd heard that he'd become a bit weary of dealing with the media and it seems to be the aspect of the job he enjoys least these days. Whatever, we did spend quite a while talking about relations between management, players and the fourth estate. At one point, he pulled me up over something I'd written when Michael Donnellan was accused of clobbering a referee. He was polite but he was firm, like the well-timed shoulder that halts the solo run. He thought I was wrong and wanted to let me know. This might be a flyer but I think the whole Donnellan controversy might have soured O'Mahony on the media. Looking back, the demands that he stop standing up for the player went against logic. Wasn't this just what Tommy Lyons was being pilloried for in connection with the Stephen Cluxton incident? O'Mahony certainly felt the GAA needed to indulge in serious thinking about the way the media interacted with players.

'When I was managing Mayo back in 1989 and 1990, the only coverage we had to deal with were the local papers up to the Connacht final. For the All-Ireland the only additions were the *Irish Independent* and the *Irish Press. The Irish Times* wasn't huge on sport then and *The Examiner* wasn't a factor up here. There was no RTÉ coverage either. Now for any game there are two or three local radio stations, a full set of national papers, tabloids, RTÉ. The game has changed totally. You have to deal with the situation. The young lad who comes into an inter-county team doesn't know the way it works. Why should they know how it works? I didn't know at first. So you have to guide them through.

'There's that whole thing of journalists coming down to the dressing room after the game. That should be formalised so that players are at least allowed to tog in and have a shower before they have to answer questions because, at the moment, it's comfortable for nobody. Maybe journalists hope players will be a bit looser in their answers but it shouldn't be done that way. We should set aside a period of time when everyone is dressed and players don't leave till the journalists have their job done.'

Amen to that. There are certain experiences in my life that I would have been happy to forego. Drunkenly downing a bottle of soy sauce in the mistaken belief that it was Coca-Cola is one. And asking players who are drying their balls with one hand and holding a cigarette in the other what they thought the turning point of the match was is another. But some reporters enjoy it.

O'Mahony was probably being slightly paranoid when he reckoned that journalists like the dressing-room interrogation because tired players may be lured into speaking unwisely. It's more that reporters think that the dressing room holds secrets that may be divulged if they rush in there while the place is still hot from the battle. It's the appeal of the forbidden they seek. That door remains closed to outsiders till the manager gives his word so matters of grave importance must be transpiring, mustn't they? They are but it's questionable as to whether anyone but the players and the management will ever really know what goes on in there, no matter what questions are asked. In the age of reality television, the championship dressing room is one of the few remaining unbreached citadels.

That was part of the appeal of Pat Comer's film (which I love). It showed team meetings and dressing-room speeches and let people think that they'd seen how O'Mahony and his players actually prepared for big games. One speech where the manager appealed to the players to use the thought of their home parishes and their families and their loved ones for inspiration really impressed viewers. Yet I knew players who reckoned the speech was hokey. It was lovely Al Pacino in *Any Given Sunday* stuff, but an inter-county manager of the calibre of O'Mahony wouldn't prepare his team in such a simplistic manner. The really interesting stuff must have been said off camera. Were they right?

'That one that was shown on the camera, I wouldn't be that proud of it. I know it made great television and it shows how comfortable we were with the camera at the time, but I wouldn't take that as an example of good management. It continued the myth of the great rousing speech that gets given at half-time but it's more important to calmly set about changing your plan when things are going wrong. There's not very much you can do at half-time, but the myth is that, if you win, you gave a great speech and, if you lose, there was a row in the dressing room. There was a rumour, after the 1999 Connacht final, that there'd been chairs flying round the dressing room and all that kind of stuff, which wasn't true. The emotional banging-the-tables stuff is going out these days. Fellas are calmer now and what's coming in is a more technical approach with someone analysing the game for you and giving you the stats at half-time, you know, so many kick-outs won, so many turnovers.'

The new technical approach has borrowed terminology from American sports. Every year the championship seems to throw up a new cliché of choice. In 2002, it was the 'impact sub'. In 2003, you kept hearing that teams were 'executing their game plan'. The idea of a game plan comes from sports like basketball and American football where the pattern of play lends itself to precise planning. Even youngsters playing a pick-up game of American football will work out a play before the scrimmage. Gaelic football and hurling don't seem amenable to an integrated plan. So you had commentators coming out with gems like, 'Their game plan is working. They're winning far more of the ball at midfield than the opposition.'

As if some misguided team might have put together a game plan that consisted of going behind early on, losing midfield and playing the match in their own half of the field. Still, maybe there was something in it.

'A game plan is a very simple thing, like a decision to play a lot of long balls. But no, there's no blackboard and XY–AB stuff because football is too fluid a game. The biggest game plan is common sense and thinking on your feet. That's where leaders come in. I'd always give players the licence to take the initiative. The worst thing is when players look to the sideline when the opposition are doing something different as if to ask what they should do now.'

Tomás Mannion was O'Mahony's ideal footballer – 'one of the greatest ever Galway players' – and leader and he worried that they hadn't replaced him properly. He talked about the 2001 final against Meath, and knowing beforehand that Galway had prepared so perfectly that he couldn't see them losing. In comparison, he'd known something wasn't right against Kerry the year after, even when they were still well in the game. And you could tell he didn't know which way 2003 was going to swing. Something he repeated a couple of times was that fans had no right to be getting on the backs of Michael Donnellan, Padraic Joyce and Derek Savage because those players had already done so much for the county that they had nothing to prove. He would say it again before the season was out.

Some people you like, some people you don't. I like John O'Mahony. I'm sure he suffers the same everyday unhappiness and disappointments as the rest of us, but there's an impressive solidity and contentment about the man. I hit off back through Ballaghaderreen, where I'd once worked with ANCO, and passed around two dozen Asians by the time I'd walked a couple of hundred yards. There is a huge Asian community in the town and nobody seems to take any great offence at this. The joke in Gurteen was, 'There was a row in Balla the other night. The guards are questioning three locals and two Irishmen.'

It was some change in 15 years. The towns of the West, which were supposed to be deserted by now, are pulling in people from all over the world. Perhaps the next great Ballaghaderreen manager was turning towards Mecca as I passed.

8

The Páidí Ó Sé–Dolly Parton Connection

13 July: Munster Senior Football Final
Fitzgerald Stadium, Killarney; Kerry 1–11, Limerick 0–9

If a Hollywood director wanted to shoot a Gaelic-football movie, he'd probably set it at the pitch used by An Ghaeltacht in Gallarus, west of Dingle. With mountains at one side and the sea at the other, it would be an ideal, picturesque setting for a film about a plucky bunch of country boys taking on and beating teams from the big towns who dared to underestimate the elemental determination of our heroes.

An Ghaeltacht are the kind of team the romantics like to think the GAA is all about. In fact, the GAA isn't all about any kind of club, but Gallarus is the kind of place that people who don't know that much about the association imagine the teams come from. It's remote, it's lashed by the elements and, a bonus point, it's in the Gaeltacht. It couldn't conform more to the stereotypical Ireland sold by Bord Fáilte and lapped up by the tourists. Our Hollywood director would lick his lips and imagine a sporting version of *Waking Ned* or *Hear My Song*.

But that pitch at Gallarus doesn't play host to some small-time outfit compensating for lack of skill with native guile and spirit. An Ghaeltacht has one of the finest senior football teams in Ireland. Two days after I visited there, five of their players –

Darragh, Marc and Tomás Ó Sé, Dara Ó Cinnéide and Aodán MacGearailt – played for Kerry against Limerick. Managing the team would be the Ó Sé's uncle, Páidí, who fate had contrived to place under pressure for reasons not entirely to do with football. If Kerry lost to Limerick, he would be packing his bags. So An Ghaeltacht was the place to be that weekend.

Once upon a time, suggesting that Limerick even belonged on the same pitch as Kerry would have had you hauled away by men in white coats, who weren't umpires. Limerick had been a bottom-echelon football team from a hurling county. The only provincial title they'd won had been in 1896 when they defeated Waterford by the princely score of 0–4 to 0–1. To put this gap into perspective, we might consider that the first aeroplane didn't leave the ground till seven years later. Limerick's last Munster football victory was closer to the 1798 Rebellion than it was to the millennium. That was Limerick football.

Or rather that had been Limerick football before the turning point, which occurred in the spring of 2000 in front of a few hundred people at Páirc Uí Chaoimh. I was one of the select few witnesses, not because of any particular perspicacity on my part but because there were three Castlehaven players on the Cork U-21 team. Castlehaven, to an extent which surprises me, has become my team since I moved to their home village of Castletownshend. The Haven people are fiercely loyal to their players so there was nothing odd about them chartering a minibus to go the city and watch a Munster championship game that barely registered on the radar. We looked forward to an enjoyable evening. Cork had a very strong team, which included Philip Clifford, the previous year's Young Player of the Year, and Fionán Murray, already a proven force at senior level. No one passed much heed on Limerick.

For about 45 minutes the game went according to expectation. Cork looked stronger and faster and far more skilful while Limerick, though resisting bravely, didn't look at all like a team who might cause a shock. Midway through the second half, Cork were five points up and probably would have gone on to the expected easy win had their players not begun to indulge in the kind of showboating that they'd become accustomed to getting away with against Limerick opposition – passing the ball around with the outside of the boot, trying to beat three men in a row, flicking passes back over their head, that kind of caper. And then a small Limerick corner-forward, Colm Hickey, got hold of the ball 50 yards from the Cork goal and set off one of those I'm-taking-on-the-whole-defence-on-my-own runs that never really work. Except this one did, he went past one defender, two, three, homed in on goal and buried a shot into the net. Cork, as often happens, found it difficult to switch out of exhibition mode and started to panic. Limerick became massively emboldened and caught Cork at the line, Hickey scoring a winning goal with a couple of minutes left. You could say this was the beginning of the Limerick footballing renaissance, except that there hadn't been much of a naissance to begin with.

That Limerick U-21 football team went on to reach the All-Ireland final before getting beaten by Tyrone. Then their manager Liam Kearns, a Kerryman, set about bestowing some kind of respectability on the county's senior side. In 2002, they defeated Kerry in a National League match at the Gaelic Grounds. I was at that game too and I don't think many league victories can have been celebrated with such fervour. The Limerick supporters invaded the pitch and stayed out there for over half an hour. It wasn't surprising. In the entire history of the GAA, this was the first team a senior football team from Limerick had beaten Kerry.

They gave Kerry a good game in that year's championship and, when last season began, were one of those teams who, while not supposed to do anything as dramatic as win the champion-ship, were expected to move another couple of steps up the lad-der. They confirmed this diagnosis in the first round of the cham-pionship when they humiliated Cork by 0–16 to 0–6. Humiliated isn't too strong a word. Cork, who included survivors of that fateful U-21 game who should have known better, once again seemed to expect the game to be handed to them. When it wasn't, they degenerated into a rabble and Limerick could have won by a few more points. One highly impressive win over Clare later and Kearns' team were in a Munster final in which they were given a reasonable chance.

Almost as surprising as Limerick's improvement was the fact of their being given a chance of beating Kerry. Because, while Limerick had spent a hundred years in the basement, Kerry were, well, they were Kerry. They were 32 championships, as many as Galway, Cork, Meath, Down and Cavan put together. They were Paddy Kennedy, Dick Fitzgerald, Jerome O'Shea, Paddy Bawn Brosnan, Mick O'Connell, Mick O'Dwyer, Jack O'Shea, Pat Spillane, Mikey Sheehy, Bomber Liston, Maurice Fitzgerald. Like Brazil in soccer, they started every competition as favourites and when they played the game well, they played it better than anyone else. They were the aristocracy of football.

Yet did the same mystique adhere to the current generation of the Kerry dynasty? Perhaps not. There had been All-Irelands in 1997 and 2000 but the semi-final trouncing by Meath in 2001 seemed to give the lie to the notion that no Kerry team would ever lie down till the final whistle. That side was supine before half-time.

Normal service looked to be resuming the following year. The All-Ireland quarter-final victory over Galway and semi-final demolition of Cork were cut from the classic Kerry pattern book. They took the field with no fear of extremely dangerous opposition, piled up spectacular scores and never deviated from football of great aesthetic beauty. In the first half of the All-Ireland final, Armagh were only trotting after them. But midway through the second half of that game, Kerry seemed to lose concentration. Armagh drew closer, levelled and went one point ahead with nine minutes left and Kerry's answer was feeble. It was so feeble that shock seemed to set in and Kerry were hardly back in the dressing room before Páidí Ó Sé was indulging in some world-class rationalisation.

Kerry, Páidí explained, were glad Armagh had made the breakthrough because of what GAA people in that county had suffered. By the time Kerry had returned home, Páidí was mentioning 'British army helicopters over Crossmaglen' and stressing how happy Armagh's victory made him. There was a protesting-too-much quality about the rhetoric that made it sound like Kerry were insisting they'd given Armagh the final out of republican solidarity, as a kind of postscript to the election of Martin Ferris. After a while, you wondered if Kerry were getting high on their own supply of hype. And when you heard Michael O'Muircheartaigh explaining that 2003 was the All-Ireland Kerry 'really' wanted to win because it was the centenary of their first victory, it was hard not to feel that the people of the Kingdom were deluding themselves and not digesting the lessons of the final defeat. The old arrogance, which had served them so well when they were the undisputed monarchs of the game, seemed to be blinding them. I nearly expected to hear them agree with the man from the pub in Newry and his story of the Irish government plot.

Still, in Kerry's minds, the championship was there for the taking. They'd even got over an embarrassing blip at the start of the season when Páidí had described some of the team's fans as 'the roughest kind of fucking animals'. That was bad enough but he then seemed to cast aspersions on the ability of team trainer John O'Keefe. It was a notably quiet time sportswise and the papers tormented Páidí for a week but no one seriously thought he'd resign. Still, it must have been unsettling even though it did provide an image for the ages when Marty Morrissey interviewed Páidí in South Africa and the manager compared his situation to that of Nelson Mandela. If anything went wrong this year, Páidí had made a mighty rod for his own back and handed it to the Kerry county board.

In Gallarus, there were a couple of pitches with underage teams, both boys and girls training on them. The numbers suggested that nearly every kid from the area was involved with the club. A junior match between An Ghaeltacht and Castleisland Desmonds was scheduled for that evening and the players waited patiently outside the dressing rooms till the youngsters had togged in.

The attendance at the junior game consisted of myself and four middle-aged women who sat in a rudimentary concrete enclosure and ruthlessly criticised every opposition foul, refereeing injustice and home mistake. They performed this function with great cheer, or perhaps it just seemed that way because it was so unusual to hear the usual litany of the hurler on the ditch being given out through the medium of Irish.

'Disaster *is ea Seán*,' sounds far less vindictive than its English counterpart.

Sometimes we take the strangeness of our country for granted. The fact that we, effectively, don't have our own language for example. It sounded downright odd to hear a game of Gaelic football being discussed in Irish and to hear players from one team cajoling, complaining and warning in the language. Yet the GAA and the Gaelic League had been set up around the same time, as part of the same programme of national cultural revival that eventually led to independence. We'd got our own country and we'd started playing our own games again but the language never really made a comeback.

I'm stumped as to why this is. Some people will tell you that the State tried to impose Irish on people and that we don't like being told what to do so that didn't help. That has to be nonsense. The Catholic Church did nothing but tell people what to do and it prospered. Or they'll blame unimaginative teaching methods except that it doesn't seem to make any difference how you teach it, the language never shows any sign of making a comeback.

You get these polls that claim that a large percentage of the population have a good knowledge of Irish, but they're nonsense too. It's easy enough to claim in the abstract that you know a good bit of Irish. Try carrying out a 10-minute conversation with someone in the language and see how easy it is. The proof that the language remains a small minority interest is that few people outside the Gaeltacht use Irish in their everyday lives. They'd no more dream of turning to each other in Croke Park and discussing the game in Irish than they would of talking about the weather in French. As a living language in the mainstream of national culture, Irish is a non-starter.

My mother is from the Connemara Gaeltacht and my father was a fluent Irish speaker. My own Irish is atrocious for no other reason than sheer laziness. Yet I'd claim, while being conscious of the contradiction, to love the language, which is why one of the most heartening trips I made last year was to the Comórtas Peil na Gaeltachta which took place at the start of the summer in the northwestern Cork village of Baile Mhúirne.

If a Gaelic League member had happened to be transported forward in time and landed in Baile Mhúirne he'd have been a happy man. On re-materialising in his own era, he'd trot round to Douglas Hyde's home and say, '*Craoibhín*, old son. I've seen the future and it works. People playing the game of Gaelic football, shouting at each other in Irish, complaining to the referee in Irish while small kids sell programmes written in Irish and ask if you've got any smaller change in Irish while an Irish radio station does commentaries in Irish. The managers discuss tactics with the mentors in Irish and the pubs nearby are full of people asking for drink in Irish. Our mission will succeed.'

The Comórtas is one of the finest spectacles sport in this country has to offer. There are top senior teams like An Ghaeltacht, An Cheathru Rua from Galway and Naomh Abán from Baile Mhúirne itself, and there are small junior teams who've had to battle through qualifying sections to get there and for whom participation is the real triumph. Last year, there was even a team of Connemara men based in London. And there is an extraordinary sense of solidarity uniting everyone there, a sense that they're a community within a community and perhaps an undervalued one at that. When I was there last year, there was great unhappiness that inter-county managers hadn't released some stars and didn't seem to realise how hugely important the event was to the areas involved. Sean Ban Breathnach, who has commentated at nearly every Comórtas for R na G (and who, by the way, is probably the best commentator in the country) was especially scathing about the attitude that anything was good enough for the Gaeltacht people.

And if there was a tinge of paranoia there, who can blame SBB or anyone else from the Gaeltacht. The place had become a slum of poverty and disadvantage in the sixties with emigration rates that would have left it deserted in a couple of generations. It took some pretty militant agitation to finally get some government money for the areas. Raidió na Gaeltachta was one result of that agitation and a couple of decades later TG4 was the reward for more well-organised campaigning. These were small gestures from governments that had done little enough for the areas in question, yet they seemed to attract a hugely disproportionate amount of media resentment. TG4, in particular, attracts the kind of oppobrium as a waste of taxpayer's money that no futile tribunal ever will.

For a sparsely populated and remote area, An Ghaeltacht has a powerful footballing tradition. Even before the advent of Páidí, 10 players from the area had won All-Irelands with Kerry and the current total of senior medals in the parish is 41. Yet, despite this glorious past, An Ghaeltacht had never achieved any real success at senior level and, in the eighties, were probably one of the weakest clubs in Kerry. At one stage, they were ranked 45th, a position that made it seem unlikely they would ever manage to be junior champions, let alone the undisputed number one team in Kerry and eventually Munster.

The man who got them started on this remarkable journey was

the main reason I was at the pitch watching a rather bad-tempered Castleisland team eke out a one point win which sent the four ladies in the stand home unhappy. Liam Ó Rócháin was one of those remarkable men who had changed the direction of a club by force of personality. He is chairman of the club now but, when he returned to his home parish in 1984 after teaching on Cape Clear Island off the coast of West Cork, he began training the club's underage teams. The crack, as they say, was about to start.

'The big change was that the motoring car had started to come in so we were able to get lads in to training. Before that, they had to train in different parts of the parish and they only got together for a game. The other difference was that I got hold of some juvenile posts so our lads were able to practise shooting properly. Previously, the idea was that Gaeltacht lads were good backs because they were hardy but they didn't have enough skill to be forwards, that was for the town players. But once they had the posts, they showed we had good forwards as well.'

There was also one of those exceptional underage teams that can often galvanise a club. Check out the history of a club winning a senior title for the first time and you'll often find a significant number of players cut their teeth on an U-12 or U-14 team.

'We had a team that started in Division Five and won the Under-12 title. That team won all the underage titles, even when they'd gone as far as the top division. Darragh Ó Sé was on that team and Dara Ó Cinnéide. There was no youngster as dedicated as Dara. He would cycle eight or nine miles back and forth to training every night.'

Liam Ó Rócháin was another one of the good guys, incredibly proud of his club and keen that I should see what they'd achieved. He said that, when they'd won the junior title in 1992, nobody had expected it. Even five years previously, An Ghaeltacht winning a county senior championship would have been unthinkable. They'd done it in 2001 (and they'd do it again in the autumn of 2003). The story was similar to that of Mayobridge in a lot of ways, years near the bottom of the pile and then a meteoric rise on the back of a couple of exceptional underage teams. Those rock-bottom years seemed to give small clubs like these an unappeasable hunger when they started to rise through the ranks. Hunger, he wanted me to know, was what characterised the club.

'Take Aodán MacGearailt and his brothers, there was one of them, P.J., playing for the juniors this evening, they live near the pitch in Gallarus and, when they were youngsters, they were never out of there. For hours every day Aodán would be kicking around in there. He wouldn't have the natural talent of Dara Ó Cinnéide but he made himself into a great footballer by pure practise.'

But no matter what any of the younger Gaeltacht footballers achieve, the most famous player from the area will always be Páidí Ó Sé. Not only because he is one of the greatest defenders the game has ever seen but because Páidí has become a media figure like few other GAA players ever have. Probably not the real Páidí either but a kind of totemic embodiment of 'Wild Man of the West' qualities. The kind of people who spend their summers towing motor boats behind their cars regard a visit to Páidí's pub in Ventry as some kind of proof that they're in touch with an archetypal common man who can still be found on the wilder reaches of the western seaboard. The great example here is Charlie Haughey, a man who seemed to have a pathological need to prove that he was in communion with the kind of older and mystical Ireland epitomised by *The Quiet Man* and Clannad's eighties' albums. So he bought himself an island off the West Kerry coast and was much photographed piloting his boat around the area, sometimes wearing a fishing cap as though entering the Tomás Ó Criomhtháin lookalike competition. He also became a great friend of Páidí. I'm not suggesting for a second that this friendship wasn't genuine, but it does remind me of a scene from the Quentin Tarantino film *Jackie Brown*.

Samuel L. Jackson walks into the office of bailbondsman

Robert Forster and picks up a photograph which shows Forster and his associate, a black man, on a fishing trip together. 'I bet it was your idea to have that photograph taken,' says Jackson.

So it is with C.J.H. and Páidí. You just know which one needs the reflected cred. Yet perhaps it's the Kerryman who's the wilier media operator. Every year, Páidí runs a club-football tournament that started off with little to distinguish it from many other small local tournaments. Yet Páidí's tournament receives huge national media coverage and, in the week beforehand, he'll usually pop up on RTÉ to do a bit of a turn, tell a few stories, run through a routine he could do in his sleep. His autobiography was another example of the facility with which the man normally played the media game. It was a textbook example of how to spend a few hundred pages revealing very little. So the 'rough fucking animals' incident was a considerable slip-up and had put him under pressure long before the season even started. The natural support and affection that would normally be his to command from the fans wouldn't be there to the same extent if things went wrong.

When myself and Liam Ó Rócháin got to Páidí's pub, the man himself was sitting at the bar drinking cups of coffee. He looked well because he'd lost a lot of weight (several locals told me with awe of the astounding mileage Páidí had covered in the local mountains over the winter) but he was also obviously a bag of nerves. Here, in his own pub, in his own backyard, the indestructible Páidí Ó Sé looked a very vulnerable man indeed.

'We'll go over and talk to him,' said Ó Rócháin.

Perhaps I hesitated. A huge grin appeared on the chairman's phizzog.

'There was a journalist down here with me a few weeks ago and he wouldn't come near the pub, he was scared Páidí would chase him out of it. That was silly. People tell all kinds of stories about Páidí, but the man would never lift his hand to anyone. He's a very decent character.'

We spent a couple of minutes with Páidí and he was polite and quietly spoken. His mother comes from the same part of Sligo as myself so we had a bit of a talk about that, he stood a drink and then we left him and he continued to swallow coffee and think. To be honest, I had been expecting some kind of reprimand. I'd written a bad review of his autobiography and there were stories of Páidí fiercely upbraiding reporters who'd crossed him. Now I felt like a considerable heel. That night with people coming over to wish him luck, offer opinions or ask about possible outcomes for Sunday's match, it would have taken a mean person not to wish Páidí Ó Sé well. You could see the prospect of the game weighing down on him. Here was a man who had been involved with Kerry for 30 years, who had been one of the finest defenders ever to play for the county, who had been outstanding in a series of All-Ireland finals, who had managed Kerry to two Sam Maguires after the longest fallow period in the county's history and people thought that he had something left to prove. It seemed not at all fair.

Being Páidí must be strange. Not only are you a public figure but everywhere you go in your place of work are reminders of younger yous. Only North Korean dictators have as many photos of themselves in their vicinity as Páidí. The pub is covered from top to bottom with them. A tremendous one of him with Jack O'Shea trooping off the pitch after an All-Ireland victory, their expressions equal parts exhaustion and jubilation, ones of him in action, ones where he receives awards, ones with team-mates, with neighbours, with celebrities, with C.J.H., with Dolly Parton. The one of Páidí and Dolly is near the bar and it's my favourite because it came to me as I looked at it that Páidí Ó Sé and Dolly Parton have a lot in common.

Look at the evidence. Dolly Parton, who came from a remote farming area, was incredibly talented from a young age. So was Páidí. But despite all that talent as a singer and songwriter, Dolly has many fans who think of her as just a kitsch icon with a big pair of breasts. And Páidí is in a similar situation. As the years go by, you hear less about his brilliance as a corner-back and a wing-back and more about his friendship with Charlie, his reputation as a wild man of the West, his appearances on television and radio. He's become a kind of kitsch icon himself. Dolly would understand. For the real Dolly Parton, you'd want to play one of the early albums that John Lennon described as 'the best music since Elvis Presley's Sun Sessions'. For the real Páidí Ó Sé, you should watch a video of the 1980 All-Ireland final between Kerry and Roscommon and marvel at a man who could defend with such a combination of ferocity and discipline.

The taxi driver who took me back to Dingle wondered what I thought of the pub.

'It's great. It's an experience.'

'It is. It's a shrine to himself. I tell the tourists that we built the church next door in honour of Páidí.'

'Do they believe you?'

'They do when they see all the photographs in the pub.'

I'd intended to stay in the Gaeltacht rather than Dingle but decided against it after:

Adventures in the Irish Hospitality Industry, Part One

I find a B & B in the vicinity of Ventry. The landlady has a single room going. Grand job.

'Would it be OK if I have a look at the room?'

'Look ahead.'

The room looks grand except there's no television.

'Have you any room with a television.'

'No, I don't.'

'I'll probably go somewhere else so.'

'You have to take that room.'

'Come again.'

'You have to take that room. When you were looking at it, the phone rang and someone asked did I have a room and I said I didn't because I thought you'd take that room so if you don't take it I'm out of pocket because of you.'

'But I only said I'd look at the room.'

'You *have* to take it and that's that.'

When I tried to walk out the door the landlady stood in front of me and, when I continued to protest, she just looked away from me as if I was some lunatic she was trying to ignore on public transport.

'OK then,' I said. As we walked down to register me, I scooted out the door, down the drive and down the boreen till I hit the main road. No, it wasn't very dignified but there was no way I was staying in that house.

This determination to skin visitors under any pretext seems peculiarly strong in Kerry. Killarney stories are common enough, but my own top Kingdom tourism experience came a couple of years ago at a well-known tourist beach, which is also close to Dingle. This beach stretches for miles and myself and a girlfriend thought it would be wonderful to do the *Baywatch* on it and drive along the beach. After a couple of miles, we got stuck in the sand. Suddenly. There wasn't any warning, no slowing down or anything, one second it was like driving on the road, the next the car might as well have been clamped. There was no shifting it so we walked back the two miles and went into the souvenir shop overlooking the beach where we explained the situation.

'There's a local man who'll tow you out with a tractor.'

'Great stuff.'

'It'll be 50 quid.'

I think we might even have laughed first before we realised that this was no joke. A tow out of the sand, the kind of favour nobody decent has any problem with, was going to be 50 quid. And there was no alternative. Along came a hefty lad with his tractor, pulled the car out and extended the paw for his 50 quid. He looked like a first cousin of the John Mills character from *Ryan's Daughter*.

'Do you get many of these call-outs?'

'I gets enough to buy a new tractor every year.'

With a day to kill before the Munster final, I had the brainwave of trying to get hold of a legendary Kerry footballer who I thought might make an interesting addition to the book. For reasons about to become obvious he will remain nameless.

Incredibly Unsuccessful Interview Attempts, Part One

'Hello, my name's Eamonn Sweeney. I'm writing a book on the GAA and I'm wondering if it would be possible to arrange an interview with you.'

'The GAA. You want to talk to me about football I suppose.'

'I do.'

'A rooter's game is all it is. There's no skill in it at all. Why would you want to talk about a game like that?'

'Do you think it's disimproved since you retired?'

'Not at all. It was always a rooter's game, a foolish carry-on. The best thing they could do is stop playing it altogether.'

'But—'

'You'll have to talk to someone else. Because if you spoke to me I'd only sound negative. A rooter's game.'

'So, you're not keen on this interview?'

'Why are you writing a book about the GAA? You're wasting your time. I didn't go to a game in years. There's no point writing anything about Gaelic football, it's a…'

A rooter's game. I know. I know. Raymond Smith never had these problems. The stars of yore would sit him down in the kitchen, hand out slices of currant cake and cups of tea and reminisce in startling factual and statistical detail about finals of 40 years ago. Anyways.

Killarney is another one of my favourite venues. It doesn't have the historical resonance of Thurles but it's another ground that is close to the town centre and the place's tourist-trap status means that there'll never be any shortage of parking spaces or pubs.

There was a real buzz around the ground that Sunday. I don't think anyone really thought Limerick would win, but the suspicion was that they would be so fired up that Kerry would have to hit top form to beat them. The combination of the two teams playing at the top of their game would then result in a classic. That's what I reckoned, and my conviction that this was going to be a special day was confirmed when I went to the ticket caravan 20 minutes before the throw-in, annoyed that I'd left it so late and would probably have to be satisfied with a spot on the terrace. The man behind the counter said, 'I've a very good ticket here if you want it.'

When I got into the ground, I found that I was right on the halfway line with the finest view of a game I was to have all year. For 15 minutes, it seemed as if I was going to witness one of the truly great GAA occasions – a Limerick breakthrough. They came out as though they'd been shot from cannon and the wing-forward Stephen Kelly made two of the most incredible solo runs I'd ever seen on a football pitch. It was very simple, he just won possession and set off in a straight line right down the middle of the Kerry defence. I don't know if young Kelly was a sprinter in his youth but you rarely see applied pace like that on a football pitch. Once he got into his stride, his pursuers melted away as though they were in a film being run at a different speed. Football had never looked so easy. This is what you do, get the ball and tear straight down the middle. No sidesteps, no swerving, no passing, no hesitation, just speed and directness. I started to think about what it would be like in Limerick that night, about how I could visit Abbeyfeale, Adare, Dromcollogher, Broadford. I was even imagining how I'd tell people in 50 years time about being there the day Limerick beat Kerry in a Munster football final.

That was before Limerick got a penalty and Micheál Reidy's shot was saved by Declan O'Keeffe. Even worse was to follow.

Stephen Kelly banged his head. Just a freakish collision, but it meant he wouldn't solo any more ball that day. They left him on for a while but he kept straying towards the sideline, wobbling on his pins like a detective who's just had a Mickey Finn slipped into his drink. He came off at half-time and, by then, the game had gone from Limerick. All the hyperactive energy of the first quarter was replaced by a determination to do things very slowly indeed and Kerry started, without playing well, to impose the dominance of a hundred years. Eoin Brosnan had suffered a cut head in a collision and reappeared sporting an enormous turban of bandage. Brosnan was no mean exponent of the sprint down the middle himself and he went 40 yards without a Limerick defender laying a hand on him before slipping the ball to Dara Ó Cinnéide.

Totally unfazed by the approach of the Buster Bloodvessel lookalike in the Limerick goalkeeping jersey, Ó Cinnéide made the goal look very easy indeed. It struck me that, when he was a young lad cycling those eight and nine miles on the lonely roads around Gallarus, Ó Cinnéide must have dreamed of being in a position like this and heard a commentary in his head.

'Dara Ó Cinnéide, he's straight through in this Munster final in Killarney. It's vital that he scores this goal. And Ó Cinnéide makes no mistake.'

Outwardly, the goal was easy enough. Ó Cinnéide didn't have to do much except take the pass and put the shot in the right place. But that move hadn't started with Eoin Brosnan in midfield, it had started with Liam Ó Rócháin and his Division Five U-12 team in the field between the mountains and the ocean. An extraordinary amount of hard work backed Dara up as he put his foot to the ball.

The second half was one of those halves that hardly seem to have happened. Kerry's Seamus Scanlon was sent off and Limerick missed another penalty. Yet, even though there were just five points between the teams at the end, it didn't seem as though scoring those penalties would have made any difference for

Limerick. Their season went precipitously downhill the minute Stephen Kelly got that bang on the head. With a five-point lead over Cork, Kerry might still have had the odd look over their shoulders, but they wouldn't countenance Limerick coming from behind to beat them. The only hope the underdogs had was to run up a big lead early on and hold on to it for dear life. Once Kelly was removed from the equation and the momentum dissipated that was never going to happen. It was a quiet crowd that left Fitzgerald Stadium. Eoin Brosnan got the Man of the Match award because GAA tradition states that any man with a huge bandage on his head has to. But the player who did most to make the game worthwhile was Declan O'Sullivan.

O'Sullivan had been Coláiste na Sceilge's star player when they engaged in the amazing shoot-out against Michael Meehan's St Jarlath's team the previous year. Nothing like the same hype attended him, but he'd come into a Munster final and sprayed the ball around from centre half-forward like a man emboldened by many years of senior success. This was what the traditional powers had over their opponents. O'Sullivan came from a small club, Dromad Pearses, with no great history of success. Yet he came on to the Kerry senior side an almost fully-formed performer, as though he'd sprung from the head of some past warrior. The previous year, Colm Cooper had done the same thing, Mike Frank Russell had arrived the same way. Next year there'll probably be another forward who'll have mastered every conceivable skill. This was the killer. Limerick's current side were probably an exceptional bunch, as were the current vintage of Westmeath and Laois. The counties would have to make the most of them because times would be hard when they were gone. Kerry, on the other hand, would always have exceptional footballers coming through.

I got a lift from Killarney as far as Baile Mhúirne. The Naomh Abán team were drinking in one of the village pubs, having just been knocked out of the championship. We watched highlights of Tyrone coming back from the dead to draw with Down in the

Ulster final. It looked like the best game of the year, five minutes of
it worth the whole lot of the strange non-event I'd just been at. No
one played football with the style and panache of Tyrone when they
were at their best. It would be more than a little ironic to hear them
decried as the destroyers of football later in the season.

A man brimming with a gregarious roguishness that made me
think of Anthony Quinn playing Zorba the Greek, introduced me
to his nephew Anthony Lynch, the finest corner-back in football
and a player who'd been idle at inter-county level since Cork had
lost their game against Limerick and a back-door match against
Roscommon. Now his club had been beaten too. To make it even
more painful, news had just filtered through that Nemo Rangers,
the All-Ireland champions had been knocked out of the Cork
championship by Na Piarsaigh, a result that no sane man could
have predicted. You could see the Naomh Abán men thinking of
that little bit extra they might have done had they known how
wide open the championship was going to become. Lynch, a
player not dissimilar to Páidí Ó Sé in style, was philosophical
enough about it but one thing he said stuck with me.

'That's another year gone.'

Even Declan O'Sullivan's inter-county career would eventually be over in a relatively short time. Like Páidí, he'd be left with
his photographs, his memories and the respect of the supporters.
But he'd be a lot longer off the pitch than on it. Retirement must
be tough for any player, but for a warrior like Páidí, someone who
played the game with an intensity most players couldn't even
attempt, at times it must be unbearable.

9

The Chatty Wee Blonde from Tempo

*19 July: All-Ireland Senior Football Championship, Fourth
Qualifying Round; Markievicz Park
Fermanagh 0–12, Mayo 1–8*

Which are the only three counties never to have won a provincial
senior title? No, I would have said Carlow as well but they actually
won a Leinster football title in 1944, defeating Dublin and almost
beating Kerry in the All-Ireland semi. Longford had their great
day out in 1968 when they beat Laois in the Leinster final. Even
Sligo and Leitrim have mustered a couple of Connacht victories.

The trio on the podium of underachievement are Westmeath,
Wicklow and Fermanagh. It's awful when you think about it.
There is no famous team for players from those counties to
measure up to, no proof that once they were the best in the
province, no faded photos in the pubs displaying an immortal 15.
And, of these three, Fermanagh are arguably in the worst position.
Westmeath's current set of players are certainly good enough to
win Leinster and, had Dessie Dolan not missed that fateful free,
they might have done it last year. Wicklow, on the face of it, don't
look too good. They're probably the weakest football team in
Ireland at the moment and they haven't even been in a Leinster
final since 1897. But demographic changes resulting from the
overcrowding of our capital city will eventually leave Wicklow

with a huge pool of players to pick from. It's not impossible. But Fermanagh...

'It's remarkable what we've achieved this year if you look at the position Fermanagh is in. It's a small county to begin with. And then 50 per cent of the population belong to the other culture so they don't play Gaelic football. We don't have many clubs, I'd say only Leitrim has a smaller pick than us. Then this year we lost our star forward, Rory Gallagher, and we've lost Shane King as well. We can't afford to lose players. But we're only one game away from the All-Ireland quarter-finals. You'd have to say Dominic Corrigan has done an incredible job.'

County secretary Dominic Houston was in understandably upbeat mood the day before Fermanagh were due to play Mayo in the final round of the back-door competition. He suggested I come up to Brewster Park, Enniskillen, where the team were meeting before they set off for Sligo. The international media would be there.

'There's a German film crew making a documentary about the team so they'll be doing interviews. They want to show them in Germany that there's more to Fermanagh than fishing and boating.'

At least they had fishing and boating. Their GAA history was one long litany of defeat. Ulster finals had been reached in 1914, 1935 and 1945 but the closest they'd come to taking themselves off that list with Wicklow and Westmeath had been in 1982 when they lost the decider by just three points from Armagh, despite a marvellous long-range goal from Peter McGinnity, perhaps the county's greatest ever footballer. I remember the huge excitement surrounding that match because some of it had spilled over to Sligo. The Sligo newspapers still carry some GAA news from Fermanagh, which borders the north of the county. And I remember our family making trips to Enniskillen every year for Christmas shopping, just before the Remembrance Day explosion made the town a byword for the pointlessness of continuing to seek a solution to the problems of the North by violence. For people in Sligo town, Fermanagh was at least as much a neighbouring county as Mayo or Roscommon.

Like many small counties, Fermanagh seemed fond of making life even more difficult for itself. At least that's how it looked at the start of the season when the news came in that Rory Gallagher, Fermanagh's best player and one of the finest forwards in the game, had fallen out with manager Dominic Corrigan and had quit playing for the county. Few counties could have afforded to lose a player as good as Gallagher, but the loss for Fermanagh threatened to be catastrophic. For years, he had been responsible for a hugely disproportionate amount of their scores and seemed, at times, to be carrying the team on his shoulders.

In 2001, Fermanagh had been full of optimism. John Maughan arrived with great fanfare and a proven track record of getting the most from teams currently hovering just below the top echelon. Hadn't he brought Clare to a Munster-final victory over Kerry in 1992 and worked wonders with Mayo? The appointment of Maughan was viewed as a sign that Fermanagh really wanted to move up in the world. But the results were disappointing, the performances fairly brutal and the relationship between Maughan and the supporters unhappy. The man from Crossmolina quit and people shook their heads and declared there was obviously nothing to be done with Fermanagh. A 24-point defeat by Kerry in the 2002 championship seemed to confirm that another long period in the cellar was nigh.

Yet here we were talking about being 70 minutes from an All-Ireland quarter-final. Dominic Corrigan, the nationally unheralded and unknown manager who'd succeeded Maughan, had performed an outstanding feat of management. First up he'd got Fermanagh as far as the National League semi-final for the first time in their history. (OK, once there they got riddled by Tyrone, but there was local history there and everyone agreed Fermanagh had an inferiority complex about their neighbours that made it difficult for them to perform.) Then they knocked Donegal out of the Ulster championship and, even after Down finished their dreams of the Ulster title for another year, Fermanagh had regrouped and given Cavan and Meath the bum's rush out of the championship. Donegal, Cavan, Meath, the tradition and the resources these counties commanded should have made them immune to defeat by Fermanagh, but Corrigan obviously had something going on. Now they just needed to beat Mayo and there'd be a trip to Croke Park. And after that? Well, they were dreaming big dreams. When you've reduced an unflappable man like Seán Boylan to near tears, nothing is impossible.

There was a lovely little bit of added spice to this Saturday-night game. Mayo's manager was none other than John Maughan, returned home after his nightmare stint with Fermanagh. They hadn't warmed to Maughan in Fermanagh and he obviously hadn't relished the one unsuccessful managerial job of his brilliant career. No one could say this match wouldn't be a little bit personal and that victory would bring vindications that wouldn't be mentioned aloud but would be savoured all the same.

My Saturday began in not particularly brilliant style because I contrived to arrive late enough in Enniskillen to miss the Fermanagh team's departure. Still keen for local colour, I decided to stroll up to the GAA grounds and promptly got lost. I hailed a man of about my own age who was walking towards me and toting a considerable hangover.

'Hello. Excuse me. I wonder could you tell me where Brewster Park is?'

He stuck the head down and kept walking. He was nearly past me. Maybe he couldn't understand my accent.

'Hello, yeah? The GAA grounds, how would I get to them from here?'

Walking a bit more slowly now but still not speaking a word and not looking too happy.

'The GAA grounds. You know, where Fermanagh play. They're around some place here.'

He stopped and spat out the best response he could think of. 'Yeah. They're some fucking place up there.'

Gesturing with his arm so I suddenly got a view of the giant Glasgow Rangers tattoo he'd had done, that made him look like a walking version of one of those Belfast murals that differentiate the stamping grounds of various loyalist gun clubs. His only crime, loyalty. It was my best encounter with the Protestant population of the North since myself and the Sligo photographer Noel Kilgallen were on the beer in Derry and heard the sound of an Orange band practising in the distance. Ten minutes later, they came in to the bar with their flute cases under their arms.

Once I'd given Brewster Park the once over and confirmed that you can't get even one sentence out of an empty ground, I thought it might be an idea to check out one of the villages that provided players to the Fermanagh team. Tempo was the first one to appear on a signpost, so Tempo it was.

Tempo was a bit like one of those settlements in *Star Trek* where the crew from the *Enterprise* beam down and wonder why there's no one on the streets. All you needed was tumbleweed blowing down the one street. Ryan Keenan was from here, a young corner-forward for whom great things were being predicted. There were a few pubs in the village but no noise issuing from any of them. In fairness, it was only 12.30 on a Saturday. I toyed with the idea of pushing on to Brookeborough but opted for a pint in the biggest pub.

There wasn't a sinner within and I was just turning to go when a small, very pretty blonde woman of around 22 stuck her head in from the back and wondered if I was all right. One pint, I thought, drink it quickly and get going. Say something.

'Ryan Keenan is from Tempo, isn't he?'

'Ryan Keenan? He goes with my sister so he does.'

And thus began one of the best GAA conversations I had all year. Or maybe conversation isn't the word for it. I provided cues, did a bit of nodding and asked the question, but when the blonde girl from Tempo got going, you might as well have been trying to take the ball of Peter Canavan. She knew plenty about football and wasn't shy in talking about it.

On that evening's match. 'I'm a bit worried. Everyone here is saying that we'll win because we beat them in the league but that was only by a point and if you look at it they kicked 20 wides mind you I suppose Mayo could kick 20 wides again.'

On John Maughan. 'Oh I really hope we win because of John Maughan. He had no respect for us up here, I mean you'd think he might have moved to Fermanagh or something. And those leggings that he wears and the short shorts, he must think he looks lovely.'

Rory Gallagher. 'He plays with a Dublin club, you see, and I suppose maybe he thought he'd get a game with Dublin but he didn't and now he sees that we can get on without him.'

Tom Brewster. 'The thing about Tom Brewster is that he'll always score one amazing point from way out on the sideline and then he won't do anything else for the rest of the game.'

Dominic Corrigan and Enniskillen Gaels. 'People from the other counties think that the only good players in Fermanagh come from Enniskillen because so many of them get picked on the county team. But there's great players in other clubs who never get a look in. It's just that Dominic Corrigan used to train St Michael's in Enniskillen so he knows all the boys from the town. Wherever you go, the country teams always get overlooked.'

Fermanagh and Tyrone. 'The only county we hate is Tyrone. It's not just because they're our neighbours but their supporters, they really rub it in when they beat you. Everyone hates Tyrone. I wouldn't care but I was born in Tyrone.'

The GAA. 'It's funny isn't it when you're a wee kid and your dad is dragging you along to the matches and you don't really want to go but you get hooked on it after a while and you're really glad you got into it when you were young. I just love football.'

I believe you. And I think I was a bit spoiled by Tempo because I started to expect the same kind of chat for the rest of the campaign when I ducked into a pub in a strange town. But this woman was sui generis.

There's a scene in *Citizen Kane* where the newspaper reporter is talking to Thatcher, the banker who'd been one of Kane's best friends, and Thatcher tells a story about a day in 1896 when he was taking the ferry from New York to Jersey and saw, just for a moment, a girl carrying a white parasol. He says, 'And there's not a day since that I haven't thought about that girl. A fellow will remember a lot of things you wouldn't think he'd remember.'

I saw a lot more games, was in a lot more pubs and met plenty of people but there wasn't a day that I didn't think about the chatty wee blonde from Tempo. I hope it always keeps fine for her.

It was time to hit for Sligo but I made one final Fermanagh stop, in Belcoo the home of full-forward Stephen Maguire. I once met someone whose aunt lived in the houses near the barracks. One morning after an explosion the previous night had killed several soldiers, she found a disembodied leg in her garden. But this Saturday, Belcoo was quiet and no different to several hundred other small villages on the island. It had been given the gift of becoming boring. The only reason you'd know you were in the North was that pubs in the Republic don't usually have posters of Hugo Duncan behind the bar, something apparently *de rigeur* in the country pubs of the six counties. And also that when you opened the local paper, as well as the GAA reports there were pictures of people enjoying themselves at Orange marches in the county. The *Impartial Reporter* was well named.

'There's rain promised,' said the landlady.

She never spoke a truer word. By the time I got to Markievicz Park, it was lashing down and black horror-movie clouds partly foretold the deluge we were going to have to endure by the second half. Only partly because no one could have imagined just how bad it was going to get.

It's not as though trips to Markievicz Park weren't depressing enough already. It may be my county ground but it's also one of my least favourite places to watch a match. I think a lot of Sligo GAA people would have a lot more affection for Kilcoyne Park in Tubbercurry or the park formerly known as Corran Park in Ballymote. Markievicz Park had many disadvantages, foremost among them being its position on the edge of a major town with only one road coming into it from the south. As nearly all of Connacht lay south of the pitch, this meant that any big game was attended by gargantuan traffic jams, 10-mile tailbacks and decisions to abandon the car and walk the last mile-and-a-half to the ground. Even when one of the teams was from Ulster, as in this case, gridlock managed to occur and, sure enough, there was the familiar sight of people streaming into the ground 10 and 15 minutes after the throw-in and some unfortunates only making it at half-time. The lack of parking around the ground also meant that people coming from the North had to ditch their cars in town and walk a mile uphill in the rain.

Add in the relatively small proportion of covered accommodation in Markievicz Park and the heart sank.

Following his midfield's destruction by Joe Bergin in the Connacht final, John Maughan had taken a huge gamble by bringing Enda Sheehy on to the team. This wasn't because Sheehy was untried at inter-county level. It was just that all his trying had been done in the Dublin jersey before he had decided to decamp to Crossmolina and Mayo.

Generally speaking, GAA followers don't like blow-in players. The idea that you should stay with your county no matter what happens almost has the status of a religious law and accounts, for example, for the enormous affection in which Declan Browne is held. Some players, like Larry Tompkins and Shea Fahy, win over the supporters by dint of extraordinary talent but there are far more examples of hurlers and footballers whose moves are disastrous. Compounding Sheehy's problems were two additional factors: one, he hadn't even played club football in Mayo yet but was being catapulted on to the county team; and, two, he was a Dub, not the most popular species among rural GAA fans.

There were so many strikes against Sheehy that even if he'd played reasonably well, he might still have been adjudged a failure by Mayo supporters. In the end, he rendered such speculation academic by having an absolutely abominable game. The unfortunate import hardly touched the ball and Paul Brewster (the very opposite to Sheehy in that he was so Fermanagh the county ground was named after his father), won everything at midfield. Brewster was one of those players who'd stuck with his county through thin and thin, and he played with an urgency born out of the knowledge that chances for famous victories were not going to occur too often.

When Brewster and his midfield partner Marty McGrath inevitably won the ball, they lashed it high in the direction of Stephen Maguire at full-forward. It was an unvarying tactic, win the ball and hump it in to the edge of the square. I don't think I've ever seen one man get so many passes in a half of football. It led to an enthralling spectacle. Maguire is a big, big man so the ball came in high. The full-back, David Heaney, is just as big and he didn't pull or drag, just contested every ball with Maguire in the air. Sometimes Maguire won, he kicked two fine points. But Heaney did well too and cleared an amount of ball. The other forwards and backs only became involved when the ball broke away from this duo.

It reminded me of conversations I used to have with old-timers who insisted that there was nothing to match the football played in the thirties and forties. 'But how could they have been great games? The scores were like 2–5 to 1–4 or 0–7 to 1–3, it must have been boring enough to look at.'

And they'd explain that the scores were almost incidental. The pleasure in the games lay in watching the individual battles between players going all out against each other. There was little combination play, breaks or off-the-ball running, you stood your

ground and when the ball came in to you, you competed 50–50
against your man and the better player came away with it. It might
seem primitive, but the old-timers swore you couldn't match the
visceral thrill of seeing two big men battling it out. That was what
the Maguire–Heaney battle was like, a throwback to the thirties
and it really was exciting stuff.

My other highlight of the first half was Tom Brewster proving
the perspicacity of the girl from Tempo. He did score an amazing
point from out on the sideline and then didn't do much else,
though in fairness that was because he had to go off with an
injury.

For all the ball Brewster had won, however, Fermanagh were
only a point ahead at half-time. They'd kicked some bad wides
and the fans near me, as only fans of weaker counties can do,
agreed dolefully that their chance had gone and that Mayo
couldn't be as bad in the second half.

They were right. Mayo weren't as bad, they were worse. And
Fermanagh, like prisoners noticing that the warder had gone to
sleep, made their break for freedom. They varied their tactics by
only hitting every second ball into Stephen Maguire. And two
subs, James Sherry and Ronan McCabe, took up the slack from
Tom Brewster by hitting two amazing points from the sideline
that he'd have been proud of. The Fermanagh fans began to relax
a bit, overlooking the fact that, if you're a small county, you have
to suffer for a bit even on your best days.

Young James Gill got fed up of looking at Paul Brewster
fielding the ball and embarked on one of the finest versions I'd yet
seen of that traditional GAA staple, the 'Fuck It Run'. The FIR
occurs when a game looks to be gone from a team, is born out of
frustration and usually ends up with the ball being lost or being
blazed wide. But sometimes it can lead to great things. Tommy
Dunne of Tipperary in the 2000 Munster final against Cork not
only scored a goal from a FIR but got another one from a 'Fuck
It Shot'. My favourite FIR is also my first GAA memory. In the

1973 All-Ireland football final, Cork were quilting Galway when the losing centre half-back Tommy Joe Gilmore (even the name is perfect) went on the FIR to beat all FIRs, bowling through the middle, swatting tacklers out of the way and eventually scoring a point, which had no effect on the course of the game but probably made him feel a hell of a lot better. For the next year in the back garden, I was Tommy Joe Gilmore.

And here was James Gill carrying on the tradition, powering down the middle with defenders bouncing off him, eating up the ground between him and the goal before smuggling the ball to Trevor Mortimer who stuck it in the net. One point in it. Seven minutes to go.

Then the rain came down. Rain like you'd never seen before at a football match. The kind of rain that half-blinded the crowd when it wasn't drenching them, the kind of rain that went through all your layers of clothing in two seconds and seemed to be soaking the insides of your bones. At the same time, Fermanagh, like some heroic marathon runner who goes into oxygen debt as he enters the stadium, suddenly looked out on their feet. Mayo owned the ball out the field and just kept coming back in as though playing a game of backs and forwards. It reminded me of watching the Ireland v. England game in Stuttgart and almost hoping that England would equalise, that Gary Lineker would take one of those chances, just to end the suspense and put us out of our misery.

Fermanagh were out on their feet except for their full-back line of Mickey Lilley, Barry Owens and Ryan McCloskey who seemed to be holding Mayo back on their own. The three defenders did something that corner-backs are often advised to do but which takes ferocious courage – they got out in front. Several dangerous low balls came winging in towards the Mayo forwards and Lilley or Owens or McCloskey would go past their man, sometimes diving full length to do so, and deflect it away from the danger zone. This was high-stakes poker because, if you missed, the man was in behind you and clear on goal. But they gambled on having the pace and, most of all, the lunatic small-county determination to win those balls and deny Mayo the chance of even a shot at a point. It was breathtaking stuff. (Somewhere along the line I'd become totally biased towards Fermanagh and would have wept bitter tears had they lost.)

The rain was so heavy now that the crowd behind the goals was shifting from side to side as if this might give some relief. We were engaged in one of these readjustments when someone noticed that Mayo had been awarded a free 30 yards out. This would have been scoring territory for any freetaker, but Mayo had Maurice Sheridan, perhaps the best dead-ball kicker in the game and someone who unkind Mayo fans sometimes suggested was their equivalent of the man who gets brought on in American Football solely to kick at goal. He had already landed a couple of prodigious frees and you'd have given 100/1 against him missing this one in the last minute. But the weather, which had caused us so much misery, came to Fermanagh's rescue. Sheridan slipped coming up to the ball, his kick only reached the edge of the square and though a schemozzle ended with Mayo scoring a point, someone had touched the ball on the ground and Fermanagh got a free out. To make life thoroughly miserable for Sheridan and Mayo, he even had time to miss another free before the final whistle.

The Fermanagh fans behind the goal went mad for approximately one second and then ran for their cars. I followed, the accumulation of water in my clothes making me move like the Tin Man in the *Wizard of Oz* (before he gets the oil). Fermanagh were in the top eight in Ireland, having survived longer than Dublin, Cork, Offaly, Derry and Meath. The crowd wasn't huge, the game wasn't great, the ground was a tip, the weather was actionable but it was one of the great days of the year. I'd say the girl from Tempo enjoyed it.

10

I Believe in a Thing Called Laois

20 July: Leinster Senior Football Championship Final
Croke Park; Laois 2–13, Kildare 1–13

I think I was on my way back home to Cork the day after the match before I realised just how much the people of Laois had invested in the Leinster final. It's customary for signs to go up outside business premises and flags to be hung from telegraph poles and planted in front gardens before teams play a big game, but I'd never seen anything like the amount of graphic encouragement that had been available to Laois that weekend. There must have been a 10-mile stretch out of Portlaoise on the road to Dublin with a wooden sign every hundred yards or so bearing a legend to spur on the team. Every single house and garage and pub bore the county colours. This was Papal-Visit stuff. It was stirring enough for an outsider looking at it, God knows what it must have been like to be a Laois footballer seeing this demonstration of just how much your performance would mean to the people of your county.

In Croke Park, the ebullience of the Laois fans mingled with the kind of frantic edge that creeps in when a county is on the verge of a previously unimaginable victory. The supporters of Clare in 1995 and Armagh in 2002 had exhibited the same kind of manic combination between total joy and extreme nervousness.

Every few seconds, they'd think of what it would be like if they confounded the odds and won the All-Ireland title and then they'd think of the let down that would follow a loss. Unthinkable joy, unbearable disappointment – the pendulum kept swinging back and forth.

Laois were a slightly peculiar case. They hadn't won a Leinster title since 1946, yet you wouldn't think of them as a weak county in the same way that, say, Longford or Wicklow or Westmeath were. In most of the unsuccessful years since the legendary Tommy Murphy had inspired them to a 0–11 to 1–6 win over Kildare, Laois would have been considered as at least dark horses in the province. No one would ever have thought of Laois football as being in crisis, they'd had plenty of good players and good teams and, if the county wasn't quite of the top rank, it would never have been placed among the no-hopers. Yet the statistics told a tale of spectacular underachievement and seven provincial finals lost since 1946. For all the fine footballers who'd come from Laois and all the promise, the county had nothing to show for it.

And now, after 57 years, Laois were on the verge of a title and the anxiety of their supporters could perhaps be explained by a very strange circumstance. They might not have won Leinster since the smoke was still settling over the capitals of Europe, but they were starting the final as favourites. Kildare had won two Leinster titles in the previous five years, but they were outsiders. It was a position Laois could hardly have imagined finding themselves in at the start of the season, and it placed fierce pressure on them. Nobody quite knew how they'd react to a situation like this. Nobody, despite that win over Dublin, still knew quite how good Laois were.

We all found out within 10 minutes of the game starting as they rattled over five excellent points without reply and quelled the nerves of their fans to such an extent that the match had assumed the flavour of a victory cavalcade before it was even quarter way through. The way Laois started showed how fully they'd absorbed the way Mick O'Dwyer thinks about the game of Gaelic football. Which is that it is a simple game – defenders and midfielders win the ball and let it go quickly and accurately to forwards who win it, turn and shoot on sight. When this was done properly, there was no meaningful counter to it. During one of the periodic inquests into the state of Gaelic football, O'Dwyer was asked about possible rule changes that might make the game more attractive. He simply said that there was nothing wrong with Gaelic football being played properly. Laois were playing it properly and looked irresistible. Kildare looked as though they'd be as well to convert their white shirts into flags and hoist one from the goalposts.

There was only one blight on that perfect 10 minutes and it will have to stand in as symptomatic of the most disappointing trend of the GAA summer. Diving, acting, rolling around in the hope of getting a man booked or sent off took off big time in 2003. Some innocents thought it had never been there at all in previous years but there were precedents. Pat Spillane became a hate figure in Roscommon, a couple of decades before he seemed to become a hate figure everywhere else, when he took a dive in the famously filthy 1980 All-Ireland final and got his marker, Gerry Fitzmaurice, booked. I interviewed Spillane when his autobiography came out and he admitted that he had dived. His reasoning was that sometimes defenders would constantly foul him when the referee wasn't looking. If he had to take a dive to alert the ref to this well that was only evening up the score. Once the defender got booked, it put manners on him and Spillane had the chance to play his game without fear of GBH.

You could understand why forwards might view diving as a legitimate recourse in a game when defenders were often allowed to pull and drag them into oblivion, but the epidemic that infected the 2003 championship was very different from what we'd seen in the past. It had nothing to do with one-on-one battles between players and everything to do with hoping to gain an unfair advantage. Time and again, a player would get a small belt from an opponent, sometimes there'd be no contact at all, and start rolling around on the ground. In the meantime, his team-mates would surround the referee and insist that punishment be administered for this disgraceful assault. Most teams had at least one player who frequently hit the deck in dramatic style. It made life difficult for referees, frustrating for opponents and annoying for spectators.

These amateur dramatics posed a problem for the GAA, not least because one of the great articles of faith in the association was that the players were phenomenally honest in comparison to those who played other sports. There wasn't a fan in the country who hadn't looked at a Champions-League match, witnessed the histrionic reactions to perfectly fair tackles and tut-tutted about how you'd never see the likes of that on a GAA pitch. David Hickey had gone on at length about it when I met him. Diving was such an abomination against sportsmanship that there would have been no complaints had the GAA followed the lead of soccer and decreed that yellow cards would be shown to any player feigning injury. But to bring in that law would be to admit how widespread the practice is, thus doing damage to the association's self-image. So the GAA hierarchy affected to believe that the only diver in Gaelic football was Damien Diver, the Donegal corner-back.

Sadly the most notable apparent dive of the season came from a team who were otherwise lacking in cynicism. Tom Kelly the Laois centre half-back had been carrying the ball out of defence in the fifth minute when Kildare midfielder Alan Barry attempted to shoulder charge him. Kelly ducked under the shoulder and then fell to the ground, rolling around and clutching his head even though Barry appeared to have made no real contact with him. Barry had already been booked so the Kildare midfielder got the red card and Laois had gained a huge advantage. Maybe I was naïve and romantic about the GAA but if Kelly had been play-acting the incident seemed totally alien to the spirit of the game.

Perhaps Tom Kelly had been hurt in some way but, from the stands and on television, it was difficult to see how.

It was 15 minutes before Kildare scored, a point that, fittingly, came from the one player to put up a fight in the first quarter, the full-forward Stuart McKenzie-Smith, a player to cherish if only because he has the most unexpected name of anyone to play at Croke Park since Paddy Rutschitzko, who captained Laois in the 1949 All-Ireland hurling final. It's as though someone called Dan Joe Buckley opened the batting for England at Lords. I know it's childish but it gave myself and a friend great pleasure to shout, 'Come on McKenzie-Smith, ya boy ya', as Stuart took on the nation's defences.

Laois could do no wrong for most of the first half, and their captain, Ian Fitzgerald, seemed especially touched by divine inspiration as he hit a series of points from positions where most players wouldn't have had a shot. These points were outrageous in conception and perfect in execution, as though Fitzgerald didn't recognise the normal laws of angle and distance. He was redeeming himself in style because, like Paul Flynn, he had come in for a disproportionate amount of criticism. Fitzgerald was one of those players who frequently essayed the spectacular and scorned the percentage ball, something that can make you look silly. Add to that the fact that his movements were deliberate and painstaking, even before he was plagued by injury, and it meant that when he was even slightly off his game, the Portlaoise man could appear to be having a terrible match.

Since he'd been a minor Fitzgerald, like Brian McDonald and several other promising youngsters, had been touted as a saviour for Laois football. He'd had to do his inter-county growing up in public and the experience wasn't always pleasant. McDonald and himself were like Gaelic football Drew Barrymores, thrown into the limelight far too early so their mistakes were unhelpfully scrutinised. Now they were finally ready to shine.

Kildare finally had a bit of luck when Laois wing-back Kevin

Fitzpatrick had a hack at Tadhg Fennin and got sent off. The foul wouldn't always have merited a red card but, by dismissing Barry earlier on, Seamus McCormack had served notice that he was going to adopt a zero-tolerance attitude to foul play. Red cards, like misfortunes, often follow closely after one another and the dismissals didn't end when Fitzpatrick took the long walk.

If this had been a movie, Kelly's game would have gone to pieces. Instead, he gave one of the best centre half-back performances seen at Croke Park in years. Just before half-time, he joined the attack and scored a point, moving with such confidence that he seemed to epitomise the change Mick O'Dwyer had wrought. Before the start of the championship, Kelly had been unknown outside his own county yet here he was carrying the ball forward, his head-up style a bit like that of the athlete Michael Johnson, with such aplomb that it seemed unthinkable anyone would be able to dispossess him. Even Kieran McGeeney, who sometimes seemed to be almost entirely composed of self-belief, didn't have the same strut about his play at Number 6.

Laois were just 0–8 to 0–6 up at half-time. Kildare had hung in there and sniped a few points near the end of the half and, at half-time, they presumably talked about making a good start to the second 35 minutes and not letting Laois pull away they had at the beginning of the game.

Straight from the throw-in, the ball was lashed upfield towards Brian McDonald who caught it, turned and drilled an angled shot into the bottom corner of the net. It was as ruthless as the pronouncement of a hanging judge, a definitive demonstration of skill and the moment McDonald changed from a great prospect to a present-day star. Probably no underage career had been attended by such hype. In four years playing for his county at minor level, which included an unprecedented three All-Ireland football finals in a row, McDonald had attracted attention at a time when most young players slipped under the radar. His nickname, Beano, became household currency and he was the first name pencilled in when the stars-of-the-future lists were being made out. You got the impression that he wouldn't be easily forgiven if all this promise led nowhere. The worry that McDonald might have a great future behind him was erased when that shot hit the back of the net. Because here was a goal that only a forward of the highest quality would have been able to score. Kildare must have been sickened, but they scored a couple of points in reply before McDonald produced his next trick.

Truly great forwards seem to have an internal calculator that works out possibilities in a different way. It's as though they see space differently and, in a second, can imagine a goal where the run-of-the-mill attacker can't see anything beyond a point. D.J. Carey is a great example of this. How often has he manufactured a goal from a position almost bereft of promise, single-mindedly pursuing the difficult option and making it look so easy that we forget the extraordinary nature of the score, the huge gamble that had to be taken? There will be 29 other players on the field and tens of thousands of spectators, yet D.J. might be the only one who thought that a goal was on. There's something innate about that, some extra sense that, perhaps, you have to be born with.

So it was when Beano picked up the ball 30 yards from the Kildare goal and the Laois crowd yelled for him to kick it over the bar. Instead, he hopped the ball and moved towards two defenders to draw them in before delivering a perfect pass to Ross Munnelly. McDonald had given Munnelly a half-chance and that was all the youngster needed. Remember this was Ross, the effervescent, manic kid who always seemed to be having the time of his life on the pitch. The ball was going nowhere else but the net. When Kelly strolled imperiously forward for another point, Laois were seven clear and people began to wonder about the biggest Leinster final victory margins of all-time. There was a Frenchman sitting next to my friend. 'This is a great game. How much are the players earning?'

'Nothing.'

'And there is this crowd. Are they mad?'

Against all the odds, we were homing in on a thrilling finish. History doesn't like being overcome and will make the long-time losers sweat before they reach the promised land. Not that the Laois fans expected this as they launched into that strange guttural chant that pronounced the name of their county in a uniquely native way. 'Ullllaois, Ulllaois, Ulllaois.'

The closest equivalent is probably the way Welsh people pronounce the start of Llanelli or Llanfairpwllgwyngyllgogery-chwyrndrobwllllantysiliogogogoch.

Kildare showed some signs of life with a couple of points before fate administered a final clatter across the head that should have killed them off. Defender Mick Wright had an innocuous dig at an opponent and became the third player to make a premature exit. Hate saying this but, if the first sending off hadn't happened, this probably wouldn't have either. For refs, as well as players, the beginning of a match can set up the rest of the game. At this stage, Kildare seemed to be trapped in a Kafkaesque nightmare. The harder they tried, the worse things seemed to get. Teams have jacked it in with far less provocation but this Kildare team kept coming back, something that seemed largely attributable to one remarkable man.

Nobody seems to try harder than Glenn Ryan, no one seems to possess quite the same competitive spirit. The first time I really noticed him was in the 1992 Leinster final when Kildare, as they were last year, seemed to be on the verge of a rout before their centre half-back took charge. Aided by some breathtakingly laissez-faire refereeing, a rampant Dublin team were outclassing a nervy Kildare outfit and looked set to finish the game before half-time. Then Ryan, looking as though he was playing Dublin on his own at times, started to dominate and, though the Dubs won comfortably in the end, they had plenty of worrying moments before the expected result transpired.

In the last couple of years, no season started without speculation that Ryan's ageing legs would not last the championship. He'd only come on as a sub in this final but he set about making it his own, performing the sort of firefighting operation that had typified his career. He had the gifts to be a centre half-back in the classic mould had he ended up on one of the strong Kerry or Meath teams of his era. Instead, his great contribution was to plug holes all over the defence, bring ball forward to support ailing attacks and generally gee up a team that was one fatal rung below top class. It was hard work and the sign of it was on Ryan's face. He had one of the classic visages of Irish sport, one reminiscent of the mugs sported by boxers in American black-and-white movies. People fling around the word iconic, but Glenn Ryan did look iconic. When he ploughed forward with the ball, the evident strain made him look like a painting of the crucified Christ. It only added to the man's appeal. It was impossible for a neutral to watch a game involving Glenn Ryan for 15 minutes and not want Kildare to win so all this effort would pay off.

Rarely had Ryan been as good as he was in that second half, picking off Laois passes, getting past two and three opponents, joining his attack and scoring an inspirational point, making Kildare's Sisyphean enterprise look suddenly realistic. A string of points went over until there was just a goal in it. Then Kildare were awarded a penalty. It really would have put the tin hat on it had Ronan Sweeney missed, but the gods relented momentarily and he crashed the ball past Fergal Byron with all the justified power of someone refusing to lie down under misfortune.

Pauric Clancy put Laois back in front but John Doyle levelled for Kildare. There were five minutes left and the pendulum had swung in Kildare's direction. The Laois man in front of me said he'd settle for a draw and another cut at it. Kildare had scaled impossible heights to get back level and then, like Phedippides delivering the news from the Battle of Marathon, their strength gave out with the mission almost complete and the final twist turned the game Laois's way.

Substitute Donal Miller kicked a fine point, which seemed to free his team-mates to play the carefree football with which they'd begun the day. Ian Fitzgerald scored and then another sub, Barry Brennan did the same. It was a fitting finish because these were three excellent good points, only good footballers would have kicked them. Given the pressure Laois must have been feeling and the feverish excitement burning in Croke Park, it was a trio of remarkable kicks. Seamus McCormack, who'd had a funny day because many felt that the sendings off had been questionable yet his willingness to let the game flow had contributed hugely to the entertainment, blew the final whistle and Laois prepared to party like it was 1946.

The proof of the silliness of the rule forbidding supporters from venturing onto Croke Park at the end of a game is that it's ignored when teams have achieved something remarkable. The Armagh fans charged on to the pitch in 2002, the Tyrone fans would do the same after they won their first All-Ireland in 2003 and there was no telling the Laois fans that Sunday that they'd have to stay and watch the presentation from the stands and terraces. They poured onto the field. There is something special about standing on a pitch where your team have just made history and it's mean-spirited to deny supporters that pleasure. Ian Fitzgerald stoked up the excitement by giving a fine speech which was a Mark-Landers special, plenty of shouting and excitement and no great worry about acoustics.

Once upon a time there was no better way to proclaim your status as an enlightened and original liberal thinker than by saying that the GAA needed to bring in an open draw and scrap the provincial championships. It was the sporting equivalent of such *bien-pensant* statements as, 'You know, like, really people's sexuality is their own business', or, 'Basically if women ruled the world we'd all be a lot better off.'

Favouring the open draw positioned you as someone who had no truck with the old-fashioned or the conservative, a dude who knew that you had to move with the times even if that meant junking a hundred plus years of tradition. Yet the celebrations of the Laois fans showed that the idea of an open draw was, to coin a phrase, bollocks. This day was special because they'd won the Leinster title for the first time in 57 years, the same way 1994 had been special for Leitrim in Connacht and 1995 for Clare in Munster, the same way it will be special for Fermanagh or Westmeath or Wicklow when they finally nail that provincial title. If there'd been an open draw, this day would never have happened. Sure, they might have reached the last eight or the last four of the championship, but this would never have anything like the resonance of a provincial victory. Sligo had a wonderful 2002 when they got as far as the All-Ireland quarter-finals. But that didn't mean one tenth as much to their hardcore fans as a Connacht final win would have. In an open-draw system, there is only one winner. While the provincial finals exist, there are five and, if a county breaks through after long years of failure, it will seem every bit as important as winning an All-Ireland. In *Alice in Wonderland*, the Dodo says (after a race involving a mouse, an eaglet and a duck, among other animals), 'Everybody has won, and all must have prizes.'

In an ideal world this would happen and the efforts of every team in the championship would be recognised. But in the real world, only a handful of counties lay their hands on trophies in any year. Why reduce their numbers with an open draw?

Perhaps the best thing about wins like the one Laois had just enjoyed is that they shine a light back on a county's history and take the tragic cast from it. For years, it had seemed awful that the brilliant Laois team that won the 1986 National League title had been ambushed by a cruelly physical Wicklow team in that year's Leinster championship and lost their heads in the game that became known as The Battle of Aughrim. That team never seemed to recover and it seemed terrible that such brilliant players as Tom Prendergast and Colm Browne had ended their careers without Leinster medals and that Liam Irwin, who in 1986 looked potentially as great as Jack O'Shea, had made only a fleeting impact on the game. The 1999 Leinster semi-final had been cruel too with Laois blowing a late lead over Dublin whose equalising point by Ian Robertson was clearly illegal to everyone except the referee. Laois had lost the replay and once more must have thought about the jinx that seemed to follow counties who could have done with good luck rather than bad.

But, on 20 July 2003, these disappointments stopped mattering so much. The story of Laois misery since 1946 had been given a happy ending and the defeats of the past were now merely bumps in the road rather than abysses that swallowed up all hope. Laois fans could pass them off with a win-some, lose-some shrug rather than viewing them as proof that the county was eternally doomed to failure. In a very real way, this title also belonged to Tom Prendergast and Colm Browne and Liam Irwin and all the fine footballers of the barren years. I imagined that the victory would have taken the edge off the disappointments they'd suffered. You'd have to hope so anyway. They'd deserved better than fortune had given them.

It was a special day in many ways. For one, it completely changed my mind about Kildare football. They'd suffered from the sendings off and the terrible start and kicked 17 wides for bad measure, but they never stopped believing and it was their doggedness that had pushed Laois to the heights. A mere six days later, fatigued and now decimated by injuries, they gave an equally brave effort against Roscommon in the final game of the backdoor section. Once more they stuck at it when the cause seemed hopeless only for Roscommon's Frankie Dolan (cousin of Dessie) to equalise with almost the last kick of the game, a shot from a distance and an angle that would have been close to impossible at any stage but which defied belief when produced at the time it was. Battered, shattered and unbowed, Kildare were despatched in extra-time, their bravery almost totally unrewarded.

Now consider the wonder of Mick O'Dwyer. He played in his first All-Ireland final 45 years ago and managed in his first one 29 years back. Football has undergone massive changes in that time period and, just as importantly, so has the country. The young players O'Dwyer is dealing with now grew up in a very different Ireland from the one he knew, or indeed from the one that spawned his great Kerry team of the seventies and eighties.

O'Dwyer's huge achievement in making the generational leap should not be underestimated. I remember in the mid-nineties when a former inter-county great took over as manager as one of football's major teams. His spell in charge was a disaster and the best theory as to why came from one of the most perceptive GAA reporters on the national newspapers who'd followed the sorry saga. 'The problem was that he'd been watching the games with his cronies and they'd all been going on about how the present-day players got it too soft and weren't all they were cracked up to be. So, of course, when he took over the team he wanted to prove this and just alienated all the players. They knew that, at the back of it, he just didn't like them.'

In a country where it's become increasingly common to denigrate the young and suggest that morally and socially we're somehow going to hell in a handbasket, the generation gap can be a destructive force. It's tough for someone who grew up in the Dev era to connect with lads who wouldn't believe you if you told them that, 20 years ago, you had to get a prescription from your doctor to buy a packet of condoms. It's a bit like trying to arrange a duet between Bridie Gallagher and Snoop Doggy Dog ('The Homies of Donegal', anyone?). A large age gap between managers and players doesn't seem to be ideal. Yet this doesn't seem to bother O'Dwyer. The young Laois players he took on had a considerable reputation as party animals but there is obviously a great mutual affection between them and their septugenarian boss. That alone says remarkable things about Micko's qualities as a man manager.

More remarkable still is the way, after all those years, that O'Dwyer's approach to football is characterised by a kind of innocence. Other teams bang on about stats and percentages and the necessity of gamesmanship and persistent fouling because nothing matters except the result. O'Dwyer wants to win too but he believes in winning with panache and style and allowing players to express themselves. You don't hear him talking in grim terms about the pressure on his team and the need to win at all costs. That simply has nothing to do with the way he views football. You could dismiss him as naïve and idealistic if he wasn't the most successful manager in the history of the game.

By bringing first Kildare, after a 42-year gap, and then Laois to Leinster titles, Micko should have silenced forever the doubters who suggested that anyone could have won All-Irelands with the Kerry team that racked up eight All-Irelands in 12 years. Sure, they were talented, but there have been other teams blessed with the same kind of ability and none of them ever managed to stay on the go for anything like as long. Anyone else would have been tempted to rest on his laurels after that incredible period but O'Dwyer is different.

It must have been strange too to switch from Kerry to Kildare and Laois. Someone told me once that one reason Jack O'Shea wasn't a success as manager of Mayo was that it was difficult for him to understand why players of average ability couldn't grasp skills that were automatic to him. It reminds me of the time that my father, a fanatical lover of traditional music, decided he should learn the flute and asked the great Gurteen musician Jackie Coleman how his father had taught him to play the instrument.

'It was like this, Joe, he came in one evening and he played me a tune, "The Plains of Boyle" I think it was, and he said to me to have that learned by the next day. And the next day, he came in and played me another tune, and that was how I learned.'

My father never learned how to play the flute.

I imagine that coaching Mike Sheehy or Jack O'Shea or Pat

Spillane must have been a bit like using the Jackie Coleman method. They wouldn't have needed to be shown anything twice. But going to Kildare would have been a huge change, a culture shock that might have tempted a manager used to dealing with geniuses to throw up his hands in despair. Instead Micko soldiered on. There are plenty of heroes in the GAA today but, for my money, Mick O'Dwyer is *the* hero.

If this match had been sublime, the post-match shenanigans smacked of the ridiculous. Joe Higgins, the Laois corner-back who had an outstanding year, had decided to bring his twin sons, six-year-old Jack and Kevin, into the pre-match parade. They were mascots and wore the Laois jersey. It was a beautiful touch, something to be admired. Unless, that is, you were one of the people at the helm of the GAA who decided that this was against association rules and merited a €1,400 fine for the Laois county board.

If there's one thing that would drive you mad about the GAA, it's nothing to do with opening up Croke Park to other sports (they've a perfect right not to, they don't have to get the FAI out of the pit it's dug for itself), their attitude towards the GPA (it's not ideal but there are reasons of principle underlying it) or their tardiness about repealing Rule 21 (they took their time but it was a sensitive issue and the GAA needed to be sure it didn't end up a horribly divisive one). These are all grist to the mill of GAA bashers but what probably gets the goat of the ordinary fan is the association's love of petty bureaucracy and rules that only seem to be there so some martinet can have the joy of enforcing them.

When asked about the reason for the fine, Croke Park said that there was a rule against it and that was that. They, and some benighted apologists, seemed to view this as sufficient explanation, something that would make everyone, even Joe Higgins, nod their heads and say, 'Aha, now I understand, there was a rule against it.'

Whereas this was beside the point. Obviously there must have been a rule against it. No one was suggesting that the GAA had fined Laois because they bore a personal grudge against Joe Higgins. The point was that (a) the rule was a silly one; and (b) sometimes rules should be waived and the circumstances taken into account. This is called common sense, cop on, going with the flow and it is something the association's politburo do not do well. Already that summer, they'd refused permission to representatives of the Special Olympics to carry a banner before a match in Croke Park. Why? Because 'there is a rule against it'. After the Omagh bombing, there'd been a plan to play a match between Manchester United and the local soccer team. The only ground in town big enough to cater for the projected crowd was the GAA pitch but Croke Park wouldn't give permission for it to be used. There was a rule against that too. Some high-ranking association officials couldn't refrain from boasting that the GAA had raised more money for the victims than any other sporting body. This was another prime example of missing the point. The bombing had affected both communities in Omagh and surely shouldn't have been just another opportunity for saying that our side did better than their side.

Nobody in their right mind could have thought that fining Joe Higgins was right and Gerry Ryan made a fine gesture by offering to pay the €1,400. Yet the president of the GAA, Seán Kelly, defended the decision. This was odd because, anyone who's met Kelly knows him as a warm, enthusiastic, generous man with the potential to do wonders for the association's image. So why did he stand four square over a decision so obviously insensitive and daft? Probably because of the mentality prevalent in big, monolithic organisations which insists that, unless you support every single action, you are against them. Which is why the hierarchy of the organisation makes decisions like the Joe Higgins one, the Special Olympics one and the Omagh one. If everyone who criticises you is an enemy, you're never going to be wrong.

While Laois had been making history, Tyrone had destroyed Down in the Ulster final replay with probably the best team display of attacking football seen in the championship. There was a neat symmetry about the fact that the same day Steven McDonnell gave the best individual attacking performance, scoring three superb goals in *Waterworld* conditions as Armagh just rolled over a clearly demoralised Limerick team.

Oh, and I decided to arrange an interview with one of the Laois players. I rang him on his mobile.

'Hello Mr— my name's Eamonn Sweeney. I'm writing a book about the GAA season and I wonder if I could meet you and talk about what winning the Leinster title means to a Laois player.'

(There is much clanking of pint glasses and various bacchanal noises in the background.)

'Fuck off out of that, horse.'

'Sorry?'

'I fucking know who that is. You're not fooling me, horse.'

'I'm not codding you. My name *is* Eamonn Sweeney and—'

'Ah now, you're not fooling me, horse. You're that cunt from Meath ringing to wind me up.'

'No, I'm writing—'

'Don't, I know who you really are. I know your wife too, horse. I know your wife well.'

'Seriously, I don't know who you think—'

(Aside) 'It's this fucker from Meath taking the piss.'

'Listen, I'll give you my number and you can ring—'

'Come on, horse, you have to be up early to catch me. How are they all in Meath anyways, horse?'

They're grand I suppose, horse. Do you believe me now?

11

I Want to Take You to a
GAA Bar, GAA Bar

27 July: All-Ireland Senior Hurling Championship
Quarter-finals; Croke Park
Wexford 2–15, Antrim 2–12; Tipperary 2–16, Offaly 2–11

Have you ever seen 40,000 people sleep standing up? Neither had I till I went to the All-Ireland hurling quarter-finals. There were about 15 minutes left in the second half between Tipperary and Offaly and the game had become as one-sided as the US invasion of Iraq. Not even the most triumphalist Tipperary supporter could extract much joy from the stroll his team were enjoying. The Offaly fans looked resigned to it all. Tipp were going to win without having to play particularly well and the next quarter of an hour would drag like one of those Open-University documentaries that surprise you from your couch-bound slumber at three in the morning. This was tedium.

How could this be? Hurling was, by general consensus, one of the most exciting sports in the world and here were two of the country's strongest teams playing for a place in the last four of the championship. Yet there was something anti-climactic about the game that had been there since the start. Tipperary had scored a facile win over Offaly in the previous year's championship and never looked in danger that day. Now here we were enduring a repeat, which showed just how preordained the hurling championship seemed these days.

It would have been different if Antrim had beaten Wexford, but nobody had really believed that Antrim would win – even when they were three points clear with about six minutes left and playing really well. It was like watching a Hollywood thriller and suddenly realising there was no suspense about the scenario at all. The good guy wouldn't come to any harm and the bad guys would lose. It always panned out that way.

Not that Antrim hurlers were bad guys. They were the plucky little team that everyone wanted to do well. An Antrim win over one of the big counties would turn the shape of hurling from a triangle into a square. But lately an Antrim victory, never likely with just two in 60 years, seemed even more far-fetched than ever. They'd been beaten by Derry and Down in Ulster and there had been some horrendous canings for teams from the province in Croke Park. In 2002, there had been predictions of the worst rout yet when they came up against Tipperary. Instead, they led for a good portion of the game and kept their defeat to within a respectable margin without ever really convincing anyone that they might win. Their manager Dinny Cahill, a Tipperary man, was obviously astute and when Dunloy reached the All-Ireland club final before getting trounced by Birr, there was some talk of an Antrim revival.

Antrim hurlers are the epitome of a team that travels hopefully yet will probably never arrive. Their history shows just two championship victories over major counties, one of which (their 1944 All-Ireland semi-final against Kilkenny) was perhaps the greatest shock result in the history of the game. For a start, there was the role played by Adolf Hitler, not usually known for his contributions to GAA history. Antrim were considered too weak to play senior hurling and normally played in the junior championship, which happened to be cancelled because of petrol restrictions necessitated by the Second World War. They had never even managed to reach the final of the junior competition but they were allowed into the senior championship to give them some match practise. Their quarter-final win over Galway had been noteworthy but the defeat of Kilkenny defied all logic. On the bumpy Corrigan Park pitch in Belfast, Antrim won by 3–3 to 1–6. When the Kilkenny team returned home, they were accused of having been drunk during the game. Cork showed what an aberration Kilkenny's performance had been by hammering Antrim 5–16 to 0–4 in the final.

It took 45 years for the next shaft of light to break through the gloom. There was nothing fluky about Antrim's semi-final win over Offaly but, once more, they were brought back down to earth in the final, Tipperary administering the punishment this time. Since then, nothing. They'd even had to endure speculation that the GAA were thinking of making them play in the Munster championship, though why the more convenient alternative of Leinster wasn't being considered remained a mystery. An Antrim official had wondered aloud if the powers that be could make them travel any further.

Poor old Antrim. Against poor results, official indifference and geographical inconvenience, they strove mightily. And they truly loved their hurling. There was no better evocation of the joy taken from hurling by a youngster than a section in Ciaran Carson's magnificent *Last Night's Fun* which remembered his days pucking a ball against the gates of Casement Park and pretending to be his hero, the great Tipperary forward Jimmy Doyle. I remember a 1988 meeting in the North Star Hotel across from Connolly Station with a gang of supporters from the O'Donovan Rossa club, which had just lost the All-Ireland club final to Buffers Alley. When they talked about going to the Munster final, they were like pilgrims describing what visiting the most sacred shrine in their religion had meant to them.

While no one ever expected Antrim to win, the fact that they were playing Wexford engendered a glimmer of hope. Flakiness was Wexford's defining modern-day characteristic, which was why they'd been such popular All-Ireland winners in 1996. Up to then, everyone had considered them a team that would provide plenty of enjoyment but inevitably bottle it when victory was in sight. Recently, their form had been staggeringly various. In 2001, they'd folded miserably against Kilkenny in the Leinster final, shocked Limerick in the All-Ireland quarter, drawn with Tipperary in the All-Ireland semi and then reverted to the miserable form in the replay. A year later, they ran Kilkenny very close in the Leinster final but surrendered to Clare the week after. Already this year, they'd been humiliated by Kilkenny before turning around and upsetting Waterford, producing in the process some of the most sublime hurling of the summer. It was impossible to predict which Wexford would turn up on any given Sunday, and perhaps they didn't know themselves. They were the jazz musicians of hurling, giving a constant impression of spontaneous, off-the-cuff improvisation. When it worked, they looked like geniuses but, when the inspiration wasn't there, all you got was a discordant assemblage of bum notes.

In many ways, Antrim's defeat by Wexford was a textbook study in how gallant outsiders are eventually defeated and left with nothing but that most useless of possessions, a moral victory. There are certain steps that seem common to many of the so-near-but-yet-so-far afternoons of the minnows.

1. *The referee does the underdogs no favours:* A couple of minutes into the game, Antrim's Liam Watson found the net after a scramble in the square. The referee disallowed the goal but it was very hard to see why. At times like this, you wondered if the goal would have stood if scored by Cork, Kilkenny or Tipperary, teams who were supposed to score goals in Croke Park.

2. *The underdogs don't strike when the iron is hot:* Underdogs often get a chance early on when the other team are busy underestimating them. Wexford started as slowly as a Morris

Minor after a night of frost but Antrim hit six wides in the first seven minutes, something powerful counties rarely did.

3. *The underdogs have no luck at all:* Liam Watson brilliantly doubled on a long delivery and the Wexford keeper, Damien Fitzhenry, didn't see the ball until it had come back off the crossbar.

4. *There's a moment when the underdogs look like winners:* Coming up to half-time, Fitzhenry fumbled a 65 into his own net and, less than a minute later, more Wexford mistakes gave Colm McGuckian the chance to score a goal. At half-time, Antrim were 2–5 to 0–6 ahead. The shock looked possible.

5. *Soon after that moment, the underdogs begin to falter:* The one thing Antrim had to guard against was giving away a goal early in the second half, but they lost concentration and, within a minute, Chris McGrath scored for Wexford. True to form, it was one that could have been avoided.

6. *The underdogs go agonisingly close to victory:* Antrim kept ahead throughout the second half and, when they brought on Aidan Delargy as a sub, he scored four points from play to leave them three clear with less than 10 minutes left. (Delargy's *tour de force* was like the way Billy Dooley had finished the 1994 All-Ireland final. No matter where he stood or ran, the ball found him in plenty of space and he made the most of it. He should have bought a lottery ticket on his way to the ground.)

7. *And that's when they get their hearts broken:* The only thing that would stop Antrim was a Wexford goal and, when they gave away a free, Paul Codd drilled the ball through a wall of players to level the match.

8. *The favourites finish like they knew they were going to win all along:* Codd stuck over a couple of points and Barry Lambert got one as well. All over the ground, Wexford fans were saying that they'd never doubted their team. Antrim fans looked like they'd been mugged. Neutrals felt silly for thinking that Delargy's fourth point had set the seal on a tremendous upset. This was how these kind of games always panned out. Pity.

Ultimately disappointing it might have been, but the match had also been pretty exciting whereas the game that followed should have been sponsored by Valium. If you had a relative who'd suffered a heart attack and been warned to avoid excitement, here was a rare opportunity for them to enjoy a day out at Croke Park. Tipp were clearly superior to Offaly, but took their time about actually showing it. Brian O'Meara got a goal four minutes before half-time and, after that, everything was very predictable. Tipp's half-back line of Eamonn Corcoran, Tommy Dunne and Paul Kelly ran the game with Dunne looking like he might really fancy his new position of centre half-back.

The way Dunne had played since his great season of 2001, when he'd been one of the main reasons that Tipperary had won the All-Ireland, was symptomatic of the team's performances. Given a bit of space, he was an aesthetic delight, looked to have infinite time on the ball and hardly ever took a wrong option. Yet when they'd come under pressure, from Waterford the year before and Clare earlier in the championship, Tipperary had folded up their tents and gone home. Dunne had been as invisible as anyone else. Yet there were constant references to him and his county as 'having plenty left in the tank'. The leisurely way they played prompted such a reading but it remained to be seen whether they could actually up the pace when they had to. The 10-goal National League final they'd lost to Kilkenny by a point was the type of loose game that suited Tipperary down to the ground. There'd been wild claims that it had been a classic match when, in fact, it had just been one of those no-marking, free-for-all affairs that regularly occur when counties play tournament games to open club grounds. The connection with championship hurling was tenuous.

Tipperary wrapped up the game with a John Carroll goal and Offaly earned a statistical respectability they hardly deserved when they got two goals in the last few minutes. The second, from substitute Neville Coughlan, elicited much glee from the supporters. In one movement, Coughlan collected a short pass from a free, turned and buried the ball past Brendan Cummins from 30 yards. Cummins was the best goalkeeper in hurling, but he hardly got a chance to raise his stick. Coughlan had hit undoubtedly the best shot of the year, one that was totally unstoppable. And he'd hit it right at the end of a game that had been, effectively, over for 20 minutes. What a waste. It was no wonder that some of the Offaly fans were laughing. The chances were that Coughlan would never hit another shot like that in his career and, because of the circumstances, the shot of his life would soon be forgotten. It was God's ironic joke on Neville Coughlan.

Tipp still had a bit left in the tank and already people were talking about their semi against Kilkenny as the real All-Ireland final. But they remained notably deficient in the steel department. The wonder of this was that the greatest Tipperary teams had been founded on physically fearsome defences. Current manager Michael Doyle's father, John, had been the toughest of them all, but they seemed to have suddenly stopped breeding that kind of man in Tipperary.

It had been a hugely disappointing Sunday. Four of hurling's top six teams had failed to produce anything to disprove the notion that there were only two counties with any pretensions towards winning the All-Ireland. The hurling championship seemed an attenuated competition, ridiculously restricted compared to its football counterpart with its Laois, its Fermanagh, its Tyrone, now favourites to win their first All-Ireland, and Armagh having recently secured theirs. Why was this the case when most GAA fans, if forced to choose, would probably agree that hurling was a far better game than football and one which they held in higher regard?

Hurling, it seemed, was a bit like the Irish language. The vast majority of Irish people thought it was a great thing and were hugely proud of it, but most of them spoke English and played football. There was a tendency to portray the story of the GAA as being one of continuous incredible success. Yet, somewhere along the way, it had failed to spread the gospel of hurling and a map showing the areas where the game held sway wouldn't have changed very much in a hundred years.

If talk could have spread hurling then there'd have been no problem. Try as you might, you couldn't avoid, for example, Liam Griffin talking as though hurling was something akin to the *bushido* code of the Japanese samurai. And he wasn't the only one who spoke about the game in the same way as a Tory historian enthuses about the yeoman spirit of the longbow archers at Agincourt. There was a certain school of hurling talk that would have been best accompanied by dry ice, an Enya soundtrack and a cod Celtic voiceover filched from Michael Flatley's *Lord of the Dance*. It encouraged the notion that hurling said something special to the Irish soul and was a far more integral part of what we are than football would ever be.

Perhaps there was some truth in this analysis, but the rhetoric was at variance with the cruel fact that, even if you were generous, the game was played to a reasonably high standard in only around a third of the association's counties. Not only did it have less adherents than Gaelic football, but there were probably more people playing soccer and rugby than there were playing hurling. In around half the counties, hurling was in a parlous state and county teams played league matches where there were more people on the pitch than there were in the stands. Yet this was a game universally loved by the people and promoted by the most powerful and efficient sporting organisation in the land. When you think about it, it's nothing short of baffling that hurling is such a relatively marginal activity.

The extent of hurling's failure to take root can sometimes seem astounding. I live in West Cork, an area where the GAA is akin to a secular religion (last year West Cork teams won the senior, intermediate, junior and junior B football championships in Cork, a clean sweep of adult titles). Cork is one of the big three hurling counties yet the impact made by hurling in West Cork is negligible. There are no hurling teams in the big towns of Bantry and Dunmanway, the great Castlehaven club has no hurling section, the few hurling clubs there are play at junior level and it is inconceivable that they will ever play senior. West Cork is football country pure and simple. In fact, there is not a single senior hurling club anywhere west of the city, a huge area as big as many counties. So what hope is there for counties like Donegal, Mayo or Tyrone, far removed from the centres of hurling power?

You could, of course, say that there aren't that many football teams in with a realistic chance of winning an All-Ireland either (in the last 20 years 10 different counties have won the Sam Maguire, seven the Liam McCarthy) but what distinguishes hurling is the vastness of the gap between the have and have nots. Fermanagh can beat Meath in football, Sligo can topple Tyrone, Leitrim can beat Galway, Mayo and Roscommon in one season, Limerick can come through to beat Cork, but the teams that ply their trade in the bottom two divisions of hurling wouldn't be let on to the pitch against a decent county for fear of what might happen. When Sligo or Longford or Louth are winning Division Three of the National League, no one seriously imagines this means they are only a few years away from challenging even the Antrims or Laoises of this world. Declan Browne is recognised as one of the finest footballers in the country despite spending most of his career in the lower echelons. But even the best hurler in Division Three would find it hard to get a game with a strong club in one of the powerful counties. There are no mute inglorious Miltons blushing unseen in bottom-division hurling though it would be lovely if there were.

A friend of mine had a cousin who had been a very moderate club player in one of the strong counties. He moved to one of the weak counties and spent years top scoring for the county team and winning Man of the Match awards in county finals. The difference in standard is so great that the counties might as well be playing different sports. It's a sad state of affairs.

Or is it? There is a school of thought which holds that hurling is a game that is only properly appreciated by a select few. Its very excellence, so the line of reasoning goes, means that it will never transfer to counties that are not steeped in the tradition of the game. Hurlers aren't mere sportsmen, they're artists who can only spring up in the counties where there is a mystical transfer of skills from the greats of the past to present-day players.

The emergence of the Ó hAilpín brothers would seem to give the lie to that popular theory. Having a Fermanagh father and a Fijian mother means they were hardly born to be hurlers. They came through because they had fetched up in the stamping ground of the Na Piarsaigh club in Cork city and received excellent coaching. And coaching, more specifically the dispersal of coaches from strong counties throughout Ireland, is probably the key to a genuine hurling revival.

Otherwise the game will become predictable as the same few counties divide the spoils between them. The telling comparison between hurling and football is that, in the past half-century, only one new county (Offaly) has been added to the list of hurling All-Ireland winners. Six new football counties have come on board in that time.

There have been times when other counties have threatened to join the game's elite. Had Laois beaten Offaly in a controversial Leinster championship game in the early eighties they might have been the team to come through. Roscommon had a very good team at that time and, a couple of years later, Westmeath seemed on the verge of big things. Kerry are at that stage now, so are Meath. Laois and Dublin hover in a shadowland, not quite minnows but never contenders either. Imagine how much more interesting the championship would be if those four were serious challengers.

It remains to be seen what steps the GAA will take to try and spread the gospel of hurling. Seán Kelly mentioned it as a priority when he was elected president and must know how frustrating it is to have a game that everyone loves but relatively few people play. Just to get every club in the county fielding at least one underage team seems, at the moment, an impossible endeavour. Yet there was a concerted effort to promote the game in the late sixties and early seventies and most of the clubs in the weakest counties owe their existence to that initiative.

Sometimes it seems as though the traditional hurling counties like things the way they are and are inclined to bask in the superiority of the hurling snob. My father, a Kilkenny man, used to joke that there was no point promoting hurling in Sligo because the players would just injure each other with the hurls. This assumption is, I reckon, a pretty common one in the strong counties. Nobody is losing any sleep over the game's relative absence from large parts of the country. In a strange way, it probably even bolsters the morale of hurling folk in Cork, Tipperary and Kilkenny. The likes of Mayo and Donegal? They wouldn't be able to play our game, it would be too much for them.

Yet it would be better if the situation changed. And it can be done. OK, so the Irish language never really came back, but it was a different story with Irish music. Before the advent of Comhaltas Ceoltóirí Éireann, the Feiseanna Cheoil and the work of Seán Ó Riada, traditional music was culturally marginalised and confined to pockets of the country. Yet through dint of pure hard work, it spread out from its traditional heartlands and is thriving today. A lot of the same guff you hear about hurling attended the traditional music revival. People from outside Sligo or Clare or Donegal wouldn't be able to play properly because they wouldn't have the tradition backing them up. Irish music would be better off confined to the traditionally strong areas because it would lose its character if it moved out. The subtlety and restraint of the music meant it would always only be appreciated by the knowledgeable few. Those complaints were proved wrong by time. There are great traditional singers and musicians who didn't have the music on dúcháis. There are even fine singers and musicians from Germany and Holland and other European countries. Tradition and breeding help, but they're not the end of the story.

Something will have to be done because, at the moment, though hurling is the better game, it is football that has the better championship.

I rounded off my Sunday with a customary visit to Rea's pub in Parkgate Street, which was full of faintly bemused Offaly fans. Rea's is a place I like, firstly, because it is by far the best pub within staggering distance of Heuston Station and the train home to Cork and, secondly, because it is a classic example of that great institution – the GAA bar.

It's difficult to define exactly what makes a pub into a GAA bar. Perhaps the best test is to go in to the pub in the early evening when there are a dozen or so people perched around the bar and make some cryptic comment pertaining to football or hurling.

'Will Páidí work it this year?'

'Tommy Walsh at midfield. Jesus.'

'Geraghty is back in the wars, I see.'

If this sparks off a conversation between you, the other drinkers and the man behind the counter, then you're in a GAA bar.

Years ago, you could recognise a GAA bar because everyone in the place would be silently reading Con Houlihan's column in the *Evening Press* at about seven in the evening. As a callow youngster, I once made the mistake of interrupting the reading of a habitue in a Roscommon town GAA bar and asking him what he thought of the previous day's game.

'Whisht,' he replied. 'How do I know what I thought of it till I read what Con has to say?'

The demise of the *Press* means that there is no column with anything like the clout that Con's back-page musings once commanded. Eugene McGee is probably the closest thing to an authority figure, but the allegiances of the GAA drinkers are various now. They read Vincent Hogan or Tom Humphries or Diarmuid O'Flynn or Martin Breheny. But it's a newspaper they're reading now, whereas the Con column was holy writ.

Just sticking up photos of county teams doesn't make a pub the real thing. The bona fide GAA bar will be a bit more esoteric in its decoration with perhaps an All-Star poster from the Carroll's era taking pride of place. There might be a photograph of the owner clinking glasses with an inter-county star, a signed hurl or a framed jersey. Another giveaway is the presence of a stranger who has travelled a long distance to visit this shrine and has already engaged the clientele in conversation. The owner will usually have checked him out like so.

'What part are you from yourself?'

'Castlehaven country.'

'I see Cahalane is still ploughing away down there.'

'He is. They'll have to shoot him.'

When the stranger leaves, the owner will tell him to make sure to say hello to some GAA acquaintance of his in the stranger's part of the world. He has no doubt that they are on speaking terms. The owner of a real GAA bar knows someone from every parish in the country and probably played against most of them.

Often the owner of a GAA bar was an inter-county player. Rea's, for example, is owned by Eamon Rea who played on the Limerick team that won the 1973 All-Ireland hurling final. This gives the customers confidence. I drank for years in Collins' pub, Castletownshend, owned by former Cork player (Christy), whose son (Bernie) plays for Cork now, whose nephew (Brian) used to play for Cork, whose brother (Donal) was a selector on the Cork hurling team last year and whose six brothers lined out alongside him for the Castlehaven club. I don't think I ever left the pub without discussing the fortunes of Cork with someone. Often it was exactly the same conversation as I'd had the previous night. In a GAA bar, this is not viewed as a drawback but rather as a reassuring mark of consistency. The dread spectres of religion and politics take a backseat to the far more congenial subject of sport. Know your stuff and, to paraphrase Electric Six, 'You're a superstar, down at the GAA bar.'

Perhaps the ultimate GAA bar was Jimmy Murray's of Knockcroghery, just outside Roscommon town. Jimmy Murray was the greatest Roscommon footballer of all-time and captained his county to their only All-Irelands in 1943 and 1944. A teetotaller, he still looks as though he'd do a reasonable job if you stuck him in corner-forward. For years, the ball from the 1943 All-Ireland hung over the bar, a forbidding dark lump of a thing with the texture of a rock. There was a guest book that contained the autographs of more GAA legends than any other book ever had or will and an amazing selection of photographs and newspaper cuttings. A few years ago, the pub was badly damaged by fire and a great deal of Jimmy Murray's memorabilia was lost so the place is not quite as impressive as it once was. The match ball, however, survived the fire and still hangs over the bar. If the Earth is ever destroyed by an asteroid, I expect that ball to emerge unscathed and go on its own orbit through the galaxy.

On the Monday after the Connacht final, I dropped into Murray's for a pint. It was the afternoon and the only customers were a few lads desperately trying to regain their equilibrium after the weekend. They looked like conversation was the last thing they needed. Just as I was leaving, Jimmy Murray appeared behind the counter, as bright and energetic as ever. It was a comforting feeling to know he was still there, 60 years after he'd become a household name by tearing Cavan apart in the All-Ireland final.

That comforting feeling is, I think, the essence of the GAA bar and explains why people go out of their way to drink in Murray's or Rea's or Larry Tompkins' pub in Cork city, Lynn's in Edgeworthstown, McNamara's in Tuam, Delaney's in Kilkenny city and all their equivalents.

12

The Hairiest Man in Ireland and Moss Keane's Niece

3 August: All-Ireland Senior Football Championship
Quarter-final; Croke Park; Armagh 0–15, Laois 0–13

'I decided to treat myself to a weekend in Portlaoise.' Say that to someone and watch their reaction. Perhaps it has something to do with the fact that, for a couple of decades, the word 'Portlaoise' was invariably followed by the word 'prison' in the popular imagination. The town's name made you think of hunger strikes, prisoner protests and republicans serving long sentences.

But there was no better place to be on the long weekend of the All-Ireland football quarter-finals. Laois footballers, like Cork hurlers, were the story of the championship. They might not eventually win the All-Ireland, but chances are they'd be remembered every as bit as much as the team that did.

I booked into the Killeshin Hotel on the Sunday morning, solely because I'd got drunk there with the Roscommon football team after a National League match a decade and a half ago. Then I headed into town towards the bus stop, past the flags and banners that made Portlaoise the most decorated place in Ireland. It hadn't come down yet from the Leinster final and it would be a long while before it did.

Halfway on the road from the Killeshin, a car pulled out of a housing estate. There were two lads in the front and three in the back and huge blue-and-white flags flapping from each window. The lads were kitted out in Laois jerseys. As they passed me, one of them stuck a klaxon out the window and hooted it. Another one let a mighty yahoo out of him. Inside the car, the five of them were smiling like they'd just got the final jackpot question on *Who wants to be a Millionaire*.

It was like the perfect distillation of the spirit that makes matches so enjoyable for people. Probably, they'd gone out together the night before and talked about nothing but the match, maybe woke up in the middle of the night thinking about the time they'd have tomorrow, bolted the breakfast and thought of nothing but the match. Now here they were a few hours before the game, all anticipation and excitement and fellow feeling. In some ways, this was the best moment of the day. Games were never quite as good as you imagined when you were setting off for them with your friends in the morning. But the journey there, the crack, the outrageous predictions, the feeling that anything could happen, that was priceless. If you could bottle the feelings swirling around that car on that Portlaoise morning and analyse them in a laboratory, you'd know just why sport exerts the hold it does over people. At that moment, the quintet seemed as close to perfect contentment as any of us ever get.

As they drove past me, a small Laois flag, which had been flying from the front of the car, fell off without their noticing. These small flags made it big in 2003 at inter-county and club level. At times it seemed as though the majority of the motoring population were driving around with the flags fluttering the way Star Spangled Banners used to fly from the cars in presidential motorcades. I picked it up and filed it as a souvenir beside the Mayobridge top and the tickets and programmes I'd picked up on the odyssey so far. My baby daughter, Emily, played with it incessantly for what remained of the summer. Nobody, it seemed, could resist Laois.

It was one of those days when good things happened. I was several hundred yards from the bus stop when the express to Dublin pulled away from it. On the off-chance, I stuck out my thumb and the driver pulled in to the side of the road. 'Come on, hop in. Are you going to the match?'

I love this about Ireland. Strictly speaking, the express should only stop at a few designated spots. But it took a bad yoke of a driver to stick to this rule. The bus system might be a disaster, but the men who actually pilot the vehicles are unsung heroes. Pick up an oul' lad in the middle of nowhere and then stop for his neighbour 50 yards further on? No problem. Let schoolkids off right on their doorstep? Sure thing. Ignore the express rules because it's raining? Right on. Talk away to the disturbed character who can't stay in his seat? Sure what else would you be doing? I'm not being sarcastic, there is an easy-going humanity about this kind of attitude that it would be awful to lose. For years, people had railed against the ah-sure-it'll-do outlook that was, apparently, holding the country back. But I was fond of it. I'm an ah-sure-it'll-do kind of guy myself to be honest.

The Laois–Armagh game was preceded by a Tyrone–Fermanagh quarter-final that had gone exactly how everyone had feared it would. Tyrone riddled Fermanagh and had 19 points to spare at the end. Fermanagh's ultimate reward for their string of heroic victories was a match against the one county who made them go all rabbit in the headlights. The way Tyrone knocked the ball around you knew they couldn't even contemplate Fermanagh giving them a game. And once the pressure was off, Tyrone were majestic. Even in the final 10 minutes they were still pouring forward and doing their best to add an extra few points to the total. A few of the Fermanagh fans reckoned that this was typical Tyrone perfidy because there was no need to rub it in. But it would have probably looked far worse had Tyrone started easing off, hitting passes with the outside of the boot, flicking passes back over their heads and doing all the condescending stuff that really drives losing teams mad. At least it remained a football match to the end.

Looking at it, you couldn't see how anyone could beat Tyrone. They'd put more than 20 points on the board for the second game in succession and they looked like the most attractive attacking side to play in the championship for years. Nobody could mark Peter Canavan, and Owen Mulligan was probably even better. Seán Cavanagh seemed able to score when he felt like it and even their corner-backs and wing-backs got up for scores from time to time. It was the day when it started to become obvious that only one team would be able to stop Tyrone and that team was Tyrone themselves. What kept the championship intriguing was that they were very familiar with the location of the self-destruct button.

I didn't think Laois had an earthly against Armagh. My conversation with Mr X just confirmed a suspicion that they would have taken their foot off the pedal after beating Kildare. The first title in 57 years, the hype surrounding it and the mere two weeks rest after the Leinster final seemed to tell against them. It would almost be unfair to expect them to reach proper competitive pitch again. No one would blame either O'Dwyer or his players if they had gone off the boil. There was even a notable lack of tension among the Laois fans. After the agonies they'd gone through before and during the game against Kildare, they were able to relax and adopt a more carnivalesque attitude. They were in bonus territory now. Armagh, on the other hand, would have been thinking of the quarter-final since they wrapped up the match against Limerick. Laois would definitely be slow out of the blocks.

Eighteen seconds into the game, Beano McDonald scored a point for the new Leinster champions and, before long, Fergal Byron made great saves from Diarmaid Marsden and Ronan Clarke to further bolster the self-belief of the outsiders. We were going to have a real game. With 20 minutes gone, Laois were 0–3 to 0–1 ahead and Armagh were looking for ways to slow the game down. The game became a battle of wits with Laois trying to keep the ball moving so everything could be done at pace while Armagh took their time over frees, kick-outs and sidelines so the match returned to the speed they felt comfortable at. Aidan O'Rourke, the Armagh wing-back who never got a headline but never seemed to do anything wrong, bombed over one great point and John McEntee did the same thing. Laois wing-forward Gary Kavanagh tormented the Armagh defence by running at them, Colm Parkinson came on as a sub and flopped his hair about menacingly. At half-time, the teams were level at seven points apiece, and the Laois crowd had begun to work themselves into the frenzy of belief they'd showed all the way through the Leinster final.

It was a good game. You had the feeling that this Laois team would never be in anything but good games, they were so open and lacking in cynicism. Yet, in 10 years' time, what the spectators will remember won't be any of the fine points kicked in Croke Park, it will be what happened at half-time.

Laois bounded back on to the pitch when the break ended and took their positions. Then they waited. Armagh didn't show. One minute went past, two, then five. The crowd got restless. The Laois players started to lose concentration, you could see them wondering what the hell was going on. Still no sign of Armagh. Mick O'Dwyer got on to the ref about the delay. The Laois lads were wandering about now, doing stretching exercises, gazing over at the tunnel. Gerry Kinneavy, the referee, finally decided to go towards the dressing room and rout Armagh out. After some whistling, they deigned to appear. By now, the bound had gone out of Laois. Whatever thoughts they'd had in their mind coming out of that dressing room had gone. A middle-aged Laois man in front of me summed the whole caper up pretty well. 'When they beat Kerry in that All-Ireland final, we were all delighted for them. Now look at that shit, I've no respect for Armagh now. How could you have respect for them after that?'

It was the lowest and dirtiest trick of a football championship that witnessed too many low and dirty tricks. Afterwards, Joe Kernan would claim that Armagh hadn't noticed the time passing and that, anyway, they'd had to get their stats ready and work on injured players and really the allocated interval wasn't enough for them to do everything they had to do. Those were poor and unconvincing excuses and few people believed them. Armagh, it appeared, had left Laois stewing on the pitch because they thought there might be an advantage to be gained by hanging on in the dressing room. And gaining an advantage had apparently become sacrosanct to Kernan and his team. The spirit of the game could jump in the lake.

Armagh had become caught up in the mythology that portrayed them as the ultimate purveyors of an only-results-matter outlook. When they'd arrived at the top level in 1999, they were actually a hugely attractive attacking side and their games with Kerry a year later were classics of open football. Yet, follwowing their All-Ireland win in 2002, they seemed determined to attribute their success to planning and grim determination. They began to talk as though they were the first team ever to win an All-Ireland. Kerry, Galway and Meath had dominated football for the previous six years but Boylan, O'Mahony and Ó Sé rarely gave lectures on how the Sam Maguire could be won. Brian Cody, the most successful contemporary GAA manager, was charmingly dismissive about his role with Kilkenny. But, through the winter and spring, there was a deluge of articles pinpointing the absolute perfection of Armagh's approach. A team that had won a single All-Ireland by a point had suddenly become a paragon.

Sometimes the stories were odd. Take the oft-repeated tale of Joe Kernan and the All-Ireland losers medal for example. At half-time in the 2002 final, Kernan was supposed to have taken out his losers medal from the 1977 final, brandished it in front of his players, thrown it against the wall, and asked them if they wanted to be going home with one of those. Inspired by this, Armagh were a changed team in the second half. Yet, on the day of the match, RTÉ's match commentator Ger Canning had revealed that Kernan would be doing this if Armagh were behind at half-time. The gesture, then, was premeditated and the Armagh management team had felt it necessary to tell RTÉ about it in advance. That was odd.

Post-victory there had been something grim about Armagh. There were stories about players going out training for the 2003 championship the day after Armagh had won their first All-Ireland or vowing not to get married until they'd won sufficient titles. Enjoyment wasn't a word that was mentioned often, instead there was talk about hard yards and vital inches and winning being all that counted that called to mind the English rugby manager Clive Woodward.

Occasionally, the post-mortem emphasis on Armagh's status as the most cunning and devious team of them all became ludicrous. There'd been one newspaper article that began by blaming Armagh's quarter-final draw with Sligo the previous year on the Ulster team getting caught in traffic on the way down. The cunning back-room boys of Armagh, so the story went, resolved never to be caught in traffic again and rang the gardaí to check the least troublesome route into Dublin. They sorted this out and stayed the night before to avail of this convenient way into the city. Thus they were in perfect condition for their next game. There were a few small inconsistencies in this story but one big one killed it stone dead: Armagh's replay against Sligo hadn't been played in Dublin, it took place in Navan.

Such were the results when people fell in love with mythology. If the 'teleological fallacy' was the perpetual overarching myth of the championship, the 'invincibility of Armagh' was the big one of 2003. Armagh had apparently such reserves of tactical nous and competitive spirit that it was physically impossible to beat them. They were being talked about as a great team on the strength of just one All-Ireland title. They'd already been awarded the championship in 2003 and that was being taken into consideration too.

Hype accounted for this misreading. The GAA had never been so central to national life and the media responded by devoting unprecedented space to the games. Yet, as anyone who'd covered the championships knew, it was difficult to come up with something new every week. Still, players had to be interviewed and enthusiastic journalists had to pretend that there was something extra-special about today's subject (I've done this myself, I'm not judging at all). When tied in with the increasing tone of certainty that pervaded the coverage, this led to an odd phenomenon. Every interviewed player was apparently poised to prove the doubters wrong, show the enormous depth of his character, put right the mistakes of the past. A typical feature might end, 'Thady Quill looks out at the fields surrounding his home. A tough man. A man of courage. A man who knows his time has come. "We've lost often enough," he says through gritted teeth. This year there will be no stopping him.'

The next day, Thady goes on and plays the same reasonably effective game he always does. Luck isn't with him and his team gets beaten. His man, Matt the Thrasher, scores a couple of points. And the following Sunday? 'Matt the Trasher looks out at the fields surrounding his home. A tough man. A man of courage. A man who knows his time has come. "We've lost often enough," he says through gritted teeth. This year there will be no stopping him.'

And so it continues. The papers list hundreds of unstoppable players who've got it dead right this year. By the end of the season, no one remembers the articles anyway. It's like the day before a general election when every single party claims the reaction has been good on the doorsteps and they're expecting a great result. Papers have to be filled.

This is why, in the era of championship hype, a team like Armagh was lionised as though they possessed the very key to sporting success. They'd been written off and come in under the radar to win the 2002 All-Ireland and it looked like some journalists wanted to spend the next year making it up to them. Everything Armagh had done had been completely correct and led inevitably to All-Ireland success. They might have only beaten Kerry by a point, Dublin by a point and Sligo by two points after a replay, but the media distance between them and those teams was around 20 points.

The funny thing was that, in lauding Armagh's organisation and discipline, the real flair in the team was ignored. In 2002, they had a forward line that included five class players – Marsden, McEntee, McDonnell, McConville and Clarke. No other county had an equivalent number of quality attackers. And when Armagh really needed to turn a game, they could produce blistering spells of attacking football as they had when overhauling Kerry in the second half of the All-Ireland final. The problem was that, once they hit the front, they hauled men back into defence and left just a couple of isolated players in the forward line. This was judged to be a successful tactic because Armagh held on to their leads but, perhaps, if they'd kicked on when they got in front they might have won by more. They had the players to do it. Yet the legend of Armagh being the team who eked out every possible advantage from limited resources attained the status of an irrefutable axiom. Thus the pettiness of the half-time delay against Laois.

After the game, the general consensus was that, while Armagh's action had been out of order, it hadn't affected the outcome because the teams had stayed on level terms for the first 10 minutes of the half. But perhaps Laois were fired up to make a start like the two-goal start they'd made in the Leinster final. Who knows how the delay affected them? It certainly did them no favours.

It wasn't till around the halfway point of the second half that Armagh began to control the game. They'd been running midfield for a while but had been frustrated by the failure of their favourite attacking ploy, hit the ball to Steven McDonnell and let him display his genius. McDonnell, unthinkably, hardly got a touch because of the brilliance of Joe Higgins who gave the corner-back display of the year. It was the perfect answer to the Fine Fanatics in Croke Park. (The age of his sons showed that Higgins had been a father of twins at 17. After getting through that, everything else might have seemed a bit easier.) It took two less lauded but almost equally brilliant forwards to see Armagh through.

Diarmaid Marsden might almost stand as a cautionary tale about the increasing physicality of Gaelic football. He'd been a colleges phenomenon and scored a goal in a Hogan Cup final, a solo run past almost the entire St Jarlath's defence, which was the epitome of grace under pressure. Like Michael Meehan or Beano McDonald, he'd been expected to perform miracles in senior football straightaway and came in for a lot of rough treatment from defenders in the Ulster championship. Often left unprotected by laissez-faire refereeing, the young Marsden must have had a grim enough time. Over the years, he started to bulk up physically until, by last year, he was so comprehensively muscled that even his head looked like it could take part in a body-building contest. An odd thing about Marsden was that, when he got the ball with a bit of space and time on his hands, he seemed to find it difficult to decide which option to take. But hit him with what looked like a hopeless ball, which he had to scramble for with two or three defenders, and there was no one better in the game. Against Laois, several times he turned hopeful punts forward into excellent possession and broke the hearts of their defence.

It was hard to think of John McEntee ever having been a young star. When he'd first caught the eye, as centre half-forward and captain on the fantastic Crossmaglen Rangers team of the late nineties, I'd thought that he must be one of those wily veterans whose brilliance at club level had just never translated into inter-county success. This misapprehension was partly because he was captain and also because of the way he played, taking his time on the ball, acting as channel for most of the team's attacking moves and being the coolest player on the field when Crossmaglen needed a crucial late score. These attributes weren't something you'd have expected from a player who was barely 20, but McEntee was indeed the embodiment of that phrase about an old head on young shoulders.

He was almost an anachronism, a throwback to the days when the Number 11 jersey had gone to a team's most gifted player who acted as playmaker. While everyone was obsessing about speed and athleticism, McEntee was as one-paced as the great Brazilian midfielder Gerson who'd smoked two packs of cigarettes a day. And, as with Gerson, all that mattered was what McEntee did when he had the ball. No one kicked as many long-range points as him and no one used the ball as well. As the second half wore on, he completely mastered Tom Kelly who'd been so confidently invincible just a fortnight earlier. The point that put Armagh four points up, and more or less put the tin hat on the game, was pure Crossmaglen. McEntee picked the ball up just inside the Laois half and slowed to first a jog and then almost a walk. You nearly expected him to take the air out of the ball. He just held on and then at the perfect time passed to Oisín McConville moving up outside him. McConville kicked a superb point and once more showed the expansiveness of style that was at Armagh's disposal when they deigned to employ it.

But, once more, Armagh retreated when they'd moved four points ahead, and the last 10 minutes of the game saw Laois presented with plenty of ball but unable to get past the wall of defenders before them. They weren't helped by the subbing of Gary Kavanagh, who'd probably been their best forward. Kavanagh was suffering because of the tendency of managers in all sports to have a fixed idea as to which of their players were genuinely good enough for big contests. He'd been in and out of the team, off and on from the first 15 and even that brilliant first half hadn't been enough to persuade O'Dwyer to leave him on. Colm Parkinson completed a disappointing season by being substituted. If you'd asked most people to name Laois's best player before

O'Dwyer took over, they'd probably have come up with Parkinson's name even though he'd been in dispute with the previous management. And when O'Dwyer first took over, it was Parkinson who was picked out as the figurehead of the brave new Laois. No one reckoned he'd prove almost completely peripheral to the success story. It had been sort of the same for Damien Delaney who'd soldiered away for Laois for years and been their best player in bad years. His finally winning a Leinster championship medal had been a great sentimental story but it must have been strange for him to do it when his form had deserted him.

Ditto with Parkinson, a very good player whose profile was even bigger than his talent might have merited because of that hairstyle. The barnet mightn't have drawn a second glance on the street, but it was exotic on a GAA pitch. Lads with haircuts like that usually quit hurling and football after promising minor careers, formed bands called Marshmallow Tentacles and supplied their former team-mates with Es at the weekend.

There was a groovy-haircut motif running through modern Laois football. Hugh Emerson had also sported a luxuriant mop. My very favourite Michael-O'Muircheartaigh moment had come when, while commentating on a league match, he exclaimed 'It's hairy Hughie Emerson, the hairiest man in Ireland.' Emerson came on as a sub against Armagh but his locks had been trimmed. Like Samson, he didn't seem to be the same without them. Then again Emerson, who'd started playing senior for Laois at the age of 17, had so many miles on the clock that he kept being referred to as a wily old veteran though he was just 28 years old.

In the end, Laois's idealism foundered on Armagh's pragmatism and the all-night bacchanal celebrations I'd been optimistically looking forward to in Portlaoise looked unlikely to materialise. Once more, I took my place in Rea's to kill time before the train at seven where I met a crew from Ballacolla, a Laois village about which there is apparently a rhyme that goes, 'Up the hill and down the holla. And that's the way to Ballacolla.'

For a change, the group was mixed and the women included a niece of Moss Keane, the Irish rugby international who'd been one of my sporting heroes as a youngster. Myself and my father would watch the Ireland games on television and wait for the moment that made the whole game worthwhile no matter what the result.

'Moss Keane didn't do his run yet, Daddy.'

'Wait, he'll do it before the game is over. Look, here he goes.'

And Moss Keane would put the ball under his oxter, run straight at the opposition and keep going even though there were about six men on his back. No Brian O'Driscoll or Denis Hickie foray has ever given me the same visceral satisfaction. After the game, we'd adjourn to the back garden and my father would put a small rugby ball under his oxter and, with fierce snorting and the pulling of terrible faces, imitate the man from Currow. It was pretty cool to meet Moss Keane's niece.

13

Rossie Remembrances and Arm-Wrestling Contests

4 August: All-Ireland Senior Football Championship Quarter-final; Croke Park; Kerry 1–21, Roscommon 3–10

Portlaoise. Monday morning. Jesus. Was it my head they were using in yesterday's game? Oh yeah, Kerry and Roscommon today. But first, I'm afraid, a pint in the fine town of Portlaoise.

I didn't even have to ask the taxi driver. He dropped me right in front of a pub with wide-open, welcoming doors and a dozen hardy regulars already cured and ready for action. A small, chubby, fair-haired, tattooed lad came in and spoke far too loud for this stage of the day.

'Were ye at the match, lads?'

Two very quiet yeses from the men he'd addressed.

'I wasn't at the game. I was at the Steam Rally. Jesus, it was brilliant and they had the match on a big screen as well. Sure what would you want to be going to Croke Park for?'

They didn't bother asking him what the Steam Rally had been like. He lifted his hand up to his face. Numbers were written on the back of it, enormous numbers in blue biro.

'What's this? Oh, I know. I was at the Steam Rally and I met this woman and she was mad into me and didn't she write her phone number on the back of me hand. I must give her a ring today.'

'You're a fierce man for the women,' said one of his buddies.

'You're a holy terror altogether.'

They cackled away merrily, for all the world like Statler and Waldorf in the critics box at *The Muppet Show*. Next to him, a man was insisting to his friends that Laois had been beaten because Armagh were a far bigger team.

'But what about Pauric Clancy? He's a big man.'

'Ah not at all. He only looks big. I'd say he's just about the six foot and sure he's not filled out. He's probably only 12 stone weight. Like your man McGrane that was marking him, he'd be six-foot four and he'd be 16 stone weight. What hope did Clancy have against him?'

At the end of the bar was a man blissfully unbothered by bravado or inaccuracy. He had the kind of blond tresses once beloved by singers in bands such as Whitesnake or Europe, a moustache from the same era and arms on him like a Californian governor. His name was Sonny. I knew this because everyone greeted him by name when they came in. A slight flick of his hair was enough to order the next drink.

Cured, I caught the train to Dublin and for a few seconds wondered if I'd been standing on the right platform. The train was quiet, uncrowded and totally bereft of the buzz you'd expect on a match day. Then I remembered that this was the train carrying the Kerry fans. Kerry supporters didn't treat days out in Croke Park in the same way as followers from other counties. For a start, a lot didn't travel till the final. And, when they did travel, there was little excitement or anticipation. It was like when you manage to wangle a business-class ticket on an plane. Not being used to it, you ooh and aah over the grub and the drink, the comfort of the seats and the frequency of the service until everyone knows you don't really belong there. The businessman, on the other hand, treats all this luxury as his birthright. So it is with Kerry and big games in

Croke Park. Going to the game or coming from it, they are businesslike until they reach the final itself. You'd have to observe, however, that the neophyte in business class has a far better time.

Kingdom *ennui*, however, wasn't the reason I desperately wanted Roscommon to win. Their possible victory was important because, after my home county of Sligo, they are the team whose fortunes move me the most. The reason for this is not immediately obvious. My family connections are in Galway and Kilkenny and I've lived in Cork for the past six years. This gives me a fondness for all these counties, Kilkenny in particular for reasons I'll go into later. But Roscommon are a team, like my own county, that I start worrying about before the season starts. I comb their FBD League results to see what the auguries for the championship ahead are. I try to see what their National League results imply, I check out which clubs the lads I've never heard of before come from.

It's odd, this concern about Roscommon. When I was in secondary school in Boyle, I usually wanted Roscommon to lose. The students were evenly divided between Sligo and Roscommon and one of the highlights of every year would be a match between the two counties. We were generously supplied with county minor and U-16s and the Roscommon lads could hardly keep the ball kicked out to us. My fascination with the neighbouring county started later, when I got my first job to be precise.

Frequently over the years, the day after a big match in Croke Park was accompanied by a hangover the size of the stadium. Myself and my best friend would troop mournfully through the streets of Dublin, in search of coffee or a cure and as we shakily perused the morning papers he would say, 'It could be worse. You could have to write 6,000 words about the match for some local paper.'

'Six thousand words? God, you're right. Six thousand words on a Monday morning.'

Though the funny thing is that I remember when I enjoyed nothing better in this world than cranking out those 6,000 words and forgetting there were such things as hangovers when I was doing it.

When I landed at the *Roscommon Herald* there was no sports reporter there. As little space was given to the GAA as in any paper in the country. What made this very strange was that the long-time editor had been Michael O'Callaghan, who'd been chairman of the county board. O'Callaghan, who'd died just before I joined the paper, had been a GAA official of the old stamp. He might have been a newspaper man but he, apparently, had the suspicion that giving players too much notice in the papers would give them notions about themselves. So the *Herald* got by on meagre contributions from county and club PROs.

The irony is that O'Callaghan had been a brilliant GAA reporter in his day and had covered the great Roscommon teams of the forties. Those reports were on file in the *Herald* office and they were, once you made a very small allowance for the style of the time, excellent. He had been an exciting, evocative and engaging sportswriter and his book on the time, *Six Glorious Years*, was one I pored through as I tried to get a handle on Roscommon football. There had been no by-lines in those days so O'Callaghan wrote under the pen-name of 'Seán'. This convention has died out almost everywhere now except in my local paper *The Southern Star* where matches are still reported by 'Cois Farraige', and 'Cúl Báire'. (I've always kind of fancied one of those natty *nom de plumes* for myself. 'An Leanbh Láidir', perhaps or 'Báidín Fheidhlimi'.)

Though O'Callaghan didn't believe in giving the GAA much publicity, his attitude towards soccer was completely different. He didn't believe in giving it any publicity at all. When the Roscommon soccer league was in its infancy the then PRO rang the *Herald* editor and asked if the roundup that had been sent in a few weeks previously, had been received.

'I got it,' said O'Callaghan, 'and I burned it. And if you send me any more notes, I'll burn them too.'

Autre temps autre moeurs.

There was an opening for a keen youngster who fancied spending his weekends covering football matches. And this was why, in June 1987, I thumbed in the rain to the remote pitch at Kilmore to report on a double bill of senior championship games, Kilmore v. Tulsk and Strokestown v. St Ronan's. Like most teenagers back then, keen to make a good impression in their first job, I was wearing the kind of cheap suit a 19-year-old wore. The day was wet and the suit was like a dishrag by the time I fetched up in Kilmore, one of those tiny villages that is not on the main road from anywhere to anywhere else. I've seldom been as excited as when I waited for the ball to be thrown in to start my new career.

I have had to check back over my notes to make sure I'd got the details of the 2003 championship correct, but I can remember the first two games I ever covered in detail. Kilmore beat Tulsk 1–8 to 1–4. Gerry Connellan, an All-Star seven years earlier, got the goal for Kilmore and Paul Kelly got the goal for Tulsk a couple of minutes from time. The best player on the field was the Kilmore left-half forward Tommy Kenoy, who briefly became a national figure when, at congress, he moved the narrowly defeated motion to open Croke Park up to other sports. Strokestown beat St Ronan's 3–9 to 1–3. A guy called Martin McDermott, who was the reigning Connacht senior 100-metre champion, scored two goals and two points for Strokestown. The rain got worse and worse and, at the end, I had to thumb back home again, 20-odd miles. I was delighted with myself.

I spent that summer covering sometimes as many as four games a weekend. Nothing was too obscure for me. I must have seen every match played in the North/West junior championship for example. For these, and other efforts, I earned £50 a week. And no, it wasn't even decent money back in those days. I'd made as much on an ANCO scheme the summer before. I didn't care. What worried me was getting the teams and the scorers right in games where half the players would be wearing jerseys with no numbers on them or there would be three lads wearing a Number 24 and subs would dart in without even informing the referee, never mind the boy from the local paper. I got by because people helped me and were delighted to think that there would be reports of their games in the *Herald*. Real reports, not ones they'd had to send in themselves. I don't know if I've ever felt so useful, so welcomed.

All week I'd wonder if Castlerea's second team had a chance of upsetting St Michael's, John McGahern's local team, the next Sunday and if anyone would manage to give Clan na Gael a game. (The answers were yes and no.) During the week, I wrote a series on club histories and learned how massively important the rare red-letter days were for the smallest of teams. St Ronan's 1962 junior championship was still a huge deal down in Ballyfarnon as was Western Gaels 1978 junior win in Ballinagare. The Shannon Gaels senior title in 1964, when John Newton's father had punched two goals and the time a combination of Creggs and Oran had formed a championship-winning team called United Stars mattered as well. These simultaneously huge and miniscule triumphs, repeated countrywide, were the bedrock of the GAA. Its huge strength is at the micro rather than the macro level. And I think that's still the case. That's why I don't think we'll ever have the Champions League-type, four-month-long-series-of-games-with-county-teams-playing-every-week competition, which some commentators are clamouring for. It would be too disruptive for the club. To which some people would answer, 'But the county teams are far more important.' Whereas anyone who thinks that is guilty of misunderstanding the GAA so grievously that they might as well ask D.J. Carey how many tries he expects to score.

The nourishment spreads upwards from the roots and tampering with that would eventually kill the whole tree. There is a very real and important sense in which Muintir Bháire's first ever county junior B football title meant just as much as Tyrone's first ever senior All-Ireland a couple of months earlier. That sense is what makes the GAA special, what makes it an organisation out of the ordinary. You know this when you serve your time standing in the rain, watching games whose results won't be heeded more than 20 miles away. I still do it. I still love it. Though not with the same fervour as I did in the summer of 1987. There's something special about your first time.

All my legwork didn't go unnoticed. At the end of the summer, I was headhunted by the *Roscommon Champion*, the *Herald*'s smaller rival based in the county town. The offer was too good to refuse. Ninety-six pounds a week. And no, that wasn't great at the time either, just better than 50. And jobs weren't easy to come by. One of the first things I did in the *Champion* was a feature on how emigration had affected GAA clubs in the county. The various clubs were able to list well over a hundred players, good footballers who'd be playing with the first team if they were still at home. Yet not even the smallest club folded. They regenerated oul' lads, prematurely promoted schoolboys and kept going.

Roscommon had been knocked out of the Connacht championship early (by Sligo, hurray). So it was October before I had a chance to attain the holy grail of local-paper journalism. Inter-county football. The county had a new manager (Roscommon, Galway and Mayo just don't tolerate losing to Sligo) in Martin McDermott and he proved to be a very good one, eventually bringing Roscommon two Connacht titles after a gap of almost a decade. He was also a man of exemplary manners who put up with me ringing him several times a week to wonder, 'How's the team getting on? Who's playing this Sunday? What do you think of the opposition?' This was before the National League even started and he never once demurred. I couldn't wait till the season got started in earnest and I was able to write those 6,000-word reports, three words for every spectator.

The away games were the real thrill. There was a pub near the *Champion* office called the Lyon's Den, which was then a great GAA house. We'd ferry up pints from there when the paper was being put together on a Tuesday night (generally we didn't finish work on a Tuesday till half-three in the morning). A number of hardcore Roscommon fans drank there, including George Bannon who owned a sports shop, and Paddy Joe Burke, the local barber. It was with George, Paddy Joe, and whoever else fancied the trip, that I travelled to National League games and big club matches. The Sunday would begin with a knock on the window of the Lyon's Den where we'd be let in for a few early-morning pints to steel us for the trip to Ennis or Portlaoise, Tuam or Newbridge. We'd arrive in the relevant town a good bit before the game, so there was time for a carvery lunch and a few more pints, which ensured that the match would be watched through a benevolent haze of alcohol.

On one occasion, I arrived in Ennis and saw that the press box was at the top of a long spiral ladder. Half steamed and swaying, I somehow managed to avoid plunging to my death only to find out that this was the broadcasting area. I watched the second half from a far safer seat in the stand. After the game, we'd usually find out where the team were drinking and join them in a local hotel. The Ennis trip was a particularly bacchanal excursion and I remember that, after leaving the West County Hotel, we stopped for more gargle in Gort and played darts with a bunch of equally sozzled locals. Darts flew everywhere but the board and no heed was passed on anyone who needed to pass in front of the target area to reach the toilets. For many years, I've had a nightmare where a one-eyed Gortian tracks me down and says, as in the Edgar Allan Poe story, 'Thou art the man.'

That was also the trip during which a couple of the passengers became convinced that there was a mysterious rattle at the back of the car only for their paranoia to be mocked by the driver. When he dropped me off at my bedsit and drove away, the streetlights revealed the left rear tyre jumping in and out of its moorings as if it was just about to fall off. Probably it had been like that since Ennis, maybe even since we'd left Roscommon that morning. What could happen to us? We were the Rossies.

And when, in McDermott's first year, Roscommon reached the Connacht final against Mayo, there was no stopping the *Champion*'s sports department (or Eamonn Sweeney, as it was also known). I wrote a five-page section that was embellished by the work of the brilliant local photographer Gerry O'Loughlin, a man who went on to win several prestigious PPAI awards. There was a fierce innocence then about the interaction between teams and the press. O'Loughlin persuaded some of the Roscommon players to stand out on the road outside Hyde Park thumbing a lift in their football gear and drove Gary Wynne, the corner-back who was also a forester, out to some woods so he could pose him with a hatchet in his hand. No one refused, no one complained.

Though I boozed like Bukowski, I was a conscientious chap in those early days. One incident exemplifies the ludicrous lengths to which I'd go to protect my journalistic integrity. For the North/West senior football final between Elphin and Strokestown, I'd taken my usual spot on the sideline, halfway between the two dugouts so no one would suspect me of any bias. The weather was atrocious and got worse. Even if I'd been dressed in mountaineering gear, I'd have got a comprehensive soaking. But I was in a light jacket. People have swum the English Channel and emerged from the sea less wet than I was midway through the second half. Nobody else in Tulsk was without cover. One of the Strokestown mentors shouted to me to shelter in their dugout. But I didn't. Journalistic integrity, you see. In the end, he became so frustrated that he walked down to me, 'Will you get into the dugout. If you're bothered about looking biased, do you know what you can do? Spend five minutes in our dugout and then walk down to the Elphin dugout and spend five minutes there.'

The worst thing is that I still stayed out in the rain. Young Sweeney was one innocent boy.

In the same way that *Casablanca* wouldn't be half as good if Ilse actually stayed with Rick at the airport, Roscommon football was more attractive because of its so near-but-yet-so-far quality.

Clan na Gael were probably one of the best club teams ever to play the game, but they lost four All-Ireland club finals in a row. I was at two of those games and the air of funereal depression after the defeats, the idea that this wasn't right and that they deserved something for all the efforts was overwhelming. They did deserve better. Tony McManus, the most skilful footballer I've ever seen, deserved better. But they didn't get it.

It had been the same with the county team that won four Connacht titles from 1977–1980. They'd lost two All-Ireland semi-finals by a point and, when they finally reached the final, they lost it by three points to Kerry when they should have won. I remember someone putting on a video of that game one night in Regan's pub on the square in Roscommon town. Everyone watched the start with great interest. There was a young Tony McManus skinning John O'Keefe in the first minute and setting up John O'Connor for a goal, there was Seamus Hayden driving through for a point and John O'Gara doing the same. And then it started to go unbearably, horribly, irrevocably wrong. Before the match reached half-time, people had either walked out or were telling the barman to switch the tape off. It was far too painful to look at again.

That defeat still rankles severely with Roscommon. It is the defining game of their recent history, the way the Battle of Aughrim was for Laois until the team of 2003 enabled the past to be seen in a different light. Not until the day that Roscommon win their third All-Ireland title will that game cease to sting and goad their supporters. It was one of the classic painful losses.

I got on so well with the GAA in Roscommon that I was even asked if I wanted to become county-board PRO. I refused, citing all kinds of priggish reasons about journalistic balance and objectivity, but the truth was that I'd decided to go to England after a woman. I went and things worked out there and then we came back to Ireland and they went wrong quickly. Sometimes I wonder what would have happened if I'd stayed in Roscommon and become PRO, become a county-board member. Because, when people ask me why I went to England, I tell them a pack of lies about wanting to broaden my horizons, about wanting to get away from the stifling atmosphere of a small town, about wanting to dance to Soul II Soul, see Tom Stoppard plays and visit the Tate Gallery. But I went because of a woman and for no other reason and, if she had written to me the week before I'd planned to go and said, 'Dear Eamonn, stay in Ireland. It's not you, it's me. I hope we can still be friends. Yours, Deirdre.' I'd have been happy as Larry to stay where I was, worrying about Roscommon football and annoying Martin McDermott over the phone. That was the road not taken and all that remains of my Roscommon days is the fervent urge that they do well and someday wipe out the memory of 1980.

Even if I hadn't spent that time in Roscommon, it would be easy to have a soft spot for the county's fans. There is a certain laidback, tongue-in-cheek quality to certain of them that is attractive. You could almost call it a kind of 'stoner' vibe (and the Apostle of Hash, Ming the Merciless, is both a Castlerea native and a big fan of Roscommon). For example, some Kerry players have claimed indignantly that the bad feeling between them and Roscommon, which culminated in the 1980 hocking match, began two years earlier when the counties played a tournament game. At the time, there was a pretty brilliant punk parody (a Buzzcocks parody to be precise, listen to it after 'What Do I Get?') in the charts – 'Jilted John'. Remember? He'd been going out with Julie but Julie fancied Gordon because he was better looking than John and was also cool and trendy and when John came out of the chip shop there were Julie and Gordon standing at the bus stop which provoked John into shouting, 'But I know he's a moron, Gordon is a moron, Gordon is a moron, Gordon is a moron.'

The Roscommon fans took inspiration from this and applied it to Kerry legend Denis 'Ogie' Moran, singing, 'Ogie is a moron, Ogie is a moron.'

This, according to the Kerrymen, was the root of all the trouble. In reality, the 1980 final was probably such a bloodbath because Roscommon had some big, fearsome and ruthless defenders who had seen the Kerry forwards put 4–15 on Offaly in the semi-final and had no intention of letting themselves be roasted in the same way. They chose a time-honoured way to make life difficult for the Kingdom and Kerry responded in kind. If you unearth the referee's report, 'Jilted John' probably isn't even mentioned.

In any event, the Roscommon chant was pretty cool. How many other counties of the time had fans who were even listening to new-wave records, never mind converting them into terrace slogans? This left-field quality continues. The Roscommon GAA fan site, Sheepstealers.com, is probably the most relaxed of all the inter-county sites. (It includes, for a start, a photo of Ming the Merciless toting a Camberwell Carrot-sized spliff and the first image you see is of Boyle woman Maureen O'Sullivan in her Jane rig-out from the Tarzan films.) There is something intrinsically loveable about a site whose list of famous Rossies includes O'Sullivan, Ming, the 18th-century executioner Lady Betty, Douglas Hyde and the Lough Ree Monster, which menaced some Roscommon fishermen back in the sixties but, like an unsuccessful county team, has been out of the headlines since. And the site isn't too macho to include some of the writings of Oscar Wilde, whose father came from Roscommon.

When you see articles such as 'Green Eggs and Ham', 'Werewolves of Croker', 'King of the Muckspreaders', 'Sheep on the Beach' and 'The Hurling Dead', you get a flavour of what the Sheepstealers are about. 'Green Eggs and Ham' is a very funny reading of the eponymous story as an allegory about Roscommon football that made me think that the guy was wasted at whatever he was doing before I realised that almost every job pays better than writing and he probably had enough sense to realise that.

The county's followers are, as I pointed out, a pretty laid-back bunch but they were in a frenzied mood as they descended on

Croke Park, waving their Swedish flags in anticipation of revenge on Kerry for 1980 ... and 1978 ... and 1962 ... and even 1946 when Jimmy Murray had been playing and was having blood wiped off his face to make him look presentable for receiving the Sam Maguire when the Kingdom drew the match with two late goals. The 2003 season had already been a triumph of the unlikely. Tommy Carr had taken charge of a side that had made headlines the previous year because some players had been playing pool in their hotel while naked, vandalising the team bus and engaging in more *Ibiza Uncovered*-type behaviour back in Roscommon town.

And, when they lost a mean-spirited, first-round match to Galway, no one had expected 2003 to be any better. But then they beat Cork by a point and Leitrim by a point (with an injury-time goal). They beat Offaly in extra-time but looked doomed when Kildare led by a point with time up. Frankie Dolan hoisted an unlikely long-range equaliser and kicked a slew of other incredible points, including the best score of the season – a ball booted back over his shoulder under pressure while in the right-hand corner. The trajectory defied science; the fact he'd even attempted the shot defied logic. Roscommon were playing as though their destiny was being decided by a *Roy-of-the-Rovers* writer and, though they looked vastly inferior in almost all positions to Kerry, they believed.

The curtain-raiser proved John O'Mahony's forebodings about the quarter-finals correct. Galway trailed most of the way and only sneaked a draw with Donegal when Kevin Walsh, moving forward like a siege engine, boomed over a huge point at the death. Afterwards, O'Mahony told reporters exactly what he'd told me a couple of weeks previously. If Padraig Joyce, Derek Savage and Michael Donnellan never kicked another ball for Galway, they'd already done enough to earn the county's gratitude. It was true but hardly reassuring even if most people believed that Donegal had lost their chance.

Kerry had been lumbered with an even longer lay-off than Galway and their provincial progress had been far easier. Thus you might have expected them to clamber out of the blocks in the style of a throws expert doing the sprint section of the decathlon. Not at all. They mowed down Roscommon with the kind of start that hadn't been seen since Kerry had done exactly the same thing to Cork in the previous year's semi-final. Darragh Ó Sé would win the ball at midfield or else it would be picked up by a nimble wing-back or wing-forward and immediately be transferred to the full-forward line. The passes that came in were perfect, moving at a nice speed and a good height and so accurately directed that the forwards just had to sprint out in a straight line and take them as though executing some idealised training drill.

Not even three minutes in, and one of those perfect passes found Colm Cooper yards away from his man. Cooper flicked the ball to Declan O'Sullivan who was running past him in the direction of goal. O'Sullivan – Nineteen remember? In his first championship remember? – was faced with Shane Curran, probably the best one-on-one goalkeeper in the game. He slipped the ball into the net as quickly and casually as a postman who has a couple of hundred other deliveries to get out of the way. Cooper, who'd passed him the ball, had been the previous year's Kingdom wunderkind, just one year out of minor and apparently immediately comfortable with the demands of inter-county football. In nearly any other county, they'd have looked at Cooper's precocity and known no one like that would come along for another decade at least. Instead, there was a new phenom just 12 months later and, probably, another couple waiting in the wings.

Realism descended horribly on the Rossies in that first quarter. Their defenders were so comprehensively outpaced that they might have been U-14s from some small club press-ganged into making up the numbers in a minor match. There was a machine-like quality to Kerry's scores, an inevitability about the damage that would be wrought when Darragh Ó Sé got the ball. He was another Ciarán Whelan, a perfect Gaelic footballer, strong, brave, superb in the air, able to strike raking passes while in full stride. But, though there weren't the same amount of question marks over Darragh as there were surrounding Ciarán, and he was reckoned to be the best midfielder in the country, there were still days when Darragh didn't do it and two years in a row they'd been the days when he was needed most. In that respect, he was the opposite to his uncle, Páidí, who'd always seemed most comfortable when the roof appeared to be falling down everywhere else. Still, today against Roscommon, Darragh's play showed why Gaelic football could sometimes be called 'The Beautiful Game'. When this Kerry team moved in this fashion, they ran like a Swiss timepiece, generations of craftsmanship resulting in this exquisite and fine-tuned excellence. Hindsight made you think of how the more beautifully wrought a contraption was, the more easily its running could be upset. Grit, for example, plays havoc in the workings of a watch. And there's a special type of grit found in Ulster that can be a complete bastard.

But in those 20 minutes at the start of the game, Kerry played with an authority that didn't look as though it could possibly be countered. By the time they were 1–7 to 0–3 down, Roscommon looked set to suffer the kind of humiliation visited by Tyrone on Fermanagh. That they didn't had something to do with the character of the man between their posts who, obviously seething at the disintegration in front of him, was making furious windmill gestures for his team-mates to get into the game and the supporters not to give up the ghost. You might have thought that his fury was prompted by the impotent position a goalkeeper finds himself in, unable to influence anything much beyond the 14-yard line. You'd have been wrong, because Shane Curran had already got hold of the ball and soloed 30 yards out the field to begin the move that had led to Roscommon's first score. There was nothing unusual about that. Nothing unusual about it for Shane Curran in any event. The bizarre was one of his personal specialities.

The first time I saw Shane Curran, he was playing in the Roscommon area final of the FAI Junior Cup for Castlerea Celtic against Cloonfad United. It was a fine day in Roscommon town, and there were hardly 10 people at the game. One of them was a Castlerea man who told me that the skinny kid in goals had been on trial with Manchester United. It's the kind of story strangers spin to you on sidelines and I didn't believe it. By the end of the 90 minutes, I was wondering why they hadn't signed him. Cloonfad are a serious soccer outfit who, not too long ago, reached the semi-finals of the FAI Junior Cup and they were a lot stronger than Castlerea that day. However, the 15-year-old Curran saved a penalty and about half a dozen other shots that the average junior soccer keeper wouldn't have seen till he was picking them out of the net. Equally notably, he had no problems ordering around his much older team-mates in a voice that didn't sound like it had broken yet.

Roscommon people quickly got to know Shane Curran. He became one of the best young soccer goalkeepers in Ireland, but played his Gaelic football mainly outfield. On one occasion, when dismantling senior opposition for Castlerea St Kevin's, Curran gave a running commentary, describing what he was doing and then what he was going to do before eventually scoring a goal. Local journalists checked their dictionaries to make sure they had the proper spelling for eccentric. The 1989 Connacht minor football final showed a national audience what they'd been missing. Roscommon were a point down in the last minute when they were awarded a penalty. As the nominated penalty taker prepared for his run-up, Curran came flying in and booted the ball to the net. Roscommon had won but the goal was disallowed after the game perhaps because the GAA didn't really like that level of unpredictability. Eventually, the match was replayed and justice served by a Roscommon win.

By 1992, he was on the Roscommon senior team, opening brilliantly at full-forward against Leitrim in a Connacht championship game before being knocked unconscious accidentally, a victim of his own immense bravery. That was

Martin McDermott's last year with Roscommon and the team then entered the doldrums, Curran the Gaelic footballer was forgotten and he turned to League of Ireland football with Athlone Town. He did well there and his best moment was probably the penalty save that denied Derry City the 1995 title. I was listening to the match on the radio with my brother and, even though Stewart Gauld never missed a penalty, we knew Cake (for Curran had become known by this nickname) would save it. He wouldn't be able to resist.

Like his county, Curran went off the radar for a bit until, finally combining his talents for goalkeeping and Gaelic football. A couple of years ago, he dashed 50 yards out the field in the last minute of a league game against Donegal to create a score that put the county into the National League semi-finals. Since then, the Curran outfield foray has become a trademark. What makes it special is that it works. There were no Grobelaar-type embarrassments. And, on top of that, Curran's shot-stopping, his clearances and all the other goalkeeping basics are flawless.

It was probably the very logic of Kerry's superiority that Curran found most offensive and, although Roscommon remained well off the pace in the second quarter, they and their fans began to show signs of defiance. Still and all, Kerry were 11 points up by the 10th minute of the second half, Cooper and O'Sullivan had so much space they looked like they'd rented it from the association and anyone who'd mentioned this Kingdom team in the same breath as the 1975–1986 model wouldn't have been instantly laughed into silence.

Which was when Karl Mannion, another rare full-forward in the large-lump-of-a-man tradition epitomised by Stephen Maguire, lamped a tremendous shot past Declan O'Keeffe. Kerry, like some imperial power engaging in a quick punitive expedition following momentary embarrassment by guerilla action, chipped over a couple of quick points. It didn't stop the natives from getting restless. Roscommon worked a short free and Gary Cox scored a goal and, even though Kerry did the couple-of-points-in-reply number once more, this was beginning to look like a match rather than an exhibition.

In the last 10 minutes, Roscommon were rampant and all Kerry's elegance and poise deserted them. Frankie Dolan, who'd had one of those awful afternoons where nothing goes right because you're trying too hard and thus make things worse the more effort you put in, finally got a break and scored Roscommon's third goal. There were five points left in it now and, when Cox raced through the Red Sea-impersonating Kerry defence, there was one glorious second when I wondered if this would be the greatest comeback in GAA history. Cox, perhaps spooked by the unlikelihood and enormity of what was happening, pulled his shot badly wide and probably even Shane Curran knew that Roscommon weren't going to get another chance. Probably, but I wouldn't bet on it. The Rossies, not without reason, groaned but they also looked like supporters who were having the time of their lives. Not complaining or getting on the back of the players when things were going wrong in the first half must have made witnessing the fightback all the sweeter. And the Kerry fans? Well, they knew there was nothing to worry about. Not really though it was pretty obvious what would happen if they started the Tyrone game the way they'd just finished the Roscommon one.

Páidí Ó Sé, who'd looked in those last 10 minutes like a man watching his son wagering the family life savings at the roulette wheel, had recovered sufficiently to talk up his team's display when the reporters got to him. That old chestnut about it being a sign of a good team that they win while playing badly was trotted out. I've always been dodgy about this one since, in my early days, putting it to an English soccer manager who thought for a second and said, not unkindly, 'It would probably be a better sign if we won while playing well.'

There was also a notion that it had been good for Kerry to see their defence completely crumble when they came under sustained pressure. The, somewhat tortuous, logic supporting this theory was that Kerry might have thought they had a good defence beforehand but now they knew they didn't so the defence would play better against Tyrone. It reminded me of the statement reputed to be made by one of those Kerrymen who turn up in joke books. 'I'm glad I don't like cabbage because, if I liked it, I'd ate lots of it and I can't stand it.'

Against that, Kerry could console themselves with the flourishing of young O'Sullivan and maturing of the not much older Cooper and the attacking power that only one team in the country could come near. That team was Tyrone and, once the two teams had been drawn to play each other in the semi-final, everyone agreed the match would be a stone classic, the kind of game everyone would talk about for years. The second part of the prediction at least looks likely to come true but, for the moment, we imagined a shooting match between Russell, Cooper and O'Sullivan on one side and Canavan, Mulligan and Cavlan on the other. It would be 1977 all over again.

The Kerry fans were even more relaxed on the train down and I was glad to be checking out at Portlaoise where there might be something resembling a post-match atmosphere, even if that match had ended 24 hours earlier. In fairness to the people of Laois, they didn't disappoint me.

I landed in the sort of pub that belongs in one of those films where the hero has been driving hundreds of miles across a flat, prairie, American landscape and arrives at a bar where locals in cowboy hats are freaking out to country-and-western music while someone rides a mechanical bull on stage. Every few seconds someone says 'yee-haw', and a waitress in a short skirt cautions Billy Bob to take it easy while someone comes sliding down the counter and the barman says to the newcomer, 'Hot damn, buddy boy, you came into the right bar.'

One of the great moments of my life was discovering that these kind of bars actually do exist in the States. It was an even better moment when I found that there's one bang in the middle of Portlaoise (though probably the fortunes of the football team and the weekend that was in it cranked things up a bit).

The place was crowded and the music was so loud it was as though we were stuck inside an amplifier. And what song was on when I walked into the bar? Only the best rock-out-dudes and let's-go-crazy track of the last five years, that's what. 'Last Night' by The Strokes who, for all their New-York-Lower-East-Side-Trustafarian cool, seem to serve the same function for today's youngsters as ZZ Top did for my generation. The guitar riff, the drawled lyrics, the punters sang along to every bit. You really haven't heard people enjoying themselves till you've heard a pub full of Laois youngsters going, 'Dang a dang dang dang a dang dang, dang a dang dang dang a dang dang, Laaaaaaassssss niiiide, bazammma zamma nyah nyah nyah.'

Rock on. At the bar, they were drinking a blue liquid out of shot glasses.

'What's that stuff?'

'It's our cocktail, we made it in honour of the Laois football team.'

'What's in it?'

And she told me, but then I had four and forget the ingredients completely. What better tribute can you have if you're a cocktail? I was just ordering a fifth when suddenly there was a huge movement in the bar, the kind of enormous and sudden shift from one end to the other that usually indicates a fight has started and people either want to get away from it or cop a decent view. Everyone eventually came to a halt near a table at the front of the bar where two men lined up for an arm-wrestling contest. There wasn't a soul in the bar not watching this. On one side you had a guy in his early thirties dressed all in black and as excited as a politician who's just seen a brown envelope in his post. On the other, much calmer, was big Sonny, the solitary drinker from that morning. There was a pre-match buzz and then the two lads engaged.

The man in black wasn't content with the physical battle, he must also have reckoned that Sonny was vulnerable to psychological pressure. Every few seconds he'd shout, in an American cop-show accent, 'Come on, Sonny, you muthafucka, show me what you got. Is that all you got, Sonny?'

Sonny said nothing. They were at it for a good 10 minutes at the end of which the veins in their arms were popping up as though trying to leave. It was like the scene in *The Fly* where Jeff Goldblum tears the man's arm apart or the part in *Scanners* where an unfortunate's head blows up. It was that intense. The man-in-black's supporters roared and shouted and banged tables but Sonny's followers maintained an attitude of quiet confidence, which was justified when he eventually pinned his opponent's arm to the table. Sonny was walking back to his pint when the opposition crowd started yelling for a rematch and claiming that he'd lifted his elbow off the table. They even insisted that a bigger table should be used as the previous venue hadn't suited their lad. No problem to Sonny. Ten more minutes and he was the winner again. The cheers were even drowning out the music by now and the man in black shook his head.

'You're like a fucking bull, Sonny.'

Sonny didn't crow or caper. He just took the plaudits and went back to the counter. That was Sonny.

And that was Portlaoise. Top town.

14

The Most Exciting Match I Ever Saw

10 August: All-Ireland Senior Hurling Championship Semi-Final; Croke Park; Cork 2–20, Wexford 3–17

Fairhill and Farranree are the kind of places that took hard hits during the eighties' recession and never seemed to recover, not even at the height of the Tiger boom. The signs were there to see the evening I travelled down: lads walking Alsatians, kids hanging around on corners, security grilles, patches of waste ground and a general air of urban malaise. Areas like these are forgotten by the media, ignored by the politicians and written off as hopeless by a complacent general public. When the taxi driver dropped me off he handed me his card.

'Seriously, you don't want to be walking around here when it's dark if you don't know the place.'

The stereotypical image of a GAA heartland (and, like all stereotypes, it's partly true) is of a small village where everyone is related and most people work on the land. There was a time when you could almost be guaranteed that, if one member of a county team was a farmer, he'd be the man who would appear on television, forking bales or driving cattle before staring wistfully at the sun going down over his acres. A casual observer might think that there was very little urban input into the association and pick out Farranree as a soccer stronghold.

Yet the northside of Cork city is one of the country's great hurling areas. Roy Keane may come from Mayfield, but hurling is the number one game on the city streets surrounding his home turf. The northside is, for example, the home of Glen Rovers, probably the most famous hurling club of all. The Glen team that won 10 Cork club titles from 1932 to 1941 is reputed to be the finest club side to play the game. They produced a host of All-Ireland medal winners, including Jack Lynch, and nurtured the talent of a young man, Christy Ring, from the east Cork village of Cloyne who joined the Glen just before he began the journey that made him undisputedly the greatest star the GAA has ever seen, or is ever likely to see. In the seventies, the Glen won All-Ireland club titles and played in memorable Cork championship games against the southside giants, Blackrock and St Finbarr's. From 1972 to 1979 winning the Cork title almost guaranteed you an All-Ireland club championship (the only exception being 1976 when Blackrock lost the final to James Stephens). One Cork final was attended by 30,000 fans.

The Glen are not the force they once were but all around them are good hurling clubs. Delaneys of Dublin Hill went senior last year, St Vincent's are a fine intermediate team, Mayfield a useful junior outfit. And then there's Na Piarsaigh, the club that takes in Farranree and Fairhill and which, last summer, was the most influential team as Cork won the Munster title and prepared to challenge for the All-Ireland.

Not only did Na Piarsaigh have three players, more than any other club, on the Cork 15 but the trio were all starring. (At the end of the season they should have had three All-Stars. Seán Óg and Setanta Ó hAilpín got their awards, but there is a planet in a parallel universe where Kilkenny's Tommy Walsh contributed more at midfield than John Gardiner and, unfortunately, the All-Stars selectors live on that planet.) A fourth player, Mark Prendergast, was unlucky not to make the starting line-up but, without his outstanding contribution when coming on as a sub in the Munster final, Cork's season might have been very different. So, when I met Na Piarsaigh chairman Paddy Connery, he was on a high.

'We've never had three players starting for Cork before. We had four guys on the panel in 1986 and Tony O'Sullivan won five All-Stars, he was the biggest star we've had. But there's been nothing like this.'

Na Piarsaigh have been rewarded for their investment in facilities that would put to shame any wealthy suburban club. Cork's senior and minor teams have trained at their gym and the club complex would be impressive wherever it was situated. They have patiently climbed the ladder in Cork and are now probably the city's number two team behind Blackrock. County titles in 1987 and 1995 confirmed their arrival as a power. They also possess a powerful football club, which had knocked out All-Ireland champions Nemo Rangers earlier in the season and would go on to win a senior league title.

'Well, we listened long enough to people talking about the three superpowers in the city and we got some hockeyings from them but, eventually, we forced our way up there. There's a strong bond between people up here. When we won the county title in 1987 it was almost unique for a city team because 14 of the first 15 came from the parish. We don't get many people moving in here. It's still a family club and the same families have been involved from the start, Dalys, O'Learys, Martins. We're close-knit and we know each other so we stick together. I think the parish spirit is leaving city clubs now because that way of life is gone.'

If Na Piarsaigh don't conform to the clichéd picture of a GAA club, Connery wasn't your typical club chairman either. At a guess I'd have put him in his late thirties and there was a refreshing no-bullshit quality about him. He was proud of Na Piarsaigh, he knocked great fun out of being with the club and he reckoned the GAA was something to enjoy.

In sprawling city suburbs, the GAA is, if anything, even more important than it is in a small village. Areas like Farranree often don't have the communal areas of a rural community – one local shop, the local pub everyone drinks in, the village crossroads – so a clubhouse is one of the few places people can get together. There was a steady stream of people in and out, coming in to use the gym, to have a drink, to talk about the match. It was the same in other urban clubs I'd visited, the GAA engenders a community spirit that might otherwise be lacking in places that are too big and disparate for the old ties to hold.

Setanta and John, the two best young players in Cork, couldn't have come from more different backgrounds. John was the old-model GAA player, born to play and excel for his local club. And Setanta? Well, there haven't been many journeys like the one he's made.

'Setanta was born in Australia. They moved home from there and rented a house locally. Seán Óg came up to the club when he was about 10 years of age and at first he found it difficult to get used to the games. But there was a man, Abie Allen, and he persevered with Seán Óg and, once he got the knack of it, the other boys followed him. They're a great family, you have Seán Óg, Setanta, Teu, who's in America now but he was some hurler, and Aisaki who'll be very good too. Setanta had it from an early age, he scored a goal in a Feile Under-14 match when he was 12 and it was the best goal any of us had ever seen. He lost a bit of strength for a while because he grew so tall but you could always see the potential was there.'

Talking to Paddy Connery, it hit me that a sense of ownership is common to the people involved in most GAA clubs. The pictures of past teams on the clubhouse walls, the memories of obscure underage games, the fact that the same family names kept recurring on the team sheets, gave the club members a comforting feeling of permanence. Whatever else happened, there would always be the club to go to. It was funny but the big urban club really epitomised the special local pride that drives the association.

'It's 50 years since we won our first county junior title here and we'll be having a dinner to celebrate it, Seán Kelly is going to be down and we're hoping to have a senior hurling tournament as well. You should come to it, meet the people from the club, it'll be a fantastic night.'

High on a hill, Na Piarsaigh was like a beacon shining out a hopeful message on the northside. It was a club to be proud of and, even as I waited for the taxi the barman had called, Paddy Connery kept letting me know the special qualities of the players Na Piarsaigh had provided for Cork.

'When he was young, Seán Óg missed a lift to a match we were playing. So he ran all the way, several miles, got there and had a great game. And John and Setanta, we have camps here in the summer, training seven- to 13-year-olds, they'll turn up so they can give something back to the club. They're all nice fellas, they're all good guys.'

His parting words concerned the inadvisability of taking Wexford for granted. The you-wouldn't-know-what-those-hoors-might-do-on-the-day quality of the Yellowbellies continued to freak out opposition supporters.

Some day that week, I'd been travelling into Cork when I heard a familiar and unwelcome sound, the noise of belligerent complaint on a morning radio show. The details varied but this particular genre of crib had become something of a fixture. On this occasion, the plaintiff was a woman from Cork city whose child had been playing on their estate, had fallen out with some other kid and been slapped by that kid's father. All very unpleasant, no doubt, but hardly an earth-shattering occurrence. Yet the talk-show host was treating it as a major story. The woman, too, couldn't understand why there hadn't been more of a fuss. She'd been to the corporation, she'd been to the guards but there'd been no arrest, no eviction. It was a scandal. A host of callers seemed to agree with her.

You see, and you've probably guessed this, the man who'd

done the slapping was black. And the story of the slap sparked off a litany of complaints about the fact that they just weren't like us, they just came in here and thought they could do what they wanted, they showed no gratitude, they just looked at you when they were walking down the street like they owned the place. This particular show constantly airs this kind of story. There didn't even need to be a slap, there just needed to be someone who'd ring up and say this immigration crack had gone far enough, we'd taken our share, done our bit. Unusually, someone rang up this morning to point out that, whatever about the 'Slap of the Century', you couldn't blame every Nigerian in Cork for it. His reward was to be bullied by the host. 'Why do they come here? Why do they come here? I keep asking you people that question and I never get a straight answer.'

That statement kind of encapsulated how low the tone gets when immigration is debated on the airwaves. For the past 50 years, we've been trying to persuade the Americans, English and Europeans that this is a fantastic place to visit or even live in. We've had our tongues hanging out for any bit of praise they might drop our way. Yet it's viewed as a terrible thing when immigrants from poorer countries want to settle here. Why do they come here? What's the story? What are they up to?

When I started this book, I never thought I'd end up writing about race. But the more I travelled and the more I thought about it, the more it became apparent that it's a huge issue in Ireland at the moment. There have been two huge challenges to the people of this country in the past that we've failed miserably to deal with.

The power and arrogance of the Catholic Church should have been challenged long before it was. Instead, people put their head in the sand and the result was Magdalen Laundries, the widespread perpetration and cover-up of child sexual abuse and huge sexual repression within Irish society. Something should have been done about the blatant discrimination suffered by Catholics in the North. Instead, we left them to get on with it and then acted all shocked at the resultant conflagration. That wasn't done out of badness either, it's just that people prefer to think they're living in a decent society that doesn't need to be changed. But the indifference of the many enables the evil of the few to triumph. We're at a crossroads as regards how we deal with people from different cultures and races who've arrived in this country. Failure this time will lead to consequences just as painful as it did on the other two occasions.

What has this got to do with the GAA? Quite a lot. For a start, the GAA is more than a sporting organisation and is connected with almost every facet of Irish life. Secondly, the presence of Seán Óg and Setanta Ó hAilpín on the Cork team was a reminder that not everyone who plays inter-county hurling was born and bred in this country. Some optimists would see the huge popularity of those players as a sign that there's no real racism in Ireland. Unfortunately that's not true, the Ó hAilpíns have spoken about being racially abused as children and, on at least one occasion, Seán Óg got the same treatment in an inter-county game. The same optimists used to always present the hero status of Paul McGrath and Phil Lynott as examples of our native love of black people. But, as we've seen in England, people can like famous black people while despising the ones who live down the road.

Which brings us to Graham Geraghty. The Meathman was playing for Ireland in a friendly Compromise Rules game out in Australia a couple of years back when he called an opponent 'a black cunt'. Racist abuse pure and simple. If he'd been on an Irish rugby or soccer team, he'd have been sent home. Yet the team management merely suspended him for a week and declared themselves peeved at having to do even that. One journalist who covered the tour told me that a senior member of the party had said to him and another reporter, 'I don't know what all the fuss is about. What's wrong with calling a fella a wog?'

They decided to give the man a fool's pardon and not quote

him. Having been told the story in confidence, I won't name him either. Tours, I suppose, are fraught affairs anyway and there's probably a feeling that officials and players should stick up for each other. What was more alarming, though, was the reaction here. Papers and websites filled up with astounding amounts of folksy bullshit to the effect that wasn't this how the Irish always went on, weren't you often playing a game and someone would call you a Kildare cunt and wasn't that part of the crack and sure what Geraghty had said was no different to that and then there was another time this friend of mine didn't I call him a Galway bastard, and so on ad nauseam. By the end of it, you'd have got the impression that it was actually to our credit that we had a player who'd call someone a black cunt. Wasn't it part of what made us so special, so appealing?

It's always a bit simplistic to talk about generalised national characteristics, but one big difference between the English and the Irish is that they quite like to be hated while we're mad keen to be loved. For example, the typical English-person-abroad story is how the foreigners didn't get on with them but the English had the last laugh. The typical Irish one is about everyone really liking the Irish and going on about what fantastic crack they were. This probably explained the reaction to the Geraghty affair. Irish society is full of people who never stop banging on about how black people are inferior yet, in the same breath, insist they're not racist. It's hard to know whether the racism or the hypocrisy is worse. I don't know how often I've heard an outraged formulation which roughly goes, 'If you called him a black bastard now, they'd say you were racist.'

The problem with the Geraghty affair was the way in which people tried to pretend nothing serious had happened. Compare it, for example, with what happened when a black French rugby player accused Peter Clohessy of making racist comments after a Heineken Cup match. The player in question had bitten Clohessy and was obviously hoping to use the alleged comments as extenuating circumstances. Munster's reaction was outrage and the player was immediately forced to withdraw the allegation. The outrage was because Munster knew that there are few things lower than using racial abuse on the field. Clohessy's reputation would have been severely damaged had the accusation been allowed to stand. Geraghty's defenders, on the other hand, pretended that the comment had been harmless and affected surprise that the victim had taken offence.

The signal this sends is desperate. Whether the racists like it or not, Ireland is going to become increasingly multicultural. Black people are going to start joining GAA clubs. But, if what people purported to believe at the time of the Geraghty affair is what they really believe, a black kid playing hurling or football is going to be told that racial abuse is just part and parcel of the game. If he can't deal with it, that's his problem. GAA people often defend themselves against criticism over things like payment for players and the refusal to open up Croke Park to soccer by saying that there are matters of the association's ethos at stake that outsiders don't understand. People who compare racial abuse to a Galwayman slagging off a Mayoman come dangerously close to suggesting that racism might be part of that ethos.

Of course it's not. Joe McDonagh, who was president of the association when the hassle happened in Australia, has been involved in anti-racism campaigns and he'd have plenty of support in the GAA. But race is going to become more and more of an issue in this country and the GAA will have to be careful it's on the right side the next time a racial controversy blows up. Because one will and, next time, it will probably be a lot closer than Australia.

By one o'clock that Sunday, I was in the humour for dishing out some abuse myself. The bus I was travelling on was trapped in a traffic jam of such proportions that it seemed unlikely cars on this road would ever move again. You know you're in trouble when you're travelling from Cork to Dublin and the tailback starts the farside of Cashel and continues all the way to Dublin. Nothing against Monasterevin but I saw it for long enough that day to do me for a lifetime. The gridlock was completely unexpected. Cork hurling fans had once been like Kerry football fans, not all that inclined to travel to semi-finals. Cork people don't fancy spending money in Dublin at the best of times and a 1985 match against Galway had drawn the frankly incredible total of 7,500 spectators. But this team had caught the public imagination to an extraordinary degree and the Rebels were travelling in huge numbers. This was all well and good, but it meant that everyone's projected journey time was going to be doubled.

We rolled on in the 15-mile-an-hour cavalcade, halting at Urlingford where there's a shop that must be one of the most profitable businesses in the country. Every bus that travels from Cork to Dublin and back stops here so the driver and passengers can refuel themselves with cigarettes, breakfast rolls, bottled water and tabloid newspapers. This particular Sunday, there must have been 40 or 50 buses there. There was so much manoeuvring on the tarmac, they'd have needed a control tower to sort it out. The buses were from every part of the county, even the places where hurling wasn't played.

We left Urlingford and chugged onwards as though in slow-motion replay.

By the time we reached Dublin, the couple of buddies who'd been waiting for me had nearly given up. Thank God for mobile phones.

'Where are you?'

'Monasterevin.'

'Fuck's sake.'

Time passes.

'Where are you now?'

'Monasterevin.'

'Are you walking?'

Time passes as slowly, as in a Beckett play.

246

'What's the story?'

'Hang on. I'll just check this road sign. Oh, we're on the outskirts of Monasterevin. Hello? Hello?'

My late arrival meant that the only available tickets were high in the corner of the Hogan Stand near the Canal End. There was some good-natured grumbling from my companions. We were so far away from the action as to be simultaneously omniscient and distanced. It wasn't, in truth, the optimum position for an enjoyable viewing experience. Yet what followed proved that it doesn't matter where you're sitting if the game is good enough. Cork v. Wexford on 10 August 2003 turned out to be the most exciting match I'd ever seen in any sport. By the end we felt like we'd been granted the best seats in the stadium. It was the kind of game that would have been worth a €500 ticket. Had every other match in the 2003 hurling championship been a wash-out, this one would have justified the whole shebang.

Hurling needed a game like this. Unable to match football for the volume of games, it had begun to slacken off in quality as well, to the extent of seeming like the inferior championship. Cork and Wexford reminded everyone why an assumption like that would always be wrong. Because, when hurling is played really well, it not only outclasses Gaelic football but offers excitement the like of which isn't easily to be had anywhere in the world. This was 70 minutes of intense aesthetic bliss that left its public wandering around outside afterwards with grins plastered on their faces.

If it was going to be any kind of contest, we three agreed, Wexford needed to make a good start. So we fairly leapt out of our seats when, five minutes in, Paul Codd scored a goal. A long ball had been floated in from the left and our elevated position gave us a chance to see, long before the sliotar reached him, that Pat Mulcahy had completely misjudged it. The ball continued its trajectory, Paul Codd rose behind Mulcahy, plucked it down and then belted a shot past Donal Óg Cusack. Wexford had their start.

They built on it. Darragh Ryan mastered Joe Deane, Liam

Dunne and Larry O'Gorman played like men who'd forgotten their ages, Larry Murphy zoomed around in that inimitable headless-chicken-with-skill way he had, the two Jacob brothers, Michael and Rory, who'd previously been regarded as promising lightweights, ran the previously unflappable duo of Wayne Sherlock and Tom Kenny ragged. To cap it all, Adrian Fenlon cut a sideline ball over the bar.

The big advantage that hurling has over football is its repertory of arcane skills that pull you up short and make you wonder how someone managed that. Football, when it came down to it, had catching, kicking and solo-running, all skills you could imagine yourself performing. There was no mystery to them. Hurling had overhead striking, first-time pulling, all kinds of opportunities for logic-defying flicks. And it had the sideline cut, one of the great skills of world sport when executed properly. A man squaring up to a ball 30 yards out on a sideline, the ball dead flat on the ground, the hurl slightly curved and he manages to sweep it high in the air, travelling towards the middle of the posts, maintaining its height and flying over. It's a wonder no matter how many times you see it.

Cork could have been excused for being a bit fazed by all the Wexford brilliance. Whatever they might have said afterwards, there was no way they would have expected anything like it. But they hung on, Deane might have been outplayed by Ryan, but he got away for a good point, Setanta was having a quiet match but he did the same, sometimes the game looked to be passing John Gardiner, by but he landed a couple of great long points. Cork were only 0–10 to 1–11 behind at half-time, not a bad return considering how Wexford had played. It was hard to know what to say at the break, the pace of the match was incredible and 22 scores in 35 minutes meant you couldn't take your eyes off the game. Start talking about the score just gone and you'd miss its successor. There are often high-scoring first halves but games can settle down in the second half and I don't think anyone expected the same kind of match in the second half. But, with perfect symmetry, we had 22 scores in the second half and even more excitement.

The prognosis was that Cork would come out in the second half and quickly wipe out the lead as they had done in the Munster final. But, hang on a minute, Adrian Fenlon was squaring up to another sideline cut, about 40 yards out this time.

'Well, he won't cut that one over the bar,' said one of my friends.

He cut it over the bar and, 10 minutes into the half, Wexford were six points clear and flying. For all the skill and confidence of the Cork team, they would probably had been swamped had a special player not come up with a big goal just when it was needed. At six-foot five, Setanta was big enough, when you added in a long arm and an ability to get up for the ball, he was almost unplayable under the right high delivery. One came in, he caught it, turned, bullocked past two Wexford defenders and exhibited his Na Piarsaigh football skill by kicking the ball past Damien Fitzhenry.

We were in a new phase of the game. As Waterford had found, this Cork team were positively terrifying once they sensed any weakness in the opposition. John Gardiner struck another fine long point as Cork rattled off five points in a row to go a couple clear. Wexford, the older team, looked out on their feet and, with 10 minutes to go, another Cork attack ended with the ball falling to an in-rushing Deane 15 yards out. Almost any other forward in the country would have had a first-time shot and taken the chance of it being blocked. Instead Deane collected the ball, veered off to the side, took a step to steady himself and make an angle and only then shot to the net. It reminded me of something his father Bobby had said when I'd met him in Killeagh before the 1999 final.

'He's the kind of lad who'd never be late for work but he'd still leave it till the last minute before he got ready.'

It was a good description of how Deane functioned near goal, taking his time but making sure the job got done. It was something that most great opportunists seemed to have in common. After all Darragh Ryan's efforts, Deane had got through at the vital stage. He only needed to be lucky once.

It was pretty obvious where the game was going to go from here. Five points down with 10 minutes left and visibly knackered, Wexford would take heart from their gallant effort, fade away and allow Cork to cruise in for the expected comfortable victory. Their attack had finally run out of options, thanks to a storming performance from Diarmuid O'Sullivan who'd moved to full-back and put both himself and Pat Mulcahy out of their misery. It emerged later that O'Sullivan, rather than the manager, had made the call.

Wexford, though, were having none of it. They'd take us all for another round of the roller-coaster. Larry Murphy went to full-forward, competed with O'Sullivan and broke his dominance. Mitch Jordan, having the game of his life, bounded onto one loose ball and scored Wexford's second goal. Two points in it. Wexford brought it back to one approaching the end of normal time. Cork hit a couple of bad wides then moved two clear again. A minute into injury time, Alan Browne, who might as well have been in our high-stand seats, for all the impact he'd made up to that point, got the ball on the right sideline and from an impossibly acute angle, steered a shot over the bar, as though attempting a hurling equivalent of Frankie Dolan's point of the championship.

I was glad for Browne. If you looked at his career, he was always one of Cork's most consistent forwards, yet a certain ungainly quality meant he was often the one to be blamed by the fans when things went wrong. Now he'd got the insurance point.

There were seconds left. A long ball broke to Jordan. He was 30 yards out … 20. His pass to Rory McCarthy made the angle too tight. There wasn't much that McCarthy could do except …

The ball was in the bloody net. He'd turned and hit it, almost blind, and it had shot between the narrow gap between Donal Óg

Cusack and the post. I jumped out of my seat as if Sligo had just won the All-Ireland. There wasn't a neutral watching who didn't do the same. The referee blew the whistle and the best game I have ever seen had ended in an impossible Hollywood fashion, a fantastic goal in the last second, a goal exactly when it was needed, the kind of shot that never comes off, except in the dreams of supporters.

Cork. Wexford. Thanks. Simple as that.

We felt kind of dazed after that and watched the Galway v. Donegal football quarter-final replay on television in a trance. Galway played in a trance for most of the game until they came alive in the last quarter and missed at least four good goal chances, any of which would have rescued the game for them. The big trio of Joyce, Savage and Donnellan looked tired again, though Donnellan picked up a bit from the first game. It seemed only yesterday that they'd been as coltishly energetic as Setanta and John Gardiner. The shine was coming off players earlier and earlier. Michael Meehan had done well for a young player but, after all the hype, his season still seemed like an anti-climax. (At least at county level it had been, he quickly got down to the business of starring for his club, Caltra, as they won the Galway, Connacht and All-Ireland titles for the first time ever. We'll be hearing lots more about him.) Galway were out and, though I felt sad for John O'Mahony whose quarter-final phobia wouldn't be cured this year, I had my own reasons for being happy for Donegal, which I'll come to later.

But Cork and Wexford. Phew. I watched the highlights in the hotel that night and felt almost nostalgic for a match of such brilliance. How many of those would you see in a decade? Three? Two? If I'd known it was so good, I'd have tried to appreciate it more when it was going on.

If I'd thought my bizarre bar days were over in Portlaoise, I was wrong. Retro is a buzz word these days and what it usually means is cringey nights of seventies disco. But the bar of the crumbling suburban hotel I was staying in was retro. It was the kind of place that might once have been described as a pick-up joint, a term that now seems as quaint as garden gnomes. In other words, the type of spot we dreamed of as country teenagers. Dublin had moved on from that kind of innocent Leeson Street-style fun, but the last warriors from those days were drinking in this bar.

It was as though the heroines of those Edna O'Brien novels from the sixties and seventies, about young ones from the country who discover themselves sexually through encounters with worldly wise seducers, had come to life and were having a reunion. The glare from their short dresses and tans was only matched by the glares they'd give when one of their companions ogled one of the Filipino nurses dotted around the bar. The companions were getting on and didn't look as well as the women. They didn't need to, they looked like money. The place had a strange faded grandeur, the bon viveurs of the old days gathering to recall wild nights on The Strip when there was nothing more sophisticated than decking a bottle of wine at three in the morning as a man played Elton John on the piano in the background.

I ended the night drinking in the lobby with a hotelier, a taxi driver and a man involved in the lap-dancing industry. The hotelier reckoned I should be staying in his establishment.

'It's much better than this. You can get a late drink there.'

It was half-two in the morning and we'd just ordered another round. Sometimes you'd get the feeling this country isn't half settled when it comes to drink.

15

Tinkers, Rogues and Hotel Receptionists

16 August: All-Ireland Senior Hurling Championship Semi-Final Replay; Croke Park; Cork 3–17, Wexford 2–7

The replay of the most exciting game I ever saw turned out to be fairly lousy. This can happen with replays and there'd been a feeling of inevitability about the build-up. The old-timers on the Wexford team, and there were a fair few of them, had been able to rise to the occasion once but it was bound to have taken a toll on them. Like elderly millionaires satisfying the needs of a young bride, getting it up once was within their compass but afters weren't a likely prospect.

To continue the sexual metaphor, everyone expected an anti-climax and that's what they got. The Cork fans didn't travel in the same numbers and the match functioned as a kind of premature curtain-raiser for the Kilkenny v. Tipperary game the next day, which was being billed as the 'Real All-Ireland Final', kind of in the way Jack Lynch used to be described as the 'Real Taoiseach'.

There were other reasons to suspect a Wexford collapse second time out. Putting two good performances together had never been the team's forte, a similarly gallant underdog effort that earned them a draw in the 2001 semi-final was followed by a supine capitulation to Tipperary in the replay. And then there was the unorthodox preparation of their finest forward, Paul Codd,

253

who chose an unfortunate time to experience a rush of blood to the head. Mind you, it was hard to see who came out of the affair of the sponsored hurls with any credit.

Not many people had noticed at the time but three players, Codd and Damien Fitzhenry of Wexford and Seán Óg Ó hAilpín of Cork, had played with the first game with logos advertising the bookmakers Paddy Power on their hurls. This was apparently illegal under the laws of the association and made the GAA cross. It made the GPA very cross. And, eventually, it left Paul Codd fuming.

What got the GAA's goat was that no one had checked whether the sponsorship was legal. Their line was that allowing sponsorship on hurls undermined the deals that teams had with their main sponsor. And it probably would have though, once more, the association were in the anomalous position of stopping players earning money when they weren't actually paying the teams anything themselves. Paul Codd understandably found this hard to stomach.

The whole GAA position on sponsorship was bizarre when you thought about it. If they'd actually just got out of the way and allowed a free for all then you'd probably end up with a form of professionalism for which business was footing the bill. By stamping their foot over sponsorship, which was something they did regularly, they gave the unfortunate impression of begrudging players a few handy bob. They then proceeded to make themselves look foolish by asking Paddy Power to vacate their corporate box. They didn't go as far as evicting them, they just suggested that Paddy Power should recognise that the GAA wanted them out on a point of principle and do the decent thing. It was a bit reminiscent of disgraced Prussian army officers being handed a bottle of brandy and a revolver and being urged to take the manly way out. Paddy Power declined the offer. They probably knew that the odds on the GAA actually kicking them out were very long indeed.

The GPA got in on the act when their head honcho Dessie Farrell bemoaned the fact that the players had not arranged the deal through them. The gist of his argument was that the GPA had been trying to behave responsibly and couldn't do this if players went off on their own to set up personal deals. He also seemed to suggest that the €750 they'd each received was on the low side and that Paddy Power were verging on the exploitative.

Farrell's reaction was also understandable, but he was caught in a contradiction as well. The GPA was by far the best representative body the players have ever had. It is the only one they've had, if you discount the one set up by Croke Park that was similar to the works committees set up by companies who didn't want to deal with anything as independent as a trade union. Yet it was a cross between a trade union and an agency. It spoke about the welfare of the players but it took a slice of their endorsement money. Admittedly, and anyone represented by an agency knows this, that sum was probably far less than the additional money they'd earned in negotiations. But the three hurlers did have a right to go off and strike deals on their own. The healthiest situation of all would be if there were several agencies representing the country's players, which would maximise the sponsorship money they'd make. Yet that would undermine the trade-union aspect of the GPA, which is also important. The GPA was a victim of the strange status of GAA players in the modern era. They weren't professionals but they had the potential to earn a lot of money off the field. That put them in a unique position and made Farrell's life difficult when something like this happened.

The Paddy Power line was that €750 was plenty and that they hadn't gone through the GPA because they preferred negotiating with the players personally, a line that echoed shyster employers down the ages. ('You don't want to be bothering with those old unions, son. I'll look after you well.') Yet they did make the one decent gesture of the whole caper by paying the players €2,250, the amount they'd have earned if they'd sported the logos in the replay and the final. And they got the players out of a hole by not insisting that the deal was honoured once the GAA kicked up.

Which leaves Fuming Paul Codd. While Fitzhenry and Ó hAilpín were keeping their heads down, FPC threw a couple of cans of petrol on the blaze by describing the GAA as 'tinkers and rogues', the kind of phrase that hadn't been heard in public since the heyday of J.M. Synge. He got in a few more digs against officialdom and concluded by observing, 'Everyone is getting money out of the games except the players.'

The general prognosis was that FPC had gone too far and let the side down and there was much tut-tutting and shaking of heads. True enough, the language had been choice and suggested that any members of the travelling community camping on the full-forward's land would get short shrift. But, underneath all the compliments-pass-when-the-quality-meet stuff, he was probably right. How often did you hear commentators say that the great thing about a big GAA match was that the players weren't getting a penny out of it? This was supposed to leave the audience with a big Ready-Brek glow in the pit of its collective stomach. But what was so great about it? The commentator was getting top dollar, the journalists, the security guards, the waiters in the corporate boxes, the girls working the hot dog stands, everyone involved in running the show at Croke Park was getting paid. The 30 guys on the pitch weren't. It wasn't surprising that someone would throw the head when they found their €750 being portrayed as a danger to the fabric of the association.

The problem was that, if Codd had been wise, he might have left these observations to another time. And the lack of sympathy for him was connected to a certain self-pitying tone that could creep into his interviews. Not long before, he'd laid into his county's supporters for being insufficiently appreciative. The problem with spectators, said FPC, was that a lot of them only went to a match for a few drinks and an enjoyable day out and didn't put in the same effort as the players. It conjured up a wonderful vista of Wexford fans being forced to attend training camps to earn the right to support their team. The amount of money they had to pay out for a big day in Croke Park seemed to have passed Codd by.

The upshot of all these high jinx was that the mind of Wexford's best forward and one of the best forwards in the country was not fully on the match he had to play at the weekend. It wasn't all that surprising when he had a stinker and was subbed early in the second half. An added cruel twist was that the game probably denied him an All-Star, which he still deserved – €2,250 must have seemed a poor reward for that double disappointment.

Codd wasn't the only man who wasn't in the best of form that weekend. I now present:

Yet more adventures in the Irish hospitality industry

I book into a hotel near Bus Áras. I am given a key and use it to open the door of my room. Oh very nice, they leave out a pair of deck shoes for you. And, hang on a minute, a wardrobe full of clothes, and money and keys beside the bed. Back down the stairs to reception.

'Sorry, you gave me this key. There's someone already staying in the room.'

'Yeah.'

'Well, I'll need another room.'

'You'll need another room?'

'There's someone staying in the room you gave me.'

Silent exasperated shake of the head from the young one on duty. Jesus, she thinks, there's always someone complaining.

'So, like, you want another key, yeah.'

I wanted to check out, but it was getting perilously close to throw-in time.

'Another key would be an idea all right.'

Eventually, muttering away, irritated at my awkwardness, she gave me another key. There was no one staying in this room though, I don't know if anyone else was shown it while I was at the match.

Did I complain? No, I didn't say a word. Why not? Because I'm a Paddy. We're grateful that people actually allow us to pay them money to stay in hotels. We think they're doing us a favour. And so do they. The tale doesn't end yet.

Next morning. I'd arranged to meet a friend at a quarter-to-one in a pub in Parnell Street. I'd bought the papers that morning and wanted to finish them rather than lugging them around Dublin with me.

'Hello, is that reception?'

'Yeah.'

Different young one. Same charm school.

'I'm just wondering if I could extend my check-out time from twelve to half-twelve.'

'No.'

'It hardly makes any difference.'

'Check-out time is twelve. Bye.'

I'd hang on anyway. Five-past twelve.

'Hello, Mr Sweeney. Check-out time is twelve, you'll have to leave the room now.'

'Is there someone waiting for the room?'

'I don't know but check-out time is twelve.'

I hung on till half-twelve and didn't answer the two phone calls to my room. I waited for the knock at the door like a Soviet dissident during National Purge Week.

And do you know something? If she'd asked me how I'd enjoyed my stay, I'd have said very much thank you. If she'd handed me one of those comment cards and asked me to please take a few minutes to fill it in I'd have ticked the top mark in every category.

In the game, Wexford were so far off the pace that even two jammy goals in the first 15 minutes, the type of goals that make you think it's going to be a team's day, didn't do much for them. A couple of fluky ricochets ended up leaving Mitch Jordan straight through and he scored the first, the second came when Donal Óg Cusack blocked a shot from Larry Murphy that might have been going over the bar and it dropped down into the net. It didn't make any difference. Cork responded to the second goal by doing the most demoralising thing possible, the routine that lets the other team know their best shot doesn't even hurt. They scored their own goal within a minute through the maligned Alan Browne.

Diarmuid O'Sullivan had once more motioned Pat Mulcahy to the corner. O'Sullivan had cut a cumbersome figure at corner-back, he'd even looked a bit nervous, astounding for someone whose self-belief normally rose off him like a heat haze. At full-back, he was the one player in the country who lived up to that favourite coinage of the sports journalist, 'colossus'. There was something larger than life about him in his favourite position, an expansiveness about the way he struck the ball, about the catches he elected to make. Challenges were dismissed with the disdain of Jonah Lomu walking over Mike Catt and Tony Underwood. He seemed to be playing in a different game where everything was done on a larger scale. And he did it with the relief of a man released from prison. You could see why Larry Tompkins had misguidedly imagined he could make an inter-county footballer out of O'Sullivan, even though the Cloyne man's skills were rudimentary. In his pomp, he looked like he could do anything he set his mind to.

The game effectively ended in the 25th minute when Niall McCarthy cut through the middle of the defence in the same way he'd done all through the championship and put Timmy McCarthy in on goal. Seeing Timmy McCarthy one on one with the keeper was a strange thing and evoked peculiar emotions because there was probably no player more marginal or derided in the inter-county game. He had been brilliant for Cork against Waterford in 1999 and miserable in every game till the final when he won the Man of the Match award. Since then, he hadn't played a good championship game for his county and, a lot of the time, his displays had seemed woeful. Yet, as someone pointed out to me, four different managers had picked him in their starting 15 for Cork and they couldn't all be deluded.

Timmy McCarthy obviously contributed something of value but it was hard for the casual observer to see what it was. The fans groaned when he got the ball and soloed 20, 30 yards, everything going well until he lost it or passed it to an opponent or sent a shot way wide. It had got to the stage where any score he got was regarded as a bonus so it was hard not to feel happy for him when he beat Fitzhenry with a shot as calculatedly accurate as any Joe Deane might have mustered.

You wondered how he must feel. All those championship games looking for your true form, eager to shine again, all those substitutions, all the bright hopes turning to disappointment. It showed character to keep getting on the ball and making those solo runs that once had led somewhere but now did not. Some day it might all go right for him and he'd score six or seven points from play when it mattered. For the moment, he was on the most thankless path in inter-county hurling.

After the goal, we were back in the snoozy territory of the Tipp v. Offaly semi-final. Cork had a bit of target practice, Ben O'Connor did a few spectacular things and Joe Deane was lucky once more with the third goal of the game. Cork, the team that had begun the season in disarray, the team with something to prove, the team with all those exciting youngsters – Setanta, John Gardiner, Tom Kenny, Ronan Curran – were in the final for the first time in four years. Ooh to be a gggrebilll.

16

Young Kielty Sprang across the Goal
to Tip It Deftly Wide

17 August: All-Ireland Senior Hurling Championship Semi-Final; Croke Park; Kilkenny 3–18, Tipperary 0–15

Around nine minutes into the second half of this semi-final, Kilkenny decided to brook no further resistance from Tipperary. They cut the Tipp defence apart but Brendan Cummins made a great save. From the rebound, he made another. Then another. Then Tom Costello cleared the ball off the line. Finally Tommy Walsh put Tipp out of their misery by drilling a shot past Cummins. It was as emphatic as a full stop. Cummins could perform all the wonders he wanted, but Kilkenny would keep coming after him. It just didn't seem fair.

In the corporate area of Croke Park was one very relieved Kilkennyman, Joe Sweeney. My father had spent the week before frantically texting me with his worries about the game. Tipperary had such a good record against Kilkenny traditionally, they'd come so close in the last two meetings of the sides, Kilkenny were coming off a long lay off, D.J. wasn't getting it together, after two National League finals and an All-Ireland, Kilkenny had to lose a big game some time. He had, he said several times, a bad feeling about this game. The night before the semi-final, he texted me to say that he was very worried about how it might turn out. Why hadn't they picked Andy Comerford? Was Peter Barry the same player he'd been the year before? And what about young Walsh from Tullaroan?

Lots of people worry like this before their county play big games. The difference with my father, I know now, was that he knew he was dying. The reason he was texting me was that his speech had become incomprehensible over the phone because of the throat cancer that had been winning its battle with him over the previous months. They had tried radiotherapy, chemotherapy, some of us even tried prayer. Cancer kept coming after him. It just didn't seem fair.

The first GAA match I ever saw live was in Conlon's Field in Gurteen where Eastern Harps, our local team, beat Geevagh by a couple of points. I was four, maybe five, and it seemed more impressive to me than any All-Ireland final or *Match of the Day*. My father brought me to it.

By 2003, we'd gone our separate ways, but we met a couple of hours after Kilkenny had destroyed Tipperary and given perhaps their best performance under Brian Cody. He was delighted, though he couldn't say much about the game. It was easier to communicate with him when you were a couple of hundred miles away. Texting across a table would have seemed strange. He lived to see the All-Ireland final, but it's his delight after the semi-final that I'll always remember. He'd grown up in an era when Tipperary regularly put the kibosh on Kilkenny's hopes of glory. Kilkenny's record against Cork, a couple of blips notwithstanding, was far more impressive. He never doubted that they'd win the final, but he thought Tipperary might stand in the way of his fervent hope that he would see Kilkenny win one more title. My father knew he wouldn't be around for any subsequent championships.

The last time I saw him alive was on a Saturday in Beaumont Hospital. We talked about books for a while (at this stage he had a wipe-free writing pad and a marker and employed them frenetically), and then got on to the Australia v. Ireland World Cup match that had been played that morning. He was delighted at how well Ronan O'Gara had played and was a partisan supporter of the Munster man's claims over those of David Humphreys. Matt Molloy had come in afterwards, they'd talked and Matt had played a few tunes. It had been a perfect morning for my father – sport and music, his two great passions. A few days later, he was dead.

I remember the first day I saw him when he was undergoing radiotherapy. His beard and moustache had been shaved off and his face was as red as if he had fallen into the fire. There was a tube going into his neck and one attached to his stomach. He could not speak or eat or drink. He had an expression on his face that was oddly familiar to me, a mixture of a resigned smile and a pained grimace. For months I couldn't remember where I'd seen it before. The day he died, I remembered. Adolf Eichmann, on trial in his glass booth in Jerusalem, wore the same look. The look said, 'Fuck it, I'm not going to get out of this one.'

The day after I saw him, I was due to appear on *The View* on RTÉ. I went on the beer instead and never turned up. It just seemed the height of irrelevance to go on and talk about art while my father was suffering like this. Art meant nothing to me that day and, as my father got worse, fewer things meant anything to me. I thought of abandoning this book, wondered what was the point of the football and hurling championships in a world where people died painful deaths. The only thing that prevented me from quitting was the thought that my father might enjoy the book, that it would cheer him up in his sickness. I didn't think he'd die, you see. None of us, I think, really believe that someone close to us is going to die until it actually happens. Sometimes, I still think of ringing him to talk about something that has caught my eye – a match, a book, a political event – so we can set the world to rights over the phone. And then I remember that there won't be any more of those conversations. Not ever. The last word has been spoken.

Plenty of people died while the championships were going on.

Many of them were younger than my father. Teenagers were killed in car crashes, kids died in domestic accidents, babies suffered cot deaths or were lost shortly after birth. The accumulated total of all that pain almost defies the imagination. Every death was the end of the world for someone and felt like the end of the world to several others. The grieving must have thought, for a while, that it was obscene for the country to carry on as it had with matches being played, shopping being done, dancing going on.

When someone dies and they are connected sufficiently closely with the GAA for the death to make the sports pages one stock phrase is usually trotted out. 'This puts Sunday's game into perspective.'

You can't argue with that. But death doesn't just put sport into perspective, it puts everything into perspective. In fact, it puts life into perspective. As Woody Allen once said, no matter how good your life is you're never going to get out of it alive.

In the end, the fact that there's so much pain and suffering in the world doesn't make sport unimportant. It's because there's so much pain and suffering that sport, like art, is important. It takes our mind off the abyss. While Kilkenny were playing Tipperary, and in the run-up to the game, my father got some relief from his illness, there was something else to think about, something a world away from sickness and dying.

I remember Pat Mulcahy, the Cork full-back/corner-back, playing a county final for Newtownshandrum the week after his father died. His brothers were on the team too. The Mulcahys were outstanding, Newtown won and Pat was Man of the Match. At the time, I didn't have a clue how they must have felt. Now that my own father has died, I have some notion because there are experiences that can only be understood after you've gone through them yourself. Hurling wouldn't have taken away their pain but, for 60 minutes, they'd have been able to transcend their grief, even to direct it in a way that could honour their father. That's something sport can do for us.

I thought I'd look back on the 2003 championship in years to come and think of it as the one I wrote the book about. Now, last year will always be the year my father died and the games will be tied in with that.

Why have I written about him? Because I'm a writer and this is what we do. If I was a stonemason I could have built him a headstone but he'll have to settle for this. Ladies and gentlemen I present the 20 great GAA moments of the late Joe Sweeney.

1. Though he read a great deal, my father had no particular facility with words. He was, however, responsible for one of the crowning glories of Irish literature. This was the ballad he composed after Eastern Harps had won their first county senior title in 1975 by defeating Craobh Rua 1–8 to 0–5. It appeared in the *Sligo Champion* and he spent a while blasting it out in the pubs of Gurteen, Keash and Culfadda. In later years, I'd try to get him to sing a few verses when we were both jarred. He couldn't remember much of it but the one line that tickled him concerned a penalty missed by Craobh Rua at a crucial stage in the second half. The line from the song went, 'Young Kielty leaped across the goal to tip it deftly wide.' He confessed that Frank Kielty, a brilliant young keeper who would have been a Sligo player but for injury, probably didn't touch the ball at all. But he liked the line, so in it went. This taught me an important lesson about artistic creation. And lying.

2. Perhaps the first man in Sligo to possess a video camera was our local publican Paddy Conlon. Paddy's camera was a gigantic contraption, which ran off a huge battery and produced pictures whose quality was around the same as that produced by video phones in the Iraqi desert. Nevertheless it was in great demand at local sporting events and my father sometimes provided commentary. The broadcasting team were on the sideline at Kilcoyne Park, Tubbercurry, at a first round Sligo championship game between Eastern Harps and Shamrock Gaels when an enormous row broke out that eventually led to spectators invading the field for a free for all reminiscent of a 19th-century faction fight. A couple of burly Shamrock Gaels men spotted the camera and told Paddy and my father to switch it off and fuck off out of the ground. My father wisely fled but Paddy was possessed of the true CNN spirit and continued filming. The highlight of the video is when a Harps mentor finds himself cornered by several Gaels men and retaliates with the only available weapon. There is a strange formal beauty about the sequence as a Lucozade bottle glints in the sun and descends several times on the heads of the enemy.

3. Markievicz Park, as noted previously, is famous for its pre-match traffic jams. In 1981, we found ourselves stuck in one on our way to the Connacht championship game between Sligo and Roscommon. As usual, there were people trying to cut in, driving on the wrong side of the road and employing the usual means that can gain you a few seconds. When one car swerved across us, my father beeped the horn loudly and jumped from the driver's seat. Out of the other car leaped Rory Tansey, an Eastern Harps player not known for taking nonsense from anyone. My father improvised and pointed to a car a few yards down the road. 'Did you get the number of that fella, Rory? He's a disgraceful driver.'

4. My father was an excellent black-and-white photographer and there are dozens of photos of Harps matches at home. But the best shots he ever took came after my mother's club, Michael Breathnach from the far side of An Spideal, had won the Galway minor final against Corofin in the mid-seventies. My mother's cousin, Máirtín Beag Ó Cualáin, was Man of the Match and scored the winning point in the last minute. There's a shot of him holding the cup in the car window to us kids that I love. And there's a shot of a group of Michael Breathnach men, among them my Uncle Ned, standing around a celebratory bonfire that says everything about community pride in victory.

5. Though there was no hurling club in Gurteen, my father splashed out on a couple of Ollie Walsh hurls in an effort to teach myself and my brother, Eoghan, the rudiments of the

game. (He insisted that 'hurl' is the only correct English word for a camán. Hurley he dismissed and I once saw him nearly faint when he heard someone in a pub mention 'hurley bats'.) He would have been as well off giving them to the dog. I don't feel too bad about this now as I've realised that part of the point of getting us the hurls was so he could nostalgically hammer 21-yard frees past us and remember his glory days on the green at St Francis Terrace. At least we were spared the green plastic Wavin hurls, the mention of which can cause many a youngster to clutch their elbows with remembered pain. The Wavin hurl, you see, was brilliant until you hit the ball. Then it delivered a juddering aftershock through the whole of your body. It was like touching an electric fence.

6. The first All-Ireland final my father ever went to was the 1957 match in which Kilkenny beat Waterford. It was the final in which Kilkenny had 16 men in the pre-match parade. This was because an English film, *Rooney*, was being made and the climactic scene involved the hero playing in the hurling final. The actor John Gregson marched in the parade so the director would have some authentic-looking footage. Following the Joe Higgins affair, the GAA should, in the interests of fairness, impose a retrospective fine on Kilkenny for their blatant rule breaking. *Rooney*, which gets shown from time to time at the IFI in Temple Bar, is actually great crack, though no one is ever going to mistake it for *Citizen Kane*.

The eponymous hero is a Dublin dustman who marries into a posh family who don't approve of him hurling. In the end, he goes back to the game he loves and keeps the woman as well. Val Doonican sings the excruciating title song, which I remember singing along to in a kebab shop on Coldharbour Lane in Brixton one late drunken night. It had come on the radio and when it was finished the Turkish lad who owned the place, raised his eyebrows and said, 'Is that what Irish music sounds like, mate?' The same man found endless fascination in my Christian name as the only other Eamonn he'd ever heard of was Eamonn Andrews. Every night when I went in, he'd roar, 'Eamonn Sweeney. This... is... your... kebab.'

7. The first All-Ireland final my father and mother went to together was the 1966 All-Ireland hurling final between Kilkenny and Cork. Kilkenny were hot favourites but Cork hurled them off the pitch. The story was that Kilkenny had been given sleeping pills the night before the match but had taken too many and were half stoned in Croke Park the next day. The team were described for a while as 'Pilltown' by their followers, Piltown being a club in Kilkenny. My mother probably wasn't too worried, she was back a few weeks later to see Galway complete their three-in-a-row of football titles. I interviewed Mick Waters, who'd played midfield for Cork that day, before the 1999 final. He'd joined the priesthood and the 1966 game was his last game for Cork. Shortly afterwards, he departed for the missions in Africa and was still working there when I spoke to him 33 years later. The change it involved – Croke Park celebrations one day, Africa the next – must have been mind-boggling and would probably have made a far better film than *Rooney*.

8. My father left Kilkenny when he was 17 and never lived there again. Like many exiles, however, he was roused to extreme local patriotism by the GAA. The change in his accent on the day of a Kilkenny match was incredible. The team were 'de byz'. D.J. was 'Deeja'. The great nineties midfielder Michael Phelan became, 'Mickey Falen'. He spoke about Lory Meagher as though he'd seen him playing. But his favourite player was 'Eddie Care'.

9. Once he had the opportunity of seeing his beloved Kilkenny playing on Sligo soil. Sligo football had sunk to such a low ebb that we had drawn Kilkenny, the worst county in the country, in Markievicz Park. It was 1982 I believe, the depths of winter and there were about a hundred people at the game. Kilkenny had hurling stars, such as Joe Hennessy, Dick O'Hara, Mick Brennan and Christy Heffernan on the team. With the exception of Mick Brennan who scored a goal, they looked ill at ease with the big ball. Full-back for Sligo was Denis O'Hara of Eastern Harps who was marking Christy Heffernan and didn't give him a ball. At the time, Heffernan was the deadliest forward in hurling and my father got great joy out of telling people that we had a player in our club who'd held him scoreless no bother. He didn't mention that it had been in football. Sligo won easily enough. This game was also covered by the Paddy Conlon video unit and, at one stage, there was the following exchange between cameraman and commentator. 'Johnny Stenson kicks an untypical wide for Sligo.'

'Aye, he'd typically kick it a lot further wide.'

'Jesus, you can't say that, they won't let us in the next day.'

'Don't worry, it won't come out on the tape.'

10. Big Kilkenny games in Croke Park usually drew my father's Uncle Neddy to the capital. My father would meet him in Gaffney's pub and they'd set off to the game together. Uncle Neddy had once been All-Ireland champion on the mouth organ and had been a wild man before finding religion late in life. When my father spoke to him, their Kilkenny accents became completely incomprehensible to outsiders.

11. The recently maligned Johnny Stenson deserved a bit more gratitude given that he'd been Man of the Match on one of the two greatest days in the history of Sligo football, the 1975 Connacht final replay win against Mayo in Castlebar. Myself and my father were at that game and at the first match in Markievicz Park. My memory of the games is patchy but then my experience of them was patchy as well. It was the heyday of hawkers and, every couple of minutes, my view of the action would be obstructed by someone proffering apples, crisps and minerals. Such are the joys of being four-foot tall. There is a cruel tale circulated about the Sligo people getting off the train in Dublin for the semi-final and coming to a dead stop because nobody knew where Croke Park was. In that semi-final, they were annihilated by the Kerry team who'd go on to become the greatest side in the history of the GAA. Sligo had a team full of big, strong and not particularly mobile men accustomed to playing good, old-fashioned catch-and-kick football. Their defeat by Kerry was one of those moments when the old is overwhelmed by the new, as when the Polish cavalry tried to take on German tanks in the Second World War or when stone axes were replaced by weapons of bronze.

12. My father's people, on his father's side, came from Tullaroan, who had been the original kings of Kilkenny hurling and had probably been the greatest club in Ireland at one stage. In the days when club teams represented counties, they'd won All-Irelands in 1904 and 1912. In the twenties, they produced Lory Meagher, probably the greatest ever Kilkenny hurler and the finest midfielder to play the game. Tullaroan lost their dominant position over time, but they returned to the top in 1994 when they won the county final against Dicksboro. My father was overjoyed and described a particular long-range point by Liam Keoghan for the next year. My father's cousin Bobby Sweeney, a veteran at that stage, came on as a sub to share in Tullaroan's victory. Bobby had enjoyed a fine career, which included scoring the winning goal for Kilkenny against Cork in the 1975 All-Ireland final. In recent years, my father had been keeping an eye on Bobby's son, Ned, who had impressed at underage level for Kilkenny and St Kieran's College. My father's people on his mother's side came from Coone. Coone's lack of GAA success perhaps explains my father's lesser interest in the area.

13. Cyril Farrell and Ger Loughnane were wont to go on about the superior attitude of the traditional hurling powers. The ultimate two fingers to this perceived disrespect was Anthony Daly's famous, 'We are no longer the whipping boys', speech after the 1997 Munster final. The attitude does exist and my father could assume it at times. After the 1992 All-Ireland semi-final, when Kilkenny came late to beat Galway, he met myself and a friend of mine from Galway coming out of the game. 'Ye gave us a little bit of a fright there,' he said and patted my friend on the head. He wasn't forgiven for a long time.

14. He should have known better because, in 1986, the whole family went to Thurles to watch Kilkenny hammer Galway. That was the plan anyway because no one gave Galway a hope. He warned my mother on the way down not to be too disappointed when Galway lost and not to complain about it. Galway stuffed Kilkenny and the journey home was largely silent, punctuated only by my father complaining to my mother about a belt Sylvie Linnane had given Liam Fennelly. You'd have sworn it was my mother who'd drawn the blow. This was one of our last family outings. I'm sure the result has nothing to do with that.

15. Arrogance is hard to shake. My father's main worry before the 1999 All-Ireland final was that Kilkenny would have the match won by half-time and thus the second half would be a bit of a bore. He expounded on this theory at great length in Gaffney's. At around half-one, he spotted an acquaintance of his from Galway leaving to see the minor final between Galway and Cork. 'Look at him,' said the oul' fella, 'going off to see his matcheen.' Four hours later, Kilkenny had been shocked by Cork and the Galwayman had returned to Gaffney's. 'We won our matcheen, Joe. How did yours go?'

16. In 1998, I read at the Kilkenny Arts Festival. My father had a one-man show there. As a painter, he was a fine amateur though never good enough to break through into the world of gallery shows and reviews in the arts pages. Yet, now that he'd quit his job, the idea that he was a full-time painter was a great consolation to him. We were in a pub watching the All-Ireland semi-final replay between Clare and Offaly and Ollie Baker was putting in some typically vigorous challenges. Baker is a garda so my father shouted at the screen, 'Hit him again, Ollie, you'll make sergeant.' The man on the next stool turned around, stared us down and snarled, 'It's harder to make than that.'

17. Every year, Dermot Crowe gave my father a couple of good tickets for the Leinster final. My father would give Dermot a bottle of whiskey. Dermot came up trumps again when I wanted tickets for my father for last year's semi-final, though someone else offered the oul' fella a rare seat in the corporate box that he took instead. Ingratitude being what it is, Dermot Crowe was not my father's favourite hurling reporter.

That honour fell to Enda McEvoy of the *Sunday Tribune* whose excellent history of hurling in St Kieran's was one of the books my father read in his final days. Enda would visit the Kilkenny one-man show every year and apparently announce that he'd come for his free glass of wine. There'll be no more free wine.

18. With perfect timing, we both missed Sligo's greatest victory since 1975. On the day in 2002 when they were trouncing Tyrone in Croke Park to reach the All-Ireland quarter-final, we were on Cape Clear Island for the christening of my daughter, Emily, whose mother, Siobhan, comes from Cape. We did manage to catch the game in Ciarán Danny Mike's pub and, by the end, were leaping around the place in amazed disbelief. When my father got the boat back to the mainland that evening he said, 'They say you've done all right if you see your children's children. I can go now.' I think we laughed at the improbability of such a demise, unhealthy and all as he was. Yet it made me think of the James Joyce poem, 'Ecce Puer', which he wrote the year both his daughter was born and his father died, when Joyce asks for forgiveness for forsaking his father. Did I forsake him when he was dying? Should I have seen more of him? You ask yourself these things when someone you love dies. Forsaking was on his mind too. On the Sunday before he died, he apologised to one of my siblings for leaving home. There was no need for apologies at that stage.

19. On that final Saturday, his scribbling on the wipe-free pad became so animated it was exactly the same as if he was holding forth on the Ireland v. Australia match in a pub somewhere. 'Keith Wood is the best player in the world. They won't appreciate how good he is till he's gone.' You're right, Daddy. 'He was a hurler first, you see.' I see.

20. I remember playing an U-16 match for Eastern Harps. My father came along to watch and, at the end, I asked him how I'd done. 'You're the same as I was. You're good, but you're cowardly.' It was probably a fair assessment. Our common

cowardice was a running joke between us. Like me, he had a fear of flying and, after September 11th, told people that this kind of thing was always likely to happen to you on planes. He had a reputation for hypochondria too and I remember him shaking with fear when I brought him on a tour of my old haunts in Brixton one time. Like Woody Allen, he probably exaggerated his timidity for comic effect. Perhaps it was this idea of himself as a mild man that gave him such an affection for the tough guys of Kilkenny hurling. He loved the likes of Pa Dillon, Pat Lawlor, Dick O'Hara and Eddie O'Connor. Yet, when he spent those long months with the cancer racking his body and the prescribed treatments proving more painful than the disease itself, he never complained. There was no self-pity, just a stoical acceptance of what he was going through. On the last day I saw him, he was more bothered about keeping everyone else's spirits up than about his own predicament. A friend of my father's, a doctor who'd visited him almost every day, said he'd never seen anyone bear terminal illness with such fortitude. Joe Sweeney proved to be a brave man in the end.

One of my father's favourite movies was *Touch of Evil*, an Orson Welles thriller that stars Welles himself as a corrupt cop, Janet Leigh as his wife, Charlton Heston as a Mexican detective and Marlene Dietrich as a brothel owner. At the end, after the Welles character has been shot dead, Dietrich drawls out his epitaph, 'He was some kind of a man.'

What more can you say?

17

Panic in the Game of Football, Will Life Ever Be Sane Again?

24 August: All-Ireland Senior Football Championship Semi-Final; Croke Park; Tyrone 0–13, Kerry 0–6

'They kept coming in the same way all the time, inviting us to foul them when they should have switched the plan of attack and gone for long-range points. To win an All-Ireland, you have got to be prepared to hit your opponents hard. We hit them hard that day, within the rules. There's no room for softness or sympathy when you are in there battling to win a place in the All-Ireland final or battling for the title itself.'

Not, as you might imagine, a comment by Mickey Harte about Tyrone's semi-final win over Kerry but the words of Kingdom legend Joe Keohane on his county's semi-final win over Antrim in 1946. That match was one that assumed legendary status for a generation of football followers. Kerry's tactics were so rough that Antrim appealed the result to central council and only lost by 19 votes to 10. Breandán Ó hEithir is scathing about the way Kerry played that day in his book *Over the Bar*. There were two ways of looking at it. Either Kerry had bludgeoned a wonderful Antrim team into submission or the fancy approach of the Ulster champions have come unstuck against the no-nonsense approach of the Munster men. It was a game that remained controversial for many years.

I think the semi-final between Tyrone and Kerry will assume legendary status too. Already, an accretion of myth and misinformation has begun to cling to the encounter. So it's worth trying to work out what exactly did happen and why there was such a fuss made about the match. (Another Joe Keohane comment, in response to Roscommon complaints after the 1980 All-Ireland final was, 'We never blame anybody in Kerry. If we lose, the only people we blame are ourselves.' That quotation might draw a few wry smiles in Tyrone.)

Most of the people at Croke Park that day were expecting a classic, high-scoring, free-flowing match. This optimism was not foolish. The Tyrone and Kerry attacks had looked irresistible on occasions during the year and the two teams had played the most attractive football of the championship (with the possible exception of Laois's Leinster final performance). Equally important, both had looked vulnerable at the back, with Down pulling Tyrone apart in the drawn Ulster final and Roscommon making lanes through Kerry in the All-Ireland quarter-final. This combination of powerful attacks and suspect defences led people to believe that the umpires would have a busy day. In the end, it was referee Gerry Kinneavy who was overworked.

To make the match even more appealing, there was the prospect of an exceptionally rare occurrence – a direct clash between the two outstanding players of their generation. Nobody had matched Peter Canavan and Seamus Moynihan for consistent excellence over the past decade and the idea that they'd be taking each other on in a game of this magnitude was almost too perfect, like some 'Fight of the Century' put together by Don King. Canavan had looked almost as good as ever, though few forwards have ever been as good as he was in 1995, while Moynihan's reputation for rising to the big occasion was unrivalled. The outcome of the duel between them, almost everyone agreed, would be the decisive factor in the game.

The contest was impossibly close to call because no one could remember Moynihan coming off second best when it really mattered to his team in Croke Park, while there was something inexorable about the way Canavan was closing in on the All-Ireland medal, which only a couple of years before had seemed destined to elude him. They were both vastly experienced and awesomely competitive and the only difference between them might be that Canavan was playing in his favourite position while Moynihan was manning a position he'd taken up as stopgap three years earlier and was unable to escape from.

In interviews, Moynihan is extremely courteous and extremely diffident. I remember speaking to him a couple of years ago in Killarney at a press day and he managed to deflect questions with the same facility that he blocks kicks. His dealings with the press are apparently inspired by the Seamus Heaney line, 'Whatever you say, say nothing.'

Yet it was still obvious that Moynihan was tired of filling in at full-back, of spending the final years of his career in a position that didn't suit him. He'd won Footballer of the Year at Number 3, which said volumes about his adaptability and general attitude. But he could have dominated games from centre half-back and employed his considerable footballing ability in a constructive role. As it was, Moynihan was limited to occasional dashes out from full-back. He'd go 30 yards, maybe 40 and then have to transfer the ball to a team-mate and run back to the edge of the square. It was one of the saddest sights in Gaelic football, like watching a lion pacing inside a cage as it remembered what it had been like to roam free across the savannah.

Perhaps GAA fans were just projecting their own desires onto the figure of Moynihan when they suspected that he burned with frustration at the constant necessity to curb his natural instinct for the swashbuckling break forward, the incision deep into enemy territory. Because his confinement to the edge of the square didn't just inconvenience the player, it prevented the supporters from seeing the player given free rein. Further encouraging the calls for his redeployment was the belief that he'd begun to struggle at full-back.

Cork's Colin Corkery had given Moynihan a torrid time in the previous year's Munster final replay and then Armagh's Ronan Clarke had taken three points off him from play in the All-Ireland final. The doubters said that he would always struggle against big, strong full-forwards because he was smaller and lighter than most inter-county full-backs. The travails of the Kerry full-back line against Roscommon did nothing to silence such quibbles.

He was in an unusual situation. Great players normally shone because they'd been given the opportunity to make the most of their talents. Eoghan Liston hadn't been forced into an inter-county career as a midfielder while Nicky English might have been considerably less famous had he spent his best years doing a job for Tipperary at centre half-forward. Nobody had told Picasso he could only use crayons. Yet Moynihan was spending years of potential greatness in a position where the full range of his talents could only be displayed fitfully.

Earlier in the year, it had looked as though he'd be released. Barry O'Shea, the man whose injury in 2000 had lumbered Moynihan with the full-back job in the first place, got a run in the National League and Eamonn Fitzmaurice was there when Kerry had faced Tipperary in their first championship match. Moynihan was back at centre half-back. But not for long as a shaky start by Fitzmaurice resulted in a switch. Just when Moynihan thought he was out of the full-back racket, they'd dragged him back in. And that was where he'd stayed. But if he couldn't cut it at full-back anymore, Peter Canavan was the ideal man to find him out.

Darren Fay of Meath was the outstanding full-back of the modern era, and a man who'd always looked born to fill the position. I decided to ask him if he thought Moynihan was a busted flush as a full-back.

'I think there's too much fuss made about Seamus playing at full-back. He's a brilliant full-back and any team in the country would like to have him playing there, you've got to be strong at the back and lead it from there. The idea that he wasn't playing well there seemed to start in Kerry, but I'd put it down to the fact that some people would prefer if he was playing in a different position.

'People forget that height doesn't come into it anymore. As a full-back, I know that you get very little ball to catch over your head. What you have is full-forward lines moving from side to side and a lot and players out the field looking to play precise ball into them. That's how Tyrone play and it will suit Seamus because, although he's not that quick, he's a phenomenal reader of the game, which helps him intercept those kinds of passes. Anyway, there's been a lot of media hype about Canavan, but he's been mainly pulling strings · around the half-forward line. Owen Mulligan has been doing far more damage.'

Seán Counihan, who'd managed the East Kerry team that Moynihan had inspired to three county titles in a row between 1997 and 1999 thought differently.

'He's so exciting with the ball in hand that you wish he had more freedom. I even thought, at one stage, he'd end up at centre half-forward. Imagine if he was given the licence to follow Brian Dooher on Sunday, he could score two or three points and really give Mickey Harte something to think about.'

Personally, I reckoned that Moynihan was beginning to look a bit marooned at full-back but that Picasso with crayons was still Picasso. I couldn't see him having a bad game, yet I couldn't see Canavan not making a major contribution. Nobody could have predicted how it actually panned out on the day with the two outstanding players of their generation largely reduced to irrelevance.

There was plenty of feigned shock after the match, but the first 20 minutes were genuinely startling. It was shocking how sharp, how hungry, how good Tyrone were from the first whistle and it was equally shocking how flat and slow Kerry looked. The two teams were operating at completely different levels from the start and this seemed to be forgotten later when all the caterwauling began.

Tyrone's display in those first 20 minutes was breathtaking. They played the best football seen in the whole championship, treating Kerry like they'd treated Down in the Ulster final replay and Fermanagh in the quarter-final. They just rolled over the opposition and it was pretty obvious that, when this team hit top form, no one was going to live with them. They were too fast, too focused, too skilful. Nobody else played football like this. They won every breaking ball in the first 20 minutes, every pass found a free man, every flick went right, every player in possession had a couple of options, they murdered Kerry for pace with players just running past their men. At the end of that golden spell, Tyrone were seven points to no score up, and three of those points could have been goals. One of them was harder to put over the bar than under it. Had a couple of goals gone in, I think we could have been in for a rout of unprecedented proportions because Kerry were wandering around in shock and didn't look to have the wherewithal to put up any serious resistance.

The moment that everyone remembered was when Darragh Ó Sé found himself surrounded by Tyrone players. He was completely isolated, there must have been four of them in his way. Yet there was no support forthcoming from his team-mates, in fact a couple of extra Tyrone men arrived to make his life even more unbearable. It was like the scene at the start of the greatest Western ever made, Sam Peckinpah's *The Wild Bunch*, when a bunch of children watch a scorpion being tormented by ants. The ants kill the scorpion in the end and Darragh Ó Sé had to admit defeat too. He lashed at the ball aimlessly and it went to a Tyrone man. For a marvellous footballer, Ó Sé could be very easily upset and he never seemed to be on his game after that. But it was just one of many incidents in which Kerry crumbled under pressure while Tyrone fattened on it.

Tyrone's midfield duo of Kevin Hughes and Seán Cavanagh

weren't the most fearsome fielders in the game and Ó Sé would have been expected to dominate in the air. Tyrone would have to break the ball and hope for the best. Yet there were clean catches taken around the middle of the field and a Tyrone man was coming up with them. Gerard Cavlan from Dungannon, a player who had everything (size, skill, accuracy, intelligence) but consistency had picked his moment. He plucked balls out of the air with ease and prevented Kerry from getting out of their own half of the field.

Seán Cavanagh didn't do a lot of fielding in the middle of the park but, over the course of the championship, he'd almost redefined the midfielder's role. Intelligent footballers sometimes find loopholes in the way the game is set up and Cavanagh seemed to have worked out a flaw in the way midfielders play Gaelic football. The average midfielder spends a great deal of time inside the opposition half, often in scoring positions. Yet no one specific is delegated to pick him up. The midfielder playing against him will contest high ball and keep an eye on him, but a Number 8 or 9 going forward is not marked the same way an attacker is. This means that a midfielder who is bold enough in his runs forward, and accurate enough in his finishing, could score some useful totals. Cavanagh had been doing it all year with three points from play against Derry, a couple of points against Down and 1–2 against Fermanagh. Against Kerry, he scored just one point, though it might have been a goal, but those runs from midfield were something else the Munster champions couldn't cope with at all.

Meanwhile, Brian McGuigan was playing puck. He'd been a fine underage player and they rated him in Tyrone but, everywhere else, he was Brian McGuigan, son of the legendary Frank, who'd been the greatest ever Tyrone player before Peter Canavan emerged. Frank had been a big, striking man with an unruly mop of hair and a flamboyant style. Brian couldn't have been more different. He was a playmaker who went about his work as though he was operating undercover. Yet in the drawn game against Down, Tyrone would have been sunk without his passing. And in the first half against Kerry, he orchestrated waves of attacks and purloined two points for himself. Frank McGuigan, who'd won a hellish battle against alcoholism, must have been a proud man and realised that soon the county's youngsters would be asking him if he really, really was Brian McGuigan's father.

Owen Mulligan had been at the centre of everything good Tyrone had done in their previous games. No one seemed to be able to cover the runs he made and, when he got an opening, he invariably made the most of it. You'd have expected him to share in the plunder of that opening 20 minutes but he was fairly well subdued by Kerry's Michael McCarthy who was doing a good impersonation of the little Dutch boy with his finger in the dyke. McCarthy must have felt as though he was playing a game of backs and forwards, he'd clear the ball and, within a minute, Tyrone would be on the attack again. The Kilcummin man probably did more work in that first 20 minutes than he'd done in the whole of the quarter-final. On a day when Kerry reputations plummeted faster than internet company stocks, he got away almost unscathed.

Yet Mulligan still produced the move of the game against McCarthy. The corner-forward had no business throwing such an outrageous dummy against the best man-marker in the game when he got the ball on the end-line – but he did and it worked. Mulligan cut in and popped the ball up, like a volleyball player, for Enda McGinley who was running in and met it about 10 yards out with his fist. That the ball went over rather than under the bar had nothing to do with Kerry defensive work and it was a let-off they hadn't deserved.

So what about Canavan and Moynihan and the expected epoch-defining battle? Like the bloody house-to-house battle in the streets of Baghdad, which had also been forecast that year, it hadn't really happened. The first thing Canavan did was to throw himself against the back of Michael McCarthy and go down as though he'd been picked off by a sniper on the grassy knoll. McCarthy didn't get booked and Canavan went off, re-emerging with a small bandage around his head. Moynihan cut out the next ball that came in the duo's direction, reading the intentions of the passer perfectly, as Darren Fay had predicted he would.

They were running together for a 50–50 ball when Canavan appeared to get his legs tangled up and Moynihan came away with possession. The Tyrone man crashed to the ground again and there were some booes. The forward who cried wolf and all that. Except this was serious. Canavan's ankle was banjaxed and he had to be stretchered off. There were only 13 minutes gone when the incident had occurred but it did not have the slightest effect on Tyrone's play. Yet the general consensus about the young team had been that they relied on Canavan far more than any of the other contenders depended on a single player. Their ability to not just overcome, but apparently ignore, their nightmare scenario bespoke an extraordinary maturity.

If Canavan was having an awful afternoon, Moynihan wasn't much happier. He'd looked like the old focused Seamus while his rival was on the field but when Stephen O'Neill came on as a replacement, the story changed. It was hard not to feel that Moynihan had been thinking about this clash with Canavan since the draw had been made, that he'd been working out how he'd play him, studying the other man's game, building himself up for the challenge entailed by the Tyrone captain. The signature Moynihan performances had come against players who'd entered matches in the very best of form. Padraic Joyce in 2000 and Colin Corkery in 2002 had proved unmarkable all year. Yet Moynihan, who always came across as one of the most thoughtful of footballers, seemed to have worked out exactly how to play them. Psyched out, neither Joyce or Corkery could make any impression against him. Presumably, he'd given Canavan plenty of thought, yet now the man was gone and Moynihan had a relatively unknown quantity to deal with.

To make matters worse, the relatively unknown quantity was the kind of player who troubled the Kerry full-back – a big, rangy player who was good in the air and difficult to knock off the ball. To make them worse again, O'Neill had a huge amount to prove. Three years previously, he'd looked like the heir to Canavan, the new golden boy of Ulster football, an All-Star miles ahead of the likes of Cavanagh, McGuigan and Mulligan. But he'd been subbed in his first two games of the championships and hadn't figured since. Moynihan would be playing on a hugely talented man who had nothing left to lose. Perhaps it wasn't surprising that O'Neill soon got the upper hand and maintained it to the finish. After all the pre-match hoopla, both Canavan and Moynihan had suffered their worst ever day in Croke Park.

Kerry managed to put together a few attacks near the end of the first half, but the usual smoothness wasn't there. Tyrone were 0–9 to 0–2 up at half-time and completely in command. I expected them to kick on from there and win easily. They just needed to keep doing what they'd been doing in the first half and Kerry would suffer the same fate as Down and Fermanagh.

Instead, they immediately fell back in numbers at the start of the second half, their midfielders lying deep, their half-forwards coming back the field to form a barrier so that Kerry had two lines of players to contend with before they even engaged the Tyrone defence. Why Tyrone felt they had to do this is unclear. Maybe it had something to do with the way they'd lost a big early lead to Sligo the year before. They were just 35 minutes away from an All-Ireland final, something that might panic any team. My own guess, and it's only a hunch, is that they had too much respect for Kerry whose footballers have always been heroes in Ulster. Tyrone couldn't believe that they were this much better than a Kerry team. There had to be some twist in the tale. They couldn't go on running them off the field. It was as well to be cautious.

Neither Gaelic football or hurling are particularly good games in which to try and hold on to a lead. It's far easier in soccer where

a goal is so difficult to score. But give away territory and possession in football or hurling and you'll generally be caught out.
That was how the greatest team ever, Mick O'Dwyer's Kerry, had
been tumbled when they were just a few minutes away from the
first five in a row in the history of the game. They'd begun to
retreat, Jack O'Shea was playing in around his full-back line and
they invited Offaly onto them. The other greatest, Muhammad
Ali, got away with lying on the ropes and letting his opponents
take their best shot. Kerry didn't. Seamus Darby scored the goal
that probably put paid to the idea of the five in a row till the end
of time.

Just three years previously, Armagh had made the same
mistake. Leading Kerry in the second half and playing well, they
tried to defend their lead and were eventually beaten in extra time.
Tyrone's strategy was, on the face of it, extremely risky. Yet it
worked because Kerry continued to play badly and didn't raise
their game at all. With Tyrone not coming out to play, and Kerry
unable to play, the game understandably degenerated into a bit of
a yawner. The pattern was that Kerry would try and attack, take
far too much time on the ball and either kick it away or lose it in
a challenge. Tyrone had plenty of ball with which to counterattack but they had so few men up front, they inevitably gave the
ball back to Kerry. And so the cycle continued. It was stasis city.

The only way Kerry could have troubled Tyrone was if the
Ulster champions had begun to disintegrate defensively and this
was never going to happen in a back-line anchored by two men
whose presence in the central berths said a great deal about the
perspicacity and courage of Mickey Harte. Cormac McAnallen,
like Stephen O'Neill, was earmarked as a star of the future. He
was reminiscent of Derry's Anthony Tohill, a physically dominating centre-fielder who used the ball well and could get up and
down the field at will. The odds on him winning an All-Star award
at midfield in the near future would have been short. He had
minimal experience at full-back, he was one of those midfielders

who looked like attack rather than defence would be their second preference, yet Harte had moved him there after Dan Gordon took Chris Lawn to the cleaners in the Ulster final.

McAnallen did very well on Gordon but it looked like a horses-for-courses move, one big man marking another. Still, Harte kept him at Number 3 for this match and the move worked. So did bringing back Gavin Devlin at centre half-back. Devlin had played there all through the National League campaign before being caught on camera stamping on Laois's Colm Parkinson in the final. He got a three-month sentence, which probably reflected the public nature of what he'd done rather than its seriousness. In the previous championship season, Clare's Gerry Quinn had his hand broken and a Derry player broke Gerard Cavlan's jaw. No one served a day's suspension for those crimes, but Devlin missed the guts of the championship for a quite superficial offence. After three months out of the game, he shouldn't have been match-fit but Harte took a chance on his preferred Number 6. Like McAnallen, Devlin delivered.

The Tyrone manager did things his own way. It is a truism that you can't do too much tampering with a team once the championship was underway. Even if players weren't going well, it was the lesser of two evils to keep a settled team with the strugglers *in situ*. Harte figured differently. The entire full-back line that played in Tyrone's first championship match had been scrapped by the time the All-Ireland final came round. And only seven players played in the same position all through the campaign. In all, 29 players appeared for Tyrone along the way. That wasn't supposed to be how it was done. It is hard to escape the conclusion that Mickey Harte is a very clever man.

One of the canards expounded after the game was that Tyrone had been so negative that it was impossible for Kerry to get the necessary scores against them. According to this line of reasoning, no team could have managed to break through the massed white ranks. It just wasn't fair. Yet Kerry, for all their sluggishness, had plenty of chances. Kickable frees were missed and they had enough chances at scoring points to get right back into the game. The task was scarcely impossible. The Kerry of 2000 or Galway of 2001, would have chiselled out the scores.

As it was, Kerry managed to cut the lead to four points entering the last 10 minutes. Mind you, they could have been dead and buried if Declan O'Sullivan had not got back to take an Owen Mulligan shot off the line. What O'Sullivan, a full-forward, was doing back there we'll never know, but he had got his side out of jail, for the moment anyway. Yet it was all a bit like the Munster final. There was something plodding about Kerry and you always felt that it was in Tyrone's power to put the game away.

Ryan McMenamin's point was crucial. If Seán Cavanagh had slightly expanded the role of midfielder over the season, then McMenamin had thoroughly redefined the possibilities for a corner-back.

Gaelic football positioning had become less rigid over the years. Teams brought in wing-forwards to crowd midfield, pulled out full-forwards to leave space for the two corner-forwards inside, and Armagh's Joe Kernan had come up with one of the most brilliant strokes yet in the way he deployed Tony McEntee. But there were still some pretty hard-and-fast rules. One was that the corner-forward, unless he'd been specifically deputed with a roving role, stayed within scoring range of the opposition goal and the corner-back stuck close to him. When the ball was in the other half, the players jogged around, perhaps made some mild attempts to intimidate each other and didn't get involved in the play till the next attack was mounted.

Ryan McMenamin's worldview was a bit different. There were plenty of attacking wing-backs in football but he had decided to become the first ever attacking corner-back. In almost all of Tyrone's games, he'd bombed forward from defence to give his team yet another attacking dimension. This took tremendous athleticism (it was a long way from the corner-back position to the attack) and self-belief (it was a long way back from the attack to the corner-back position). Yet McMenamin managed to make an attacking impact without his defensive duties suffering. It remained to be seen whether this was a meaningful tactical innovation or just an improvisation by one gifted player. If it was the former, then it had the potential to change the game of Gaelic football profoundly. A game where the corner-backs regularly attacked would be flexible in the way that soccer was. There would be no respite for the corner-forwards, who would have to think about defending as well as attacking, something they hadn't had to do in the previous 120 years of the sport.

Now, in a tight game with a huge amount at stake, McMenamin took the risk again. He sprinted forward to join an attack, took a pass, kept going and slotted a superb point over the bar. The damage to Kerry's already battered morale was incalculable. You think you have everyone covered and who comes up to kick the ball over the bar? The corner-back. That is just not supposed to happen.

The wild celebrations that greeted the nail-in-the-coffin point which followed probably had as much to do with the identity of the scorer as the importance of the score. For eight seasons, Brian Dooher had been ploughing up and down the field as a Tyrone wing-forward. Ploughing was the word for it, as Dooher always seemed on the verge of collapsing through tiredness. His running style had all the grace of John Treacy's. Like the Olympic medallist, he always got there in the end but there were many doubters who reckoned that Dooher had little to show for all that running. Colm O'Rourke, the most economical of footballers, who never wasted a run because his knee injuries didn't give him the luxury of doing so, had taken a bit of stick for saying that Dooher wasn't a class inter-county player, but he wasn't exactly bucking common wisdom. There had been a series of ultrapowerful, super-classy Tyrone underage teams with forwards who were as stylish as they were effective. Surely Dooher's day was gone. Yet here he was, the skinny fella galloping up the field and arrowing a shot over the bar. Tyrone finished with three points in five minutes and confirmed that they could have pulled away and put a big score on Kerry if they'd had the self-belief. A seven-point margin was massively flattering to the losers.

The celebrations among the spectators and on the field suggested that Tyrone really reckoned that the All-Ireland was in their grasp now. Previously they'd suspected, now they believed, almost knew. There is, when all is said and done, something special about a win over Kerry in the championship and Tyrone had never done it before.

Out on the pitch, one player stood out. Owen Mulligan with his dyed-blond mop and the huge Celtic symbol tattoos on his arms gave the lie to cutesy ad campaigns where players were all broth-of-a-boy country lads who wouldn't have been out of place in *Waking Ned*. The Cookstown boy was the Gaelic footballer as Limp Bizkit frontman.

I'd been sitting at the match with a man from Caherciveen and he didn't express any outrage about the way Tyrone had played. As far as he was concerned, Kerry had been lousy, the second half had been boring and he wished Tyrone the best in the final. There didn't seem to be much outrage among the Kerry fans outside the ground either. It took a while for the idea that Kerry had been cheated and that Tyrone's display constituted some kind of nadir for Gaelic football to gain currency.

The backlash began, I think, when Pat Spillane referred to the game as 'puke football' on RTÉ.

It was one of those phrases that will probably haunt the speaker for some time to come. Funnily enough, I spoke to Spillane later in the week about an unrelated matter and he was far more considered about the game. He didn't reckon Tyrone's blanket defence was impossible to play against, for a start the Kerry team he'd played on would have handled it easily enough. Kerry could have surmounted the problem by either kicking points from long range or by playing a big man who could have acted as a target on the edge of the square. Incapable of doing either, they were doomed.

Of course, those reasoned comments aren't as memorable as a phrase like 'puke football' and, by the next day, there was a gaggle of pundits queuing up to describe how upset their delicate stomachs had been by the way Tyrone played. It was the biggest championship controversy since the fatwa went out on Clare and Ger Loughnane in 1998.

Why was this? The game had been dull enough for long spells, but the first 20 minutes had been thrilling because a promising team had finally come of age. Perhaps people had come to expect too much from the football championship since the introduction of the back-door system had made it a media darling to rival hurling. I remember being at a press conference prior to the beginning of the 2000 championship when, while asking Tommy, aka Tom, Carr a question, a reporter opined that the previous year had seen the worst football championship ever.

'It's always supposed to be the worst football championship ever,' replied Carr cheerfully.

But the back-door system had subsequently revived football. Exciting Kerry and Galway teams had won championships, there'd been the romantic triumph of Armagh, a Dublin revival and good runs for loveable underdogs such as Sligo and Westmeath. Perhaps falling in love with football again made people forget some of the great dour black spots of the past.

For example, the 1994 Leinster final. Dublin 0–11 Kildare 0–7, absolutely awful yet hardly criticised at all. The 1990 All-Ireland final. Cork 0–11 Meath 0–9, the acme of grim physical slogging football. The 1988 All-Ireland final replay between the same two counties had been even worse. Or what about the heinous game to top them all, the 1980 All-Ireland final when Kerry beat Roscommon by 1–9 to 1–6 amid an exhibition of dirt and bad feeling that Tyrone will probably never approach. That Kerry team is rightly venerated, but they played their part in a game that was genuinely disgraceful. And Pat Spillane, so shocked by Tyrone, was playing that day.

Tyrone had adopted a blanket defence, but they weren't the first team to have done so in a big game and they were made to look worse by Kerry's inability to open up the game or move the ball with any speed. The offence they caused was wildly out of proportion to what they'd actually done and perhaps the uproar can be attributed to an outbreak of 'Northern Bastard Syndrome'.

NBS originally evolved as a defence mechanism to lessen guilt in the Republic once it became apparent that the RUC could baton Catholics up and down the streets of Derry and Belfast and we couldn't/wouldn't/shouldn't (pick appropriate phrase according to your political affiliation) do anything about it. The condition worsened over the years as sufferers noticed that the appearance of a Northern accent on the news usually had to something to do with justifying/describing/explaining some incident in which people had been killed/murdered. The phrase commonly associated with the condition was, 'What are those Northern bastards giving out about now?'

Post-Good Friday Agreement, the attitude of us down here to them up there has improved a bit and they are now described in political speeches as 'our fellow nationalists'.

Yet it doesn't require much for the irritation of the Southern Catholic to flare up against his Northern counterpart. If you don't believe me, listen to any radio phone-in whenever there's any trouble on the streets in Belfast or Derry and listen to the callers, and sometimes the host, wondering what's up with them. Can they not just get on with each other like normal people? It's a kind of schizophrenic attitude, given that many of the people suffering from NBS would also like to be patted on the head by Gerry Adams and told that we're all in it together. But the weird situation which pertained for nearly 30 years of a war going on just up the road from a nation trying to pretend it's not happening doesn't do a lot for the national mental health.

Northern Catholics are wise to this state of affairs and we tend to describe them as being paranoid when they call us on it (as for example on Adrian Logan's GAA show). Perhaps their antennae are a bit too finely tuned but they may have a point. Look at the dark hints before the All-Ireland final that there might be crowd trouble between Tyrone and Armagh. There wasn't a bit of trouble. But the possibility of trouble at an All-Ireland final had never ever been raised before. Then again we'd never had an all-Ulster final before. NBS had reared its head again. We reckoned the crowd from up there would be capable of anything when they'd get going. NBS was, I think at the root of the complaints about Tyrone. We're not too good down here at dealing with the 'other' and our fellow nationalists still seem to count as an 'other' for a lot of people.

At times while writing this book, I've wondered whether I suffer from MBS. Well, here come Meath again. The most obvious example of a team being roughed out of an All-Ireland semi-final was in 1996 when Meath managed to injure Tyrone's three best forwards – Peter Canavan, Ciarán McBride and Brian Dooher – en route to defeating them. Tyrone were bitterly disappointed, but All-Ireland victory can legitimise dodgy tactics very quickly. The uproar about Meath quickly died down and Tyrone soon found themselves berated for not being 'streetwise' enough. Streetwise, incidentally, is a fantastic euphemism that broadly means dirty but media savvy. The 1996 debacle took Tyrone, who'd gone into this game as favourites to win the All-Ireland, a while to get over and seemed to set Peter Canavan back for a while too. It's hardly surprising that they reacted indignantly seven years later when it was suggested they'd let down the game of football.

Yet the legend of the 2003 semi-final continues to grow and the idea that a fine Kerry team were prevented from playing football by an unfair Tyrone side has gained legs. The fact that Kerry were vastly inferior to Tyrone on the day is only mentioned in passing.

Perhaps this has something to do with the defeat tolling the death knell for Páidí Ó Sé as Kerry manager. He'd finessed brilliantly after the Armagh defeat with his references to British helicopters over Crossmaglen and the game against Tyrone wasn't long over when there were 'if that's football then we want no part of it', noises coming from the Kerry camp. But his fate had been sealed and Páidí probably knew it leaving Croke Park that day. Since then, he's taken over as boss of Westmeath and everyone wishes him well, though most fair-minded people would wonder why Luke Dempsey isn't still in the job.

There was a farcical end to Páidí's time in charge of Kerry. With a few minutes left in the game, a middle-aged man emerged from the crowd, got onto the sideline and attempted to clatter him. Páidí, rather sadly, as though such a consummation was only to be expected on this woeful day, parried the man's punch rather than drawing out on him and stewards led the interloper away. I wonder if Páidí pondered the irony of it all. He'd started the season by nearly being sacked for describing some Kerry supporters as rough fucking animals. And who comes after him in his last game with the county? A rough fucking animal.

Perhaps there was another reason why people reacted so badly to Tyrone's win over Kerry. It was the second time in three years that a Kerry team had done the unthinkable and pretty much laid down in Croke Park. The mystique possessed by football in the Kingdom had been one of the game's traditions. It had been dissipated when they'd gone from 1987 to 1996 without an All-Ireland title. Yet it wasn't until 24 August 2003 that the idea of Kerry football as something special was finally buried. Until they prove otherwise, they've become just another team. Two titles in 17 years is a paltry return compared to eight in the previous 17 and five in the 17 before that.

It was enough to make a Kerryman puke.

18

Stevie from Killeavy, Mick from Kildare

31 August: All-Ireland Senior Football Championship
Semi-Final; Croke Park; Armagh 2–10, Donegal 1–9

You owe me, Michael Monahan. You owe me big time. And seeing as I'm not in a position to send around the boys with the concrete slippers and the little 'Michael, the Kildare ref, sleeps with the fishes' sign, I'll have to content myself with venting my spleen in print.

It would have come to about three and a half grand. A €100 bet at 33/1 on Donegal to win the All-Ireland football championship that I placed just after they had hammered Tipperary on the day Declan Browne gave his command performance in Croke Park.

There were a few reasons for this outlay. Donegal might not have been brilliant against Tipp, but they racked up 2–19, which is a pretty impressive score, and created enough chances to make it even better. They'd picked up speed nicely in the qualifiers and had looked very good when ending Sligo's interest in the championship. They'd gone well in the previous year's championship and might have done even better than reaching the quarter-finals had some players allegedly not celebrated their memorable draw against Dublin with such gusto that they were hardly able to walk around in the parade before the replay. They had Brian McEniff, the northwestern Micko, back in charge. And, more than anything else, 33/1 was a daft price for Donegal. I didn't really think they'd land the Sam Maguire, but it was the kind of gamble that conceivably might provide a punter with a few delusions of grandeur before it failed.

On the Monday after the game, I was sitting in a Skibbereen pub when the canniest gambler I know came in.

'Jesus, kid,' he said. 'When that Donegal goal went in, I was thinking of you and that bet. You could have done great stuff with it if they made the final, you could have laid some of it off and …'

He went on to enumerate several of those permutations that real gamblers know about and I don't. When Christy Toye scored the goal of the season for Donegal just before half-time I wasn't thinking of laying off or combinations or anything like that. But I did know that I might be about to win big.

What might have happened had a few decisions gone the way of Donegal rather than Armagh will forever remain the big intangible of the 2003 championships. Had Donegal beaten the reigning All-Ireland champions, they were well capable of causing another shock against Tyrone in the final, if only because they were the one team who'd gathered speed as the championship wore on. This was partly because they had such colossal room for improvement after an abominable defeat by Fermanagh in their first match. The promise of the year before had apparently been completely dissipated by wranglings at county-board level, managerial and coaching upheaval and the bad feeling caused by a county championship that had finished half a year late after ending up in the courts. Had they been kayoed by Longford in the first back-door game, no one would have been too surprised, but they were good against Sligo and a little better in every game after that until they shocked Galway in the quarter-final. The boost of a win over Armagh would have sent them into the final in terrific shape. Tyrone, it would subsequently turn out, had already played their best football and could have been there for the taking. Who knows? It could be fantasy on my part, but I reckon that bet might just have come off.

I'm not a betting man, but I sometimes hang out with men who take the persecuting of bookmakers very seriously. A couple of them are big punters, the kind of guys whose more ambitious bets can get refused by cautious betting shops who believe that taking a chance is something that should only happen on the other side of the counter. They find it hard to watch any match on television without getting out the mobile phones and trying to extract some money from it. What are the odds at half-time? What are the odds on a draw with 20 minutes left when it's 2–0, but the losing team are coming back into it? What are the odds on it ending 4–0? These men have a personal interest, it seems, in almost every sporting fixture you watch. Sometimes I wonder if life would be more interesting if conducted in the same way. A hundred quid on the age you'll be when you get married, a double on the sex of your first and second children, a side bet on the county of origin of the man your wife runs off with (you can use the money you won on the age at which you first commit adultery).

Why not? If there's one thing you learn from knocking around with hardcore punters, it's that you can have a bet on anything. And it does make things more interesting. I recall one Friday night when, having bet on there being more than 12 corners in a nondescript football league match between Rochdale and Hartlepool, we watched rapt as a defender made a hash of a clearance and produced the 13th corner in the second minute of injury-time. No winning goal at Croke Park or Wembley was ever greeted more rapturously. The serious betting man becomes intimately involved in the fortunes of teams he hadn't heard of or cared about before the odds attracted him. I know two guys whose final leg of a huge bet involved an obscure English second-division team. Nothing would do them but to travel to the match where their extraordinary fervour shocked the home fans. The bet came up too.

The serious betting man cares about racing at Uttoxeter, Fontwell and Market Rasen, about the standings in the HFS Loans league, about American colleges football and off-season snooker tournaments in Thailand. Somewhere there is an advantage to be gained, a sloppy spread, a tip known only to a few.

I'm not a serious betting man. I dabble. But that 33/1 on Donegal would have looked very good had it come off. Finally, I would have landed a bet that would impress the pros. I would have been like some small-time crook pulling off a significant heist, like the Al Pacino character in *Donnie Brasco* finally earning the respect of the 'Made Men'. Instead I left Croke Park like the villain in *Scooby Doo* muttering imprecations after he's been foiled by Velma, Daphne, Fred, Shaggy and the titular hound. 'Curses. I would have got away with it if I hadn't been foiled by that pesky ref.'

Mr Monahan's decision to send off Donegal full-back Raymond Sweeney early in the second half not only left the team a man short, but it also banjaxed the strategy of playing two men on Steven McDonnell, which had been working well up to that. Donegal were left with two small men in the full-back line and this was directly responsible for the McDonnell goal that turned the game. The sending-off was harsh (it was for personal fouling) and looked even worse when Kieran McGeeney was allowed to commit five fouls and stay on the pitch. To make matters worse, John McEntee decked a Donegal man with an elbow at the end of normal time and was also allowed to stay on the pitch. (McEntee had been lucky to remain on the pitch against Dublin and is prone to elbowing. It seems less like malice than the kind of clumsiness perpetrated by a player without any great aptitude for tackling. Think of Paul Scholes' efforts to win the ball in midfield for Manchester United). It looked a nailed-on dismissal, but the ref let it go.

In injury-time, Armagh made the most of their extra man to add the 1–1 that won the game. Had McEntee been sent off, it's likely they would have retreated into a defensive shell and played for a draw. The inconsistency of the decisions affecting Sweeney, McGeeney and McEntee probably cost Donegal the game. No one likes to think that a referee can affect the result of a match.

This is probably because of our tendency to read every game as a little self-contained story with a moral. The winning team win because they did the right things and were always destined for victory. Luck isn't allowed to have anything to do with it and neither is bad refereeing. We're talking again about the mentality that sees All-Irelands won during famously fierce Christmas-Day training sessions or February National-League wake-up calls. Yet matches turn on small things that can upset any amount of preparation. And sometimes refereeing is responsible for those turning points.

Take the Armagh–Sligo quarter-final in 2002. Right at the death, Sligo wing-forward Seán Davey was going through when there was a slight tug on his shirt. It wasn't a clear-cut penalty, but there are plenty of referees who would have given it. And Armagh couldn't have done a thing about it if the ref had whistled. If Sligo had scored the spot-kick, they'd have won the game by a point. At that moment Armagh survived, not because of any quality intrinsic in their team, but because of the way the referee thought. And, in case you think I'm deducing a pattern of official help for Armagh, think of the All-Ireland final they went on to lose to Tyrone. The sending off of Diarmaid Marsden was a huge blow to the reigning champions and that decision was so patently wrong that Croke Park opted not to impose a suspension. Tyrone were handed a big advantage at a crucial time and it had nothing to do with their own talent. It was all down to the way the referee saw the game.

The drawn 1988 All-Ireland final between Meath and Cork is a classic example of how a split-second decision completely changes the way a season is portrayed. Larry Tompkins had kicked a massive free to put Cork ahead and they should have won by a point. Instead, Meath were awarded a hugely question-able free, which seemed to be one of the classics of the make-a-draw-out-of-it era of officiating. Yet when Meath won the replay they were canonised as a team who knew exactly how to win tight games. That Cork team were written off as a bunch of losers who were hugely inferior to Meath, a stigma they needed to win two All-Irelands to remove. Yet, had that free not been given, Cork would have been 1988 All-Ireland champions and perhaps won three titles in a row. Meath, for all their brilliance, could have won just one (though they were such a good team they'd probably have bounced back and won the 1989 championship). But that draw had far less to do with the abilities of the players than the decision made by the referee. It's the variable that not even the canniest manager can plan for. Dodgy refereeing decisions are where sport enters the realm of Chaos Theory.

There is nothing inevitable about the outcome of close matches. A referee can flap his wings the wrong way and a whole empire can come tumbling down. ·

Is any old football clip shown more often than Liam Connor pumping the ball into the Kerry goal mouth in the 1982 All-Ireland final, Tommy Doyle missing his catch and Seamus Darby turning and scoring with a shot in a million past Charlie Nelligan before doing a demented jig on the spot? Maybe it's the most famous goal in football history, the one that ensured we'll probably never see a team winning five All-Irelands in a row. Yet there are plenty of people who insist that Darby nudged Doyle in the back. It looks like he might have. Another referee might have given the free out and Kerry would have held on. Offaly would have been unlucky but they'd have been told afterwards that good teams make their own luck. Sometimes they do. And sometimes they don't.

It was the same in 1982 when Kilkenny beat Offaly in the Leinster hurling final because the referee and umpire failed to notice a ball crossing the end-line and Liam Fennelly flicked it back for Matt Ruth to score. Kilkenny annihilated Cork in that year's All-Ireland final and won another title the year after. But who knows how the fortunes of that side might have panned out had the ref been on his game in that provincial final. I'm as guilty as anyone of having overlooked the part played by human error and dumb luck in tight matches. In 1999, I extolled the enormous character of a Clare team that had earned a penalty in the very last minute of a game against Tipperary. That penalty got them a draw and I went on at length about how Clare's competitive instincts were second to none. Yet Conor Clancy probably over-carried the ball before he was fouled. Had the referee made that decision, Clare couldn't have complained and all the character in the world wouldn't have got them a draw. Refs can matter as much as any player.

I'm reminded of the old saying that just because you're paranoid doesn't mean they're not out to get you. Just because managers and fans routinely blame refs for defeat doesn't mean that sometimes they're not right. I don't want to sound like I'm getting on Michael Monahan's back about this. What's three and a bit grand anyway? He erred because he's human and mistakes will continue to be made until the GAA patents a robotic man in the middle. Even then, there'll probably be plenty of errors, as anyone who uses a computer knows only too well.

Refs astound me because they're probably the most generous people in the association. I can't comprehend why anyone would become a ref. From the day you start with underage matches, through to junior games and, if you're lucky, inter-county matches, you'll get the kind of abuse that would land the perpetrators in court if they repeated it on the street. No one ever congratulates the ref for doing a good job, no one ever bangs on about the great sacrifices they make. Sometimes the ref is in danger of physical assault to go with the verbal abuse. It's impossible to see why people would continue to do a job like that, but they do. And it's vital that they do because, without referees, there would be no games. They are next in importance to the players. In the absence of county-board officials, teams would probably hammer out some agreed fixture list and get on with things. But without neutral referees the games couldn't take place.

They're extraordinary people referees. Because there's really only one explanation for why they do the job they do. Generosity of spirit. They give up their time and take the abuse solely for the sake of the GAA. There are no local kudos to be had, nobody wants to buy the referee a pint or sleep with him (or not many people anyway). They're probably the true heroes of sport. It takes some guts to win a 50–50 ball against a back who's two stone heavier than you. But that pales into insignificance compared with the bravery required to award a last-minute free against the home team in front of a partisan crowd you'll have to walk through to get to your car. Who'd fancy that? Only a referee. Bless them all.

Armagh needed the help of Michael Monahan in this semi-final because it didn't look like their game until Raymond Sweeney was sent off. They were four points down at that stage but it could have been worse had it not been for a tactical coup executed by Joe Kernan. Like all good ideas, it was simple enough when you thought of it. But you had to think of it first. Knowing that Donegal would be keen to pick out their two star inside-forwards – Adrian Sweeney and Brendan Devenney – with long ball, Kernan positioned Tony McEntee, wearing Number 15, in front of the Armagh full-back line.

If the Donegal midfielders, half-backs and wing-forwards had been accurate kickers, a wasted McEntee would have spent most of the day watching the ball whizzing over his head. Instead, countless badly delivered balls fell short of the full-forward line and were hoovered up by McEntee. I thought of a conversation with Niall Cahalane, the great Cork player of the late eighties and early nineties, when I'd asked him if players of the contemporary era were much fitter than those of his own day. 'If they are, it's because they have to be. We were all able to kick the ball down a man's throat from 50 yards but that's gone out of the game now.'

Cahalane, in his 40th year, is still one of the best long passers of a ball I've ever seen despite an odd technique where he throws it up and almost strikes it side-on. That gave him the right to be critical and he was correct. The obsession with short passing and carrying the ball has meant that kicking the ball accurately over a distance is a declining skill. When you saw someone who was really adept, like Michael Donnellan or Darragh Ó Sé, it was an occasion of wonder. Kernan's positioning of McEntee had challenged the technique of the Donegal players and they couldn't surmount the problem.

There was some criticism of Armagh throwing a player who'd been listed at corner-forward into the defence. But, with the two-man full-forward line the height of fashion, most teams were taking a man out of the front line anyway. Often this player just ended up adding to the logjam in midfield where he could be as much use as a spare prick at a wedding. Kernan's use of McEntee in a specific and vital role showed why the Armagh man deserved to be rated so highly as manager. It had nothing to do with cheapo psychological ploys, like leaving the opposition waiting on the field or trying to upset their warm-up, it was pure football intelligence.

The McEntee tactic meant that what possession came through to Sweeney and Devenney was often far from ideal. Devenney reacted by never getting into the game. Blessed with electric pace, a devastating shot, sublime ball skills and an elegant economy of movement, he was one of the most frustrating players in the game. Several times, he'd entered important championship matches heralded as his county's saviour and been merely peripheral. His performances against Galway suggested that a new grittier Devenney was emerging, but he contributed not a whit against Armagh.

His forward colleague's more immediately apparent attributes meant that Adrian Sweeney had been overlooked for a while. He was, in some ways, the polar opposite to Devenney. Not notably quick, Sweeney adopted an odd crouched posture when he was in possession and often looked to be taking too much out of the ball just before he arched a shot over the bar from an unlikely angle. The other difference between the players was that Sweeney seemed to play his best football when Donegal most needed him. The previous year, with Donegal a point down against Dublin and out on their feet, Sweeney had won a ball on the right touchline and shaken off the challenge of All-Star Coman Goggins through pure force of will before cutting in and getting the game-tying score. He needed all his resilience in this game because he was about to embark on a mighty battle with the redoubtable Francie Bellew.

Mention Bellew's name to most football fans and a fond look will grace their faces. Since he'd made the Armagh team, the Crossmaglen man had been regularly tipped for impending embarrassment and destruction. Bar a hairy first half on Mike Frank Russell in the previous year's final, this fate had not transpired. (Though, if my Newry informant is correct, Francie owed his second-half renaissance that day to Anglo-Irish politicking. If he was correct, the peace process must have been in terrible trouble altogether in Tyrone last year for Kerry to make such a sacrifice. And they'll be in for even more severe embarrassment should there be any mutterings of republican discontent from Fermanagh in the near future.)

In the days of sleek, gym-toned players with trendy haircuts, Francie Bellew is a bit of a throwback. He has a mop of fair hair, a reddish complexion and a body that doesn't immediately summon the phrase 'physical conditioning', to mind. He is like the man you see filling in for your local club at full-back in a March county league game and doing well. But when you ask why the man in question doesn't play more regularly, you're usually told, 'Oh sure, if that man was bothered about football, there'd be no stopping him. But he's very busy with the farming. Anyways, he'd be caught out when the ground gets hard.'

It was probably Francie's physical resemblance to someone of this ilk that led to the frequent predictions of his imminent exposure as an imposter at inter-county level. In fact, he was a very good corner-back indeed. Most modern-day footballers are fine athletes who could do a job for their team in several different positions if required. Francie would be out of his depth if he'd moved anywhere outside the full-back line. But it doesn't matter. He doesn't have to play anywhere else and is well versed in the arcana of the position, can read the game, knows the wiles by which a crafty defender can frustrate an attacker with a far higher skill level.

One of the intriguing aspects of Gaelic football is the way in which players of relatively limited ability can find a niche in which to thrive. So it is with Francie Bellew and corner-back. There is something heartening about a game whose other outstanding corner-back of the year was Ryan McMenamin, a marvellous athlete who played the game completely differently. There is a place for both of them.

Francie did, however, benefit from the latitude afforded to him by Michael Monahan. Whenever a ball was played into Sweeney, the corner-back would grip him and there would ensue a brief, high-intensity wrestling match as the forward endeavoured to free himself and Bellew held on like a rodeo cowboy gripping a bucking-bronco's ears. That Sweeney didn't get a few frees was just another indicator that interpretation plays a huge part in the art of refereeing. In between the pulling and the dragging and the switching, there was some football and some woeful shooting by Armagh, who hit 12 wides in the first half. The teams were strangely tentative and it looked as though nothing memorable would happen till Donegal scored the goal of the season. The move started in their own half and seemed to gather momentum with every pass, each player getting the ball away just as an Armagh man closed in on him. It ended with Christy Toye getting the final pass 20 yards from goal, taking a few steps forward and, as if saying 'Ah, why not?', putting a blistering shot across Paul Hearty and into the corner of the net. Donegal were that goal clear at half-time.

Soon after the restart, Donegal went four points clear and

were playing with the confidence of winners. And then Oisín McConville cut in from the left, Raymond Sweeney fouled him and Michael Monahan decided the game needed a sending off.

They might have raised their game, but Donegal were hardly good enough to win playing almost an entire half with 14 men. Armagh had been let off the hook and they knew it. They got completely on top at midfield and piled forward. Except their shooting wasn't any better in the second half. There was another string of wides and the fans in the orange jerseys around me on Hill 16 started to look faintly sick. There were wides being kicked that verged on the unbelievable and Donegal were holding on. Then, just as it seemed that the 14 men might tough it out, came the second great goal of the day, one that spoke volumes about the grace under pressure that Steven McDonnell possesses.

McDonnell had been the best forward in the country the previous year and he'd looked even better in Armagh's victories over Dublin and Limerick. Then his form had completely deserted him. He'd hardly kicked a ball against Laois and hadn't been much more influential against Donegal. It reminded me of an Armando Ianucci sketch on BBC about a day when sportsmen mysteriously lose their talent (boxers tell their opponents to stop hitting them because it's sore, footballers run away from the ball, that kind of thing). McDonnell suddenly didn't look himself. It was typical that he came out of the slump by scoring his most vital goal of the season, albeit one that owed a great deal to the dismissal of Raymond Sweeney.

The Tony McEntee move had enabled Donegal to play a couple of defenders in close proximity to McDonnell at all times. All three were quick, but only Sweeney was physically a match for the Armagh man who is six-foot tall and has a remarkable spring in his heels that enables him to beat bigger men in the air. His departure meant that two smallish corner-backs – Niall McCready and Damien Diver – were left to guard McDonnell. And when John McEntee spiralled in a remarkable long pass from the midfield area, you could see what was likely to happen a few seconds before it did. McCready was left one on one with McDonnell and lost out comprehensively. The best forward in the game had the ball in his hand with only the goalkeeper to beat. The Armagh fans on the Hill lunged forward in anticipation. McDonnell seemed like the coolest man in Croke Park and side-stepped to make an angle for himself before drilling the ball past Tony Blake. What he'd done, winning the high ball, shaking off McCready, finding the net was difficult, but he'd made it look routine. It was beautiful, like watching an old episode of *Hands* where a craftsman matter of factly performs a function made easy by long practise.

There was the guts of a quarter to go, Armagh were level and the force was with them. Yet Donegal didn't let go. Sweeney kicked one remarkable point when he was being hounded to such an extent that it seemed impossible for him to keep possession never mind get in a shot. One great sweeping shot arrowed the ball over from way out on the left. Armagh had a remarkable score too. Paddy McKeever came on as a sub and landed a sideline ball out of his hands. Sweeney kicked a huge free and the teams were level coming into injury time. Then Michael Monahan proved as lenient with John McEntee as he'd been harsh with Raymond Sweeney and Armagh used their extra man to put in a final push for victory. Philip Loughran, unobtrusively excellent throughout, galloped up the right wing and fisted the ball over the bar. Donegal looked shattered and Oisín McConville's last-second goal from a penalty was irrelevant through beautifully struck.

We were going to have an all-Northern All-Ireland final. Tyrone and Armagh. The Armagh fans reacted to the realisation with the kind of glee exhibited by Dubbya Bush when he told Iraqi terrorists to, 'Bring it on.' It would be the ultimate local derby, one with an All-Ireland title to add to the neighbourly bragging rights.

After the game, there would be much talk about Armagh's

incredible competitive spirit and little enough mention of the man Donegal had lost. In less than a year, Armagh had begun to be portrayed as less a team than some kind of irresistible force of nature. If they won their second final in a row, it seemed, you'd be reading features wondering if the great 1975–1986 Kerry team would have been able for them. Leaving the Hill, a gang of Armagh youngsters were chanting in time to the infernal clamour of badly beaten bodhráns.

'Stevie from Killeavy, Stevie from Killeavy, Stevie from Killeavy.'

They were right. Stevie from Killeavy had made the difference. Him and Mick from Kildare.

One of the youngsters wore a black beret and a Glasgow Celtic jersey across the back of which was printed the Number 32 and the word 'siaorse'.

A French hat, a Scottish football jersey and his native language spelt incorrectly. But I'd say he felt like the most Irish person in Croke Park.

19

The Unbeatable Coolness of Kilkenny

14 September: All-Ireland Senior Hurling Final
Croke Park; Kilkenny 1–14, Cork 1–11

Two games to go, the two games that would put sense on the season, tell us what it was all about, illuminate the whole championship with hindsight. The football final would be a novelty but the hurling final would be the classic pairing.

The first All-Ireland final to be described as the greatest ever was the 1912 version. The 1939 and 1947 games came to be regarded in a similar light. All three games involved Cork and Kilkenny. Kilkenny won the three of them. The 1931 final, won by Cork in a second replay, was a legendary series of games and is credited with capturing the national imagination in a way no previous matches had. Christy Ring had given one of his greatest ever performances in the 1946 final, Cork had shocked Kilkenny in 1966 and 1999. Kilkenny had put the kibosh on favoured Rebel teams in 1982 and 1992. And, in 1972, Kilkenny had come from eight points down with 20 minutes left to win by seven points. Cork–Kilkenny finals always seemed to produce something extraordinary. They were informed by an amount of history few sporting fixtures could summon up. A final between these two counties seemed like the real thing, a triumph of tradition over novelty.

But the more the GAA stays the same, the more it changes. Even the oldest rivalries can have a new twist. Even a great county like Cork, which has been playing in finals since 1890, can break fresh ground. Which is why I hit for Grenagh, between Cork city and Mallow, a few days before the final.

Grenagh, like Mayobridge and An Gaeltacht, is a small club. Unlike them, it's not a small club that punches way above its weight. It's more typical in a way given that, for many years, its triumph lay in keeping going. Like the cat on the hot tin roof, its achievement was just staying there. In all its history, the Grenagh club had never won a county title at adult level and few people outside the immediate area would have heard of it. But it was the home club of Tom Kenny, who'd be playing at right half-back for Cork in Croke Park the following Sunday.

The ability of small clubs like Grenagh to share in the biggest GAA occasions is another defining feature of the association. Croke Park is an impressive edifice but plenty of sports have huge ultra-modern stadiums. Only Gaelic football and hurling, it seems, produce stars who play in a super-stadium but remain tied to clubs whose entire membership would hardly fill a row of seats there.

I'd arranged to meet the club secretary D.J. Linehan at the club grounds in the village and, when I landed, he introduced me to the vice-chairmen, Bertie Murphy and John McDonnell, and treasurer, Tom Kenny, father of the young man who'd been putting Grenagh on the map over the previous few months. They were a relaxed bunch, watching the junior hurling team training and a bit bemused at the club's sudden fame. It was early evening, the scene was tranquil and nothing could have seemed further away from the frenzy of an All-Ireland final than watching the local players puck the ball around between each other. The Grenagh men complimented one player on the fine suntan he'd acquired on his holidays and only became animated when they discussed the new sliotar that had been used in the championships. It wasn't the first time I'd heard this conversation. A new make of sliotar had been adopted at the start of the season, apparently without any consultation, and players had been swearing that it was vastly different to the kind they were used to. It flew further for a start and moved differently in the air. There were claims that the new model was responsible for long puck-outs by goalkeepers, which had contributed to the lack of real midfield play and that the accuracy of some top forwards had been affected. No one, it seemed, had a good word for the poor creature.

Perhaps the sliotar didn't make that much difference in the end because there wasn't much doubt that the best two teams in the country were in the final. But it seemed odd that the GAA had done something as fundamental as change the type of ball employed in one of its games without seeking the opinion of the players first.

One of the Grenagh men said he'd cut open a new sliotar and that it was completely different to the old one inside. Another man suggested that we adjourn to the Village Inn and continue the conversation in more comfort. There weren't any dissenters.

Grenagh is only about 10 miles from Cork city, but it seems as remote and rural as the Beara peninsula. A banner reading, 'Kilkenny beware, you are now entering Kenny country', had been hung. The Village Inn was one of those comfortable local joints where everyone seems at ease with their surroundings. The men from the club had been knocking around together, they knew each other's foibles, they had history between them and the triumph of Tom Kenny's son was a triumph for them all. They vied to explain how special the club's young star is.

'By the time he was playing Under-14 we knew he was going to make Cork minor at least which would have been a big thing for the club. He's always had that burst of speed and the brains to get himself out of trouble when he's surrounded. He doesn't look fast but he fairly covers the ground,' said Bertie Murphy.

'When he was a youngster, he'd just be running through the other teams. Their supporters would be giving out to them but it wasn't their fault, they were good junior players but he was a class above. He scored 3–4 for the Muskerry divisional team in a county senior championship match against Ballyhea when he was just 18,' said D.J. Linehan.

'He had those trials with Ireland too when he was Under-16. With the Brian Kerr soccer team that won the European title. He had a few training sessions with them but he missed out in the end. If he'd taken soccer seriously he'd have made it there too,' said John McDonnell.

Kenny had been an outstanding midfielder with the Cork schoolboy side Leeds, and has just missed out on a place on the history-making team that won the European Championship in 1998 and included the likes of John O'Shea, Andy Reid and Graham Barrett. I remembered him giving a Man of the Match display in the 1999 Munster minor football final against Kerry. To make a county team from a starting point like the Grenagh junior team, you needed to be exceptional. But if you were good enough, you'd get the chance. As Patrick Kavanagh said, in reference to the line in Gray's 'Elegy in a Country Churchyard', 'Mute inglorious Miltons', don't really 'blush unseen'. If you were a Milton, you'd be spotted somehow.

Through this litany of neighbourly praise, Tom Kenny senior's expression varied from one of pride to one of embarrassment. Paddy Connery in Na Piarsaigh had promised me that Tom Kenny's father would be one of the nicest men you could meet and he was right. That decency of character included an old-fashioned country modesty that made it difficult for him to listen to his son being praised at such length. From time to time, he'd interject to ask that I ask more questions about Grenagh and less about Tom junior. But it was difficult to disentangle the two.

'With all the inter-county and Fitzgibbon Cup matches and training he has, Tom will always be here to play the junior hurling and football league games for us. On the Wednesday after the Munster final, he turned up to play midfield against Cill na Mártra and nearly got the winning goal. He coaches the youngsters as well,' said Bertie Murphy.

Eventually Tom senior did manage to steer us in the direction of Grenagh. Young Tom wasn't the first man from the parish to play in an All-Ireland final. Bertie's brother, Denis, had been on the 1966 Cork team that had beaten a famously somnolent Kilkenny. But he was playing in the city for St Finbarr's at the time. His contemporary, Phil Duggan, played Railway Cup hurling for Munster but had joined civil service in Dublin by then. Like many farming areas, Grenagh saw its young men emigrate or move to the cities.

'Between 1968 and 1992, the club was in constant danger of folding. We could barely summon up enough players for a team and we even dropped down to the junior B grade. Whole minor and Under-21 teams would emigrate to America and, if it hadn't been for the struggle of a dedicated few, Grenagh would have gone under,' D.J. Linehan explained.

Over the past decade, the upturn in the economy and the building of new houses in the parish had seen the club enjoy some success. Hurler Paul Coleman and footballer Aidan Dorgan made the Cork senior team. Football began to rival hurling as the number one game in the club. Yet given their struggle to stay alive, and the fact that they had one of the smallest picks in the county, Grenagh's 1958 and 1966 divisional hurling titles and their run of Muskerry football titles in the nineties were the club's equivalent to All-Ireland club championships.

A cynic might wonder what keeps clubs like Grenagh going. They'll go unmentioned when the great GAA histories are written and you'll have to search the small print in the results sections of the national papers to see their name. Looked at coldly and rationally, the club officers might have seemed like they were wasting their time in those fallow years of the seventies and eighties.

But logic and rationality are poor yardsticks by which to measure the village GAA man. Often he's a dreamer and a romantic, a believer in the unlikely victory to come. And, sometimes, the wildest dreams can come true.

'What would you have said lads if, 20 years ago, someone had told you you'd be sitting here worrying about not having enough All-Ireland tickets because a Grenagh player was appearing for Cork in the All-Ireland final?'

They laughed at my question. Uproariously. Then they kept laughing at the sheer unlikeliness of their good fortune. And at that moment, I couldn't think of any better place to be in the run-up to an All-Ireland final.

Interview done and pints swallowed, it was time for me to head at least part of the way home.

'Where are you going?'

'I'll get a taxi back into the city and then get a bus out as far as Bandon.'

'We'll give you a lift.'

'I'll be grand with a taxi.'

'We'll give him a lift to Bandon, you'll tip along with me, Tom?'

And so D.J. Linehan, with Tom Kenny providing navigational services, drove me the 30-mile journey from Grenagh to Bandon late on a night when he was already busy fielding requests for All-Ireland tickets. (An Armagh clubman rang up to say there was no problem with swapping his club's hurling tickets for Grenagh's football tickets. 'It was two football tickets per one hurling ticket, wasn't it?' 'No,' said D.J., 'it wasn't.' 'I'll get back to you,' said your man, and he did a few minutes later with an improved offer.)

The great American journalist Murray Kempton once wrote:

I have done commentary, do it still and try to do it as best I can; but it can never be for me what going around is. The journalism that comments or pretends to explain has always been for me somehow wanting in the qualities that are most life-enhancing... the province of those who go around is the immediate, the brief, and the early forgotten. But it is a province that anyone who has ceased to go around will always miss as the ground he walked with a high and anticipatory heart when he was young.

I think that describes how I felt many times during the writing of this book and the night two men I'd only met for the first time a few hours before went out of their way to leave me to my destination I felt it particularly strongly. The travelling around and meeting people, the 'going around' is the best feature of sports-writing. There is something there that you can't get from writing in your study. This may sound like a naïve comment but one thing that's stuck with me from my travels in search of the GAA is how many decent people are out there. Everywhere I went were good people, an encounter with whom added something to me as a person. They were, as Kempton says, 'life enhancing'. When we pulled up in Bandon, Tom Kenny senior handed me a square blue book. 'This might be some use to you.'

He was right. *A History of Grenagh GAA Club* can almost stand for the history of all small GAA clubs or even small Irish communities. (He was too modest to tell me but his friends let me know that Tom Kenny senior had been largely responsible for the book, published on the club's 50th anniversary in 1984.)

There are the uncertain beginnings with teams bearing names such as The Holy Terrors, and The Green Field Levellers, playing each other locally. There is the founding of the club by an optimistic few and the penning of ballads about the team's early matches, including such irresistible quatrains as:

Jack Flynn had to see a doctor
For his lungs were tore and sore,
He never will forget that day
Grenagh played Donoughmore.

The name of the balladeer is as evocative as his verses. Many a novelist would have killed to come up with a name like Muggins

Mulcahy. There is the huge excitement caused by the first mid-Cork title in 1958 followed, a year later, by the junior league final between Éire Óg and Grenagh that resulted in every player on both teams being suspended for six months. The travails of the referee didn't end on the pitch according to his report: 'As I was about to enter my car in the village, an Éire Óg player approached me in a fighting attitude and with an empty pint-sized glass in his hand asked me why he had been put off the field.'

I wonder if he told him why. There is more glory in 1966, and I was unaccountably pleased to see that Bertie Murphy and John McDonnell had starred in that game. The Courtbrack ICA guild commemorated the victory by making a cake modelled on the pitch in Coachford where the divisional final had been played. The cake was decorated with photos of the Grenagh players. There is a farewell party for Fr Mick O'Riordan who is returning to Australia, where he had been recently buried under a house for three hours following a tornado in Bungenore. There are details of that forgotten part of the GAA repertoire, the Scor competitions. Going by results, the people of Grenagh were no slouches at the set dance. A few pages later came a possible explanation. Grenagh is the native parish of the Donal Ring Céilí Band, 'The Kings of Irish Dance Music'.

The history is a volume, like all the other painstakingly compiled club annals, which it is impossible not to regard with affection. It's the story of not just a different Ireland but a different GAA.

We all know that the country has changed in many ways since the days when every club match could find a balladeer to commemorate it. The final few days before the hurling final confirmed just how great those changes have been. They also showed that not all change is progress.

D.J. Carey had been atypically peripheral in the championship. The year before, he'd been as good as ever when he came back from a lay-off to play a crucial supporting role to his successor as best hurler in the country, Henry Shefflin, in the final two games of the season. But he'd hardly pucked a ball in the Leinster final against Wexford or the All-Ireland semi against Tipperary. For once, D.J. wasn't the main topic of conversation coming up to an All-Ireland final.

That all changed when word leaked out that the GAA was finally going to be dragged into the world of gutter journalism, and it was the association's biggest star who was being targeted by the sleazehounds. Almost overnight, everyone in the country knew that D.J.'s marriage was in trouble and that huge tabloid exposés were primed to detonate on the weekend of the final.

Looking back, it's strange to see how much of a damp squib the affair turned out to be. There was wild talk doing the rounds of big cheques being handed out and of squads of English reporters schooled in dustbin dragging and doorstep heroics trawling Kilkenny in search of smut. In the end, the stories never really materialised on the scale they were supposed to. But a boundary had been crossed and there were stories about the star's personal life, some of them under the guise of concern. It was a disorientating experience for many people. There are still a couple of generations in this country for whom the phenomenon of marriage breakdown is disturbing. Those same generations also regard privacy as one of the primary values. Seeing the troubles of one of the most respected sportsmen in the country being discussed in the media must have made them wonder if there were any standards left in Ireland.

And you didn't need to be a natural conservative to find the whole caper disturbing. It overshadowed the final itself, to the extent that, on the Monday afterwards, D.J. was still the big story even though he'd once more been peripheral in the game.

There were some odd contradictions about the way the story was approached. The *Sunday Independent* ran a lead story about D.J. being under siege from the tabloids and rounded off the piece with a strange paragraph about how much the man was respected by everybody. *The Dunphy Show* the night before had been just as determined to have its cake and eat it. On came Liam Griffin and Ger Loughnane to say what a disgrace it was that D.J. Carey was being hounded by the media. They went on about this at length – on a prime-time television chat show. They seemed so upset about the stories that silence wasn't an option for them.

Both Griffin and Loughnane took a tack that proved popular as the discussions dragged on over the weekend. They went on at length about the fact that D.J. was an amateur sportsman much loved by the public and also a very nice man. This wasn't in dispute but neither was it particularly relevant.

The truth is that D.J. got off relatively lightly. Not long afterwards another one of the great Irish sportsmen of modern times figured on the front page of the tabloids. Paul McGrath had got drunk on a Friday night in Dublin, staggered around the place and been refused admission to a nightclub. This was reported in lurid detail. One paper published a photo of McGrath urinating in an alley. The people who'd ochoned about the awful treatment of D.J. Carey were nowhere to be heard. Their silence seemed to imply that Paul McGrath deserved this kind of treatment. On the weekend of the hurling final, Griffin and Loughnane had said that the Irish people would never forgive the tabloids if they printed anything about D.J. Carey's personal life. Well, Paul McGrath was another great sporting hero and I didn't notice any huge bundles of papers being burned the weekend he was dragged through the mud.

Why was this? McGrath's drinking is as much his own business as Carey's marriage is his. Papers used to be able to pretend that it was in the public interest when he was playing for Ireland if he went off on the tear. But McGrath is retired now, he's a private citizen fighting a very tough battle against alcoholism. His private life doesn't deserve to be splashed all over the papers anymore than D.J. Carey's does. Yet, the tabloids humiliated him with impunity.

Mentioning D.J.'s amateur status was a total red herring. Soccer players or members of Westlife or even the Taoiseach are paid wages to do their jobs. They're not paid to be trailed around and hunted down by the scum of the press. They have a right to privacy the same as D.J. Carey. Nobody's personal life is the business of the newspapers unless they want it to be. Not D.J. not Paul McGrath, not George Best, not Nicky Byrne and Georgina Ahern.

The moral outrage about media behaviour seemed to belong to a different country, one where there was no appetite for the details of people's private lives. It would have been great if the outrage expressed so vehemently meant that we were so disgusted by the targeting of D.J. that we'd never again read an article which pried into someone's personal problems. It would have been great.

An opportunity was missed. By focusing on D.J.'s special status as the game's biggest star and bringing in his work for charity and his impeccable manners both on and off the field, his defenders failed to establish an important principle. With the GAA selling increasing numbers of newspapers, the private lives of its players will come under the microscope again. Only, next time, it might be a player who's known for a lack of discipline or petulance, someone with an unattractive personality. He won't deserve any less sympathy than D.J. but I wonder if he'll get the same amount.

It had been one of the weirdest ever build-ups to an All-Ireland final, but it couldn't stop you feeling the huge anticipation that only a decider can produce. A final, after all, defines a season. There is no argument with its result. Sometimes the best team in the country can lose, as Kilkenny had to Cork in 1999 and Meath did to Down in the 1991 football final. But there was no disputing that the team that beat them were true champions. That is the joy of a knockout competition. If the hurling title had been run on a league basis, Kilkenny would probably have had it sewn up with weeks to spare but they still had to win one final 70 minutes to confirm their supremacy.

Cork might have been outsiders, but the hype in the county was incredible, even for a county that has a talent for emotionalism. On the week of the final, I was walking past a shop in the city centre when a security guard shouted at me. Yes, it was me he was shouting at. I checked my pockets to make sure there were no stolen packets of glucose sweets or contraceptives on my person.

'C'mere. You're Eamonn Sweeney, aren't you that used to write about hurling for the *Examiner*.'

'I am.'

'Listen, I'm thinking of putting a load of money on Cork to win the final on Sunday. I'm just not sure about it. Someone like you now, you'd have a fair idea how it would turn out.'

'Probably no better than you would.'

'Ah now, don't be codding me. You'd know the inside story. Is it worth putting this money or not?'

He seemed like a nice bloke and the best thing to do was to tell him to save his money because betting on All-Ireland finals is a risky business. But I wanted to be helpful and, over the next few minutes, I somehow convinced both himself and myself that Cork were a lock to win the final. Thinking aloud, I assured him that Joe Deane would be the match winner. He'd have too much pace for Noel Hickey. Remembering how Deane had found his way through for a vital goal in every game, I reckoned he'd do the same on Sunday. He was a big-game player after all.

'Joe Deane will be the match winner. I'll remember that,' said the security guard.

Perhaps the first indication that Kilkenny were typically unfazed by all the confidence emanating from Cork came when I got the bus up on the day of the match. A banner overhung the main, and only, street of the great hurling village of Johnstown, home club of Pat Delaney who'd tortured Cork in the 1972 final.

'Ó hAilpíns will be Ó Hasbeens. Up Kilkenny.'

The bus driver was so tickled by this, he was on his phone the minute the bus docked in Bus Áras.

'Ó Hasbeens, boy. Did you hear that? Fighting talk.'

Securing the ticket for the final had been a nightmare, involving late-night phone calls, the invocation of past favours and a great deal of straightforward begging. What the hell, it's the same for nearly everyone. And when you finally have that ticket in your pocket, you check it's still there every single minute till you land in Croke Park. There are few feelings of gratitude like the one when you hand in your ticket at the stiles and realise that you're in, you've made it, you're one of the chosen few, you are going to see an All-Ireland final. It's a thrill that can never be staled by repetition.

The anticipatory buzz is at its greatest in the half-hour before a final. Even the new Croke Park attempt at American football-style, pre-match razzmatazz – 'Teenage Kicks' on the tannoy! Marty Morrissey! Guinness Ads On A Big Screen! Match Highlights! Marty Morrissey! 'Fanfare For The Common Man'! Marty Morrissey! Marty Morrissey! Marty Morrissey! – couldn't do much to distract the fans from playing out about 20 different match scenarios in their minds. All through the championship, the cautionary heads in either county had followed each victory by counselling that this wouldn't be good enough in an All-Ireland final, that things would be different on the second Sunday in September, that you'd want to be doing more than that if you were to win the Liam McCarthy Cup. Cork and Kilkenny had seemed destined for each other's company from a long way out, since Cork's win over Clare to be honest. Now the supporters were going to find out.

It wasn't too hard on the kind of fan who always thinks their county are going to win. But the minutes before the throw-in are a nightmare for the skin who always suspects that today is the day their team is going to be found out, the kind of person who nudges their neighbour after 30 seconds and says, 'I have a bad feeling about this one.'

As a neutral, I was in the strange position of not seeing how either team could lose. Kilkenny were not only champions but they'd brooked no resistance at all on their way to the final and against Tipperary last time out had looked as complete a team as the game had thrown up in the past couple of decades. Yet there seemed something irresistible about Cork's progress, about the excitement they generated and about the way their youngsters seemed able to rise to every challenge. It almost seemed as though their name was on the trophy. The combination of two teams with so much going for them, I figured, would probably result in a classic final. That was another mistake.

Any Cork pessimists didn't have to wait long for the bad feeling to descend on them. There were just 10 seconds gone when a ball fell to young Tommy Walsh from Tullaroan and he sent a superb shot over the bar. Walsh was being marked by Tom Kenny and, before half-time, the man from Grenagh's All-Star, which had been pretty much a certainty going into the game, had been put on hold for another year. Walsh would score three points before suffering an injury that ended his day and Kenny's torture.

It was cruel luck on Kenny. He wasn't particularly loose against Walsh but it looked desperate, his man scoring three points from play in the first 15 minutes. Yet they'd been three great points and Walsh would have been excused for missing any of them. He had required very little space to turn the Grenagh player's day into a nightmare. You could see how unfortunate Kenny had been when you compared his day with that of the Kilkenny wing-backs Seán Dowling and J.J. Delaney. They'd let their men hurl a lot of the ball early on too and hadn't been any tighter than Kenny. But Ben O'Connor was having a miserable day and his touch was off while Timmy McCarthy, as ever the epitome of honest effort, shot no better than usual. Eventually, the Kilkenny defenders stormed into the game, Delaney to such effect that he ended up being named Hurler of the Year. But if their men had been in the same devastating form as Walsh, it might have been a different story. Some days your luck is in, some days it's not.

For 20 minutes everything went right for Kilkenny and wrong for Cork. Kilkenny looked as good as they'd looked against Tipperary, Cork looked as bad as they'd looked when they were in the throes of player revolt the year before. Diarmuid O'Sullivan had entered the previous year's National League final as the undisputed Alpha Male among full-backs. His opponent was a lanky full-forward named Martin Comerford, who no one knew much about other than him being the brother of the more famous Andy. Comerford had destroyed O'Sullivan and gone on to win an All-Star. O'Sullivan had never been the same since, or at least not till the replay against Wexford. Now Comerford was getting the better of him again, he nicked two points in that opening spell and the Cork forwards and fans waited in vain for one of those Hollywood fetches and clearances O'Sullivan had patented.

The Cork attack, so unstoppable against Wexford, looked suddenly toothless and only managed a single point in those first 20 minutes. Joe Deane was tracked everywhere by Noel Hickey and couldn't find a yard of space. Cork racked up 11 wides in the first half, a good and tragic proportion of these coming from young John Gardiner's frees. It might have been kinder had Donal O'Grady excused the kid from dead-ball duties after the first couple of misses, but you could see why he didn't. The frees weren't badly struck and there was a moment when each of them seemed to be bearing in on the target before tailing off wide. They all came close enough to the posts to encourage the ruinous thought that next time might be different. Like a wife forgiving an adulterous husband, O'Grady was undone by optimism. By the end, Gardiner must have wished he hadn't got out of bed that morning but sport is too cruel to afford such fantasy solutions. He stuck out there and bravely set about rebuilding his game when switched with the equally shell-shocked Kenny.

After 20 minutes, it was 0–8 to 0–1 and the neutrals found

themselves wishing hard for some Cork scores, if only so the game didn't degenerate into a one-sided shooting match like the 2000 final. That it didn't was due to the unforeseen demolition of Kilkenny's fearsome corner-forwards by their markers. Wayne Sherlock was one of the best corner-backs in the game but Eddie Brennan had been Kilkenny's best player during the championship. Bigger, stronger and much faster than Sherlock, he should have made hay from his team's dominance on the field. Instead, he was almost as anonymous as D.J. who was completely subdued by Pat Mulcahy. Since the Munster final, Mulcahy had come in for plenty of stick and the way he'd been moved from full-back by the imperious O'Sullivan lent credence to the idea that he wasn't quite a real inter-county defender. Yet, with his team-mates freezing all round him, Mulcahy had the game of his life. Had he and Sherlock not been as good as they were, Kilkenny would likely have got in for the goal that would have converted the game into an exhibition.

Instead, they took their foot off the accelerator and Cork made tentative attempts at recovery. They even had a goal chance 10 minutes before the break. At the time, it seemed merely academic that they missed given that they were so far inferior on the day. In the light of what transpired in the second half, it might have been the moment when the All-Ireland got away from the Munster champions. Deane, for once, found space and cut in from the right wing with a defender and the goalkeeper in front of him and Setanta Ó hAilpín on the far post. On another day, Deane might have gone for a shot into the far corner of the net, but he drew the defender and flicked a pass to Ó hAilpín. On another day, the pass might have been better, because Setanta got the ball and James McGarry at around the same time. On another day, he might have used his strength to grab the ball, step inside the keeper and shoot into an empty net. Instead, the big man went for a hasty flick that McGarry touched round the post. The 65 was put wide and, from a situation of rich possibility, Cork had extracted nothing. They'd been putting away these chances all season but the final was getting to them as only a final can.

Kilkenny's defending was something to behold. One high delivery came in and Noel Hickey seemed to block three attackers at the one time while Michael Kavanagh swooped on the loose ball, made space for himself and cleared it out the field. Even Setanta wasn't getting any joy. Kilkenny had picked James Ryall to mark him, a man who was far from elegant, but who was the first corner-back to match the sensation for size and strength.

At half-time, the man in the seat next to me was jubilant. He was from Galway, he explained, and had a huge bet on Kilkenny. This explained why he'd spent much of the first half crouched in the uptight posture of a nervous flyer. Big money, he told me, really big money. Out on the field, Kila were playing and no one was listening to them. They were following in a distinguished line of Irish traditional groups. Emmet Spiceland, Donal Lunny's first band, had played at the All-Ireland hurling final 35 years earlier. And if the newsreel shown recently on *Come West along the Road* was anything to go by, no one had listened to them either. You could put on human sacrifice, or Britney snogging Mary Harney at half-time in an All-Ireland final and no one would watch it. There's too much to think about when the entire season has come down to 35 minutes of hurling.

Perhaps Cork would storm out like they had at the start of the Munster final second half and score points for fun. No. Afraid not. From 0–9 to 0–3 at the break, it went to 0–11 to 0–6 and you still couldn't see how anything resembling a thrilling finish could be manufactured from this situation.

It was time for Setanta to confirm his status as the big story of the hurling championship. He'd been obviously chafing at the lack of impact he'd had in the first half. And a man of nearly six foot six chafing is an impressive sight. The bonds imposed by James Ryall slowly began to slacken. Right at the start of the half, Setanta had embarked on one of those long-legged runs that excited the

Cork crowd so much but had blazed a shot wide of the far post, seemingly torn between the attractions of a point and a goal. Now he went on another one of those runs and set up Joe Deane for a point. Ben O'Connor scored a point and there was suddenly just a goal between the teams. More importantly, excitement had entered the game, largely because of Setanta's determination not to let Cork go gentle into that good night.

It was about halfway through the second half when a long clearance fell to Ryall. Unnerved, he hesitated and the ball broke to Setanta. A couple of giant strides brought him clear of the cover with just McGarry to beat. This time there wouldn't be any mistake. The ball was buried in the back of the net, Cork were level and, for a few minutes, that feeling that their name was on the trophy returned.

They even went ahead with the point of the game, a huge effort from Niall McCarthy who, with his two-tone retro hurling helmet, had been a surprise success for Cork. He unnerved big name Number 6s by the simple expedient of running at them with a directness that was almost disrespectful. Peter Barry is as good a Number 6 as there is but he hadn't the legs for the Carrigtwohill man. That lead point would have served as a nice example of how Cork's speed and youth had overcome Kilkenny's strength and experience. Instead, it became just one more incident, a swansong rather than an inspiration.

Because, having taken an unlikely lead after they had been in imminent danger of being disgraced, Cork didn't kick on like they had against Waterford. There were perhaps five minutes when Kilkenny seemed to be reeling but Cork could not add another score in those minutes. It wasn't as though they were short of inspirational moments. There'd been Setanta's goal, Niall's point and, receiving the biggest cheer of the day, Diarmuid's Mighty Fetch.

The great GAA moments are not all goals, points or saves. There are little vignettes whose value is far greater than can be rationally explained. Sean McMahon's intervention late in the

1995 Munster semi-final against Cork is a classic example. Playing with a broken collar-bone and exiled to the corner of the attack, the one-handed McMahon chased, harried and somehow contrived to force a Cork player to give away a sideline ball. Clare scored the winning goal from that sideline but it's not that goal that sticks in the mind, it's McMahon with his one good arm refusing to give up. That moment came to stand for the whole we'll-have-to-be-carried-out-on-our-shields ethos instilled by Ger Loughnane in Clare. Some plays just hit you right in the gut.

That's why, when O'Sullivan lost his hurl but carried on and caught a high ball with both hands football style, bullocked through a couple of challenges and won a free, the roof nearly came off the stand. It was a classic folk hero passage of play, its importance to the team and fans far greater than merely the repelling of an attack and winning of a free. And it was quintessentially Sully, no other player would have had the audacity to try something like that. He breathes self-belief like the rest of us inhale oxygen. Like the 100-yard point he'd scored against Limerick a couple of years previously, this was a moment that transcended the circumstances of the match.

The Cork faithful would insist afterwards that O'Sullivan had once more been outstanding. Yet, judged rationally, his performance had been poor. Martin Comerford had been far too good for him again and ended up with a Man of the Match award and the 1–4 tally that won the game for Kilkenny. More damaging still, O'Sullivan seemed content to let his man stray while he went in for the spectacular catches and clearances. What his manager, a fullback who was far less expansive and perhaps more effective, thought of this would determine the folk hero's future. You could even argue that the Mighty Fetch itself hadn't been that good. All right, so the catch had been a triumph of improvisation but plenty of refs would have awarded a free in for charging and Kilkenny would have been handed a point in a close game.

But perhaps judging O'Sullivan by these criteria was missing the point of the way he played the game. In itself, the Mighty Fetch had achieved little. But it had roused the crowd to frenzy and surely must have lifted every Cork player. O'Sullivan was in the process of creating his own legend. And you don't ask a legend how much his man has scored. Or do you? It's the old romance versus pragmatism argument again. O'Grady will probably hope, in the long run, for a more conservative and careful O'Sullivan. But a more conservative and careful O'Sullivan wouldn't be Sully, it would probably be Pat Mulcahy. Mulcahy is an excellent player, but folk heroes are a much rarer breed.

Perhaps O'Sullivan had missed his vocation. It didn't take much imagination to see him as a rampaging linebacker in American Football, sacking quarterbacks and doing a dance of delight as the camera zoomed in on him. The game would stop and the big play wouldn't be lost in the rest of the action. You felt O'Sullivan would have relished that kind of role, good hurler and all as he is.

The final was there for Cork in those minutes but they couldn't produce that little something extra that would have got them over the line. All-Ireland finals are agonisingly difficult to win. Teams can't just freewheel home no matter how well they've played. The day must be seized and Cork didn't manage to do it when they had the chance. Perhaps that chance had come back in the first half and a team that had shot 11 wides in 35 minutes was going to punished for its profligacy down the line. Whatever, as the game entered the final 10 minutes, Kilkenny wrested back control and began a painstaking drive for the tape.

It was painstaking. Kilkenny didn't bring their usual brilliance to the endgame, didn't hit Cork with a barrage of scores like they might have done on better days. They just steadied themselves and ground out the victory. Martin Comerford brought them level with a great angled point hit back over his shoulder and Henry Shefflin began to exert his inevitable influence.

Young J.J. Delaney might have ended up with the Player of the Year award, but no one could doubt that Shefflin was the best hurler in the game. He'd been head and shoulders above anyone else in 2002 and, though his shooting was surprisingly slack in the final two matches of the season, came good when Kilkenny needed him. At well over six-foot tall with a blistering turn of pace and a full complement of skills, he wasn't going to be easily stopped if his attitude was right. And Shefflin's attitude is always right. He scored two fine points in that final spell but, most importantly, made the incision for the goal five minutes from the finish that decided the winner of the 2003 championship.

Cork's journey had been long and dramatic, but it came to an end here. A tangle between a couple of players ended with the ball squirting loose to Shefflin who'd driven forward. He continued on and stepped past a tired challenge from O'Sullivan before putting Comerford clear. Comerford had only Donal Óg Cusack to beat and it fitted with the undistinguished nature of the day that there was nothing emphatic about his finish. He struck his shot into the ground and Cusack, set for a piledriver, was caught off-balance and could only scramble helplessly across his goal as the ball hopped tantalisingly into the net. It was just out of his reach as victory was for Cork.

After all the sparkling attacking play the champions had produced, it was their defenders who ended up scooping the awards. Delaney won Hurler of the Year and Noel Hickey landed the Man of the Match prize. All through, he had been within a couple of steps of his man, sometimes taking a chance and getting out in front of him, other times policing the Cork full-forward so Deane had no option to lay the ball off. Hickey was playing against a man with a lower centre of gravity and who was quicker than him over a few yards, but these advantages were never allowed to come into play. Diligence was the word that best described his attitude and underpinned his achievement. Brian Greene, Brian Lohan, Darragh Ryan, defenders of the highest quality, had played superbly against Deane but found him ghosting away to get the scores that took the gloss off their displays. Deane only had to be lucky once. Hickey didn't even give him that. It was a triumph of concentration and something like the way Hickey's manager, Brian Cody, had played on Jimmy Barry Murphy when the potential had been there for him to get the runaround too.

Cody was as self-effacing as ever at the finish, but this second triumph in a row had been a massive personal vindication of his selection policy. He'd taken an enormous risk by falling out with the brilliant Charlie Carter who'd quit the team during the championship. Had Kilkenny not found those vital scores in the last few minutes, Cody would have cut a rod for his own back. But he didn't crow, he didn't claim to have answered the detractors and doubters, he just mildly declared himself pleased. There were managers who adopted a stoical attitude as a pose, a different way to draw attention to themselves. Cody was different, he seemed genuinely modest, a man unlikely to become a chat-show staple in years to come.

It had been 10 years since a team had won two All-Irelands in a row. It had been Kilkenny then as well: 2002 and 2003, 1992 and 1993, 1982 and 1983 and the 1972 team would probably have won the 1973 All-Ireland final against Limerick had it not been undone by the cruellest series of injuries to ever hit a team going into a big game. A long-term bet on 2012 and 2013 might not be out of order. Kilkenny, after all, had won the minor title in the curtain-raiser. The team included an outstanding centre half-back, Donncha Cody. Yes, the manager's son. The GAA's tendency towards dynastic succession continues apace.

A friend of mine expressed his frustration afterwards at the manner in which Kilkenny had greeted victory. 'That whole it's-no-big-deal-to-us-thing with Shefflin and the boys. And the fans are the same, they just treat it like it's their right.'

I could see what he meant but that was Kilkenny's style. They took pride in not making a fuss. Win or lose, they weren't given to publicly displaying extremes of emotion. Coolness was one of the qualities that had always defined them as a team. The famous

1912, 1939 and 1947 finals had each been won by a single point and the county had probably won more close games and engineered more miraculous escapes than anyone else in either hurling or football. They'd learned the value of calm, so it wasn't surprising that they hung on to it. There were no I-told-you-sos to imaginary enemies after the game, no gloating, no huge declarations of their fanatical love for their native heath, not even the attacks on the tabloid press you might have expected in the week that was in it. No other county was able to resist a huge outpouring of emotion and that was the way it should be. All-Ireland victories are resonant moments in the histories of local communities. But it is nice to have one team who do things differently, who take it easy on the hype in an age, and a country, where hype is everything. It is admirable, old-fashioned in the best kind of way. Their treatment of the two imposters, triumph and disaster, would have warmed Rudyard Kipling's heart.

The Cork temperament is very different. The whole county had fallen in love with this young team, which had emerged from the shadow of the strike to provide more excitement than any other side over the summer. Cork was primed to explode and its fans dreamed of the cup being carried into the city, of victorious open-air drinking on the Grand Parade for the next week. Perhaps they felt like shaking the laid-back Kilkenny fans by the shoulders and asking them why they weren't more grateful. After all they'd been through together, the Cork fans hadn't really believed this team could lose. But they had. To make it worse, victory had been held out in front of them and then whipped away. The Sunday night's drinking in a capital city whose claims to pre-eminence they didn't love anyway was dark and distressed.

The crew that gathered in Rea's on Monday afternoon were like captured soldiers from a defeated army. The night before had probably taken a lot out of them, but their beaten appearance probably had more to do with the investment they'd made in their team. Whatever Paul Codd thought, some fans put a huge amount into the championship. There was the financial outlay but that was dwarfed by the emotional commitment that your local team could draw from you.

The members of the Rebel Army gathered in Rea's looked shattered. When you share the incredible highs they'd experienced – that win over Clare, the second-half comeback against Waterford, the all-time classic against Wexford, the moment when Setanta found the Kilkenny net and all dreams were on again – the lows will hit you with equal force. Fans like these identified with their team to a huge extent. They imagined what this defeat must have felt like to Sully, to Deano, to Setanta, to Wayne and it hurt them. The hurt wasn't as great as that felt by the players but it was a relation not too far removed.

Even worse were the thoughts of how different this Monday might have been. Supporters are great fantasists and they must have been imagining how unbelievably good the world would be when Cork beat Kilkenny. Imagine what it would be like in Grenagh when Tom Kenny came home triumphant, imagine the anniversary celebrations at Na Piarsaigh when their four heroes arrived with the cup. In 1999, the Killeagh people were almost scared to let themselves think of what victory would do for their village. But you can't stop yourself imagining the best. And now, on this gloomy Monday, all those fantasies had been proved to be false. Grenagh would have to wait for its glory day and victory would never be so timely for Na Piarsaigh again.

It was the last round-up in Rea's. They were getting ready to take the afternoon train and wait till next summer when the whole circus would begin again. Maybe they wouldn't even make Croke Park the next year. They hadn't in 2001 or 2002. Even the man with the sombrero, who materialises magically right beside the trophy whenever Cork win anything, looked a bit down in the mouth. A couple of guys in a corner tried vainly to rally the gathering to one mass rendition of 'The Banks'. They sang the opening about 20 times.

How oft do my thoughts in their fancy take flight
To the home of my childhood away.

No one responded and the duo weren't inclined to go on their own. By the end, everyone was looking at them as if they were a couple of lunatics. It would have been a wonderful scene if the whole pub had joined in the anthem and shown that, though defeated, the Cork fans were unbowed. But All-Ireland final defeat does bow you and there was no point pretending otherwise.

I got talking to a man from Castletownkenneigh who was sporting an enormous hangover but proudly showing off a sliotar he claimed had been used in the game. 'Do you know who was Cork's best player?'

'Wayne Sherlock?'

'No, not at all. Sully.'

Along the counter pained heads nodded agreement.

Back in Cork I was walking along the main drag when I heard the voice I'd been dreading to ever encounter again.

'Eamonn. How are you? Are you just coming back from the match?'

It was the security guard. We talked about the final for a small bit and I had to ask the question.

'Did you put that big bet on?'

'I did.'

Oh. I looked at an imaginary watch and began to mumble an excuse for leaving.

'God, Joe Deane didn't do much, did he?'

No. I'm sorry, I'm sorry, I'm sorry.

'But I suppose you can't know how games will turn out really.'

Dowcha boy.

20

The Longest Week of Peter Canavan

28 September: All-Ireland Senior Football Final
Croke Park; Tyrone 0–12, Armagh 0–9

Two weeks previously, all the talk had been about D.J. Carey's private life. In the run-up to the football final, the focus was on something else happening off the field. Peter Canavan's ankle became the most famous body part in Ireland.

The abiding image of Tyrone's semi-final victory over Kerry had been the way the players had celebrated on the pitch at the end, as though the win had confirmed their talent in their own minds. Tyrone had arrived. But the image that came to dominate as the final drew nearer was of Canavan crumpled in a heap early in the first half. The word was that he had damaged his ankle ligaments and might well miss the final altogether. Even if he did manage to play, it would be a miracle if he was able to produce anything like his best.

This was a twist so cruel that even the most sadistic soap-opera writer would have baulked at it. For over a decade, Canavan had been looking for an All-Ireland medal, in the process establishing himself as the finest forward of his generation. Now, with Tyrone just 70 minutes away from winning their first All-Ireland and looking a good bet to do so, he might have to sit out the game. No one would have dared to make it up.

If anyone deserved an All-Ireland medal it was Peter Canavan. From the moment he'd showed up in Croke Park as a Tyrone underage star, there was a special aura about him. While he was still an U-21 star with some phenomenal Tyrone teams, he was accepted as one of the best attackers in the game. And, in 1995, he had one of the great forward seasons of modern times, concluding it with an All-Ireland final performance that has rarely been matched by a player on a losing team.

Compared to the current Tyrone team that side had been pretty average. That they came within a point of Dublin in the final was almost wholly to do with Canavan's remarkable display. It wasn't just that he kicked 11 of his side's points, 10 of which came from frees, it was that he'd almost single-handedly engineered most of those frees and that, at times, he seemed to be taking Dublin on on his own. It didn't matter how many defenders surrounded him, Canavan was always able to wriggle free and create something. His semi-final display against Galway had been special too. One run, which took him slaloming past three defenders before kicking a point, was a moment of pure beauty. He could even have got Tyrone a draw in the final, throwing himself on the ground to fist a pass to Seán McLoughlin for the levelling point only for the referee to rule that he'd touched the ball on the turf. It had been another of those decisions that could have gone either way. Canavan, in 1995, was as good and as dominant as Mickey Linden had been the year before. All that was missing was a winners medal and that would hardly be long delayed. Tyrone were young and eager, their time would come.

In 1996, they won Ulster even more convincingly and Canavan looked an even more complete footballer. He was so skilful that, once he had the ball in his hand, his man was as well to give up. He had the balance of a ballet dancer and the drive of a polar explorer. For a small man, his frame would always suggest that of a minor newly arrived in senior ranks, he had a remarkable ability to ride tackles. One of his distinguishing features was the way he refused to be hurried into doing anything. Canavan took every last inch out of the ball until he was sure that he could get in the ideal shot or make the perfect pass. Allied to intelligence and patience was a massive degree of technical excellence. If there was even half a chance, he never missed. Off the ball, he moved like a world-class soccer striker, making such an amount and variety of runs that, eventually, he would get open and take it from there.

Tyrone were favourites by the time they reached the All-Ireland semi in 1996 and Canavan was well ahead on points for Footballer-of-the-Year honours. That semi-final seemed to severely damage both team and player. Meath hit Tyrone hard and didn't worry too much about the rules. Canavan was injured by a blindside hit and wasn't himself for the rest of the game. In fact, that game seemed to change his attitude for a while, to darken his sunny approach to football. He seemed to become cranky and got involved in a post-match brawl in a Tyrone club that led to at least one serious injury. There were even rumours that he'd become jaded with inter-county football and might retire. The exploits of Maurice Fitzgerald in 1997 and Ollie Murphy in 1999 made people momentarily forget just how good the small man from Errigal Ciarán was.

He played his way out of the dark days and regained the affection of the fans. But the feeling was that his chance of an All-Ireland medal was gone. Canavan became a popular answer in the pub debate about who was the best footballer never to win an All-Ireland.

Then a new crew of Tyrone wonder boys arrived on the scene. They won minor and U-21 All-Irelands and looked to be potentially the most gifted generation of footballers in the county's history. Canavan responded to the challenge of becoming the Obi Wan Kenobi to these Skywalkers with remarkable relish. In 2001, they won the Ulster title, in 2002 the National League, in 2003 the National League again.

In that league campaign, Canavan looked as hungry, as sharp

and as talented as he'd ever been. He dismantled the Fermanagh defence in the semi-final and one beautifully lobbed goal revived the debate about whether he was the best forward of modern times. It might have seemed heresy to compare him with the great Kerry attackers of the seventies and eighties but they had the advantage of playing in a team crammed with extraordinary footballers. A lot of the time, Canavan had been carrying teams on his back. At his best, he combined Mike Sheehy's skill with Pat Spillane's determination and John Egan's knack of getting the vital score when his team needed it most.

Canavan looked to be really enjoying his football in this championship. A lot of the pressure had been taken off him by the emergence of Owen Mulligan as a top-class corner-forward. But the presence of Mulligan beside him must also have reminded Canavan that he didn't have that many years left. He'd taught the blond bombshell in school. Together they combined to destroy Down and Fermanagh before Canavan had gone down in those opening minutes against Kerry. All of a sudden his dream season faced a nightmare conclusion. No one knew whether or not he'd play in the final, and this was a cause of great concern to football fans not just in Tyrone but all over the country. People liked Canavan because he was a pure footballer. Physical attributes played little part in his greatness, sheer skill had put him where he was. But, after being unstoppable for so long, Peter Canavan had finally met the most difficult opponent yet. His own ankle.

Not only had Canavan inspired Tyrone but he had contributed a huge amount to his club. Errigal Ciarán had won five county titles in the last decade and added a couple of Ulsters for good measure. They were Canavan's club and also Mickey Harte's, and had seven players on the panel for the final. Three of them – Canavan, goalkeeper John Devine and Enda McGinley – would start. Paul Horisk, Mark Harte and Peter Loughran had all made appearances during the championship. A second McGinley brother, Cormac, would have figured more prominently had he not been dogged by injury. It followed that the place to visit the week of the All-Ireland final was Ballygawley, home village of Errigal Ciarán and a place that had made the headlines for reasons other than football when Peter Canavan had been growing up.

Ballygawley was an unremarkable place. It would probably have been the same kind of uneventful country spot as Grenagh had it not been for the vicissitudes of geography and history. Geography had placed it just inside the county of Tyrone, a few miles from the Monaghan border. History had made its situation matter. When partition came around, the largely Catholic Ballygawley area was cut off from its hinterland and its people condemned to life in what Northern Ireland's first premier had called, 'A Protestant state for a Protestant people.'

The road to Ballygawley is resonant with reminders of the dark history of the past 30 years in this country. There's Monaghan town where seven people were killed by a bomb in May 1974 and are largely forgotten because the explosion took place the same day as the Dublin bombings. That it's still unclear as to who exactly planted those bombs and who helped them and why they were never caught shows that the war in the North still hasn't been properly addressed down here.

Leaving Monaghan town, you pass through the village of Emyvale where, in 1987, the funeral cortège of Jim Lynagh, one of eight IRA men shot dead in Loughgall, stopped and three IRA men fired shots over the coffin. When gardaí tried to intervene, their squad car was turned over by the crowd. A guard fired shots over the heads of the crowd and the incident seemed to confer that the writ of the law of the Irish State wasn't fully accepted by people in the border areas, at least not when it came to matters republican. After Emyvale, you cross the border into the village of Aughnacloy. In February 1988, Aidan McAnespie was making the journey the opposite way to go to a match when he was shot dead by a British soldier. For years, the McAnespie murder was the most emotive argument against the scrapping of Rule 21, which banned British Army and RUC members from joining the GAA. And, after Aughnacloy, you reach Ballygawley, which also knew plenty of death in those dark years.

The IRA killed in and around Ballygawley. They killed RUC men, British soldiers, UDR men on patrol and off-duty UDR men, one at work, another outside his shop. A building contractor was shot dead for working for the security forces, a Catholic bus driver was shot by mistake. Two RUC men were killed when the local barracks was attacked by a unit that would later be gunned down by the SAS.

And on 20 August 1988, there was the bombing that ensured that one more unremarkable Northern village would have a special place on the death list. A group of British soldiers were going on leave when a landmine was detonated under their bus. Eight of them died, they were all between 18 and 21 years of age. The youth of the combatants gives you pause. The dead IRA men at Loughgall included a 19-year-old and a 21-year-old. There is a terrible sense of waste about the whole thing.

Now that peace has come, Ballygawley is just an ordinary country place again, like Grenagh or Ballaghaderreen or Ventry. But it's pointless to pretend that the area is unaffected by what happened here in the recent past. It can't be. And that is what is most disturbing about the history of the Troubles. The killing fields are not alien or strange, like the dusty landscapes of Iraq or the urban slums of Palestine, they are familiar. Passing through them now, it's hard to imagine the sound of bombs and gunfire, the screams of the wounded, the fear and anger felt by all sides.

What did it all mean? A popular theory at the time in this part of the island was that the IRA were psychopaths. Now that the guns are silent, you don't hear that theory anymore but it was once popular currency, voiced regularly in the letters pages of national newspapers. The fear seemed to be that admitting the political roots of the violence made you complicit in atrocities. It was the extreme version of Northern Bastard Syndrome. And what nonsense it was, that belief that here in the 26 counties were normal decent, law-abiding people but once you crossed the border, that arbitrary line, you met people given to senseless violence. Monaghan normal; Tyrone crazy. They came from the same cultural background as us, they played the same sports, listened to the same music, went to the same church. Yet somehow they liked killing people and we didn't. When you think about it for more than two seconds, it is complete rubbish as a theory. Yet, prompted by my youthful reading of *Hot Press*, I believed in it for a while. Then I went to London and turned the other way altogether, oscillating wildly back and forth for a few years before eventually deciding, as Brian Friel puts it in *Translations*, that 'confusion is not an ignoble condition'.

Perhaps the key to what happened lies in the very ordinariness of the Northern villages. I was born in a small village and now I live in the countryside outside a small town. If either were invaded by a foreign army, I can imagine the local reaction. Most people would complain but do nothing, I'd be one of them. But I know that there would be people, ordinary young country lads, who wouldn't take an occupation lying down. West Cork, after all, was the scene of many deaths during the War of Independence. Political circumstances rather than local character were responsible for what happened in the North.

Breandán Ó hEithir used to say that, any time he heard someone complaining about how bad the Troubles were and how the cause of Irish freedom was being let down there, he wanted to take the complainer to Ballyseedy and show them the monument to the republicans who were tied to a landmine there by Free State troops. Nobody has clean hands. Which isn't to say that the fate of the British soldiers in Ballygawley wasn't a tragedy. As I write this, there are news of soldiers dying in Iraq, for unclear aims in a country they don't know and whose history they don't understand. And they're also wondering what they've done to deserve this after all their efforts to get on with the local population.

Thankfully the villages and towns of the North make the news for different reasons now, though the local radio station was running an item on a Sinn Féin protest planned for a policing-board meeting in Strabane the night I disembarked in Bally-gawley.

In a pub at the top of the town, a young lad wearing a top that read 'St Kieran's High School, All-Ireland Champions', served drink to a couple of men who were wondering if there was any hope of getting match tickets and if it would be worth going down to Dublin anyway on the off-chance.

'It would be. You'd have the crack over the weekend and you could watch the game in the pub down there.'

'And you could tell everyone you were at the match after-wards.'

It was the same kind of buzz there'd been in Killeagh in 1999, nervous anticipation at the possibility of suddenly becoming the centre of the sporting universe.

I felt more at home in Ballygawley than in any other place I visited, largely because the village was so like Gurteen where I grew up. Not only was it the same size and roughly the same shape, it had the same set about it. It was the kind of place where, if you stood still for a short while, a van would pull up and a couple of lads in blue overalls would jump out. One of the many journalists who visited the village that week described it as 'unlovely'. It would be more correct to say that Ballygawley looks like Ireland. Most of the country doesn't look like Connemara, the Lakes of Killarney, the Cliffs of Moher or the other highlights that we sell to the tourists and pretend somehow encapsulate the essence of Irishness. The real heartland places are the villages and small towns dotted all around the country. They're where the majority of GAA players come from.

Cathal McAnenly met me in the pub. Cathal is the chairman of the Errigal Ciarán club and was probably suffering from interview fatigue by the time he met me. The club, with Harte and

Canavan and the six other panel members, was so obviously the big story that half the country's journalists seemed to have travelled there. (The other half had gone to Moy, the Tyrone village right on the border with Armagh where local rivalry was at its most ferocious.) Yet Cathal was another one of the fiercely helpful good guys. He checked out what time the bus in the morning would be leaving and when we got to Kellys Inn checked if they had a spare room and advised me to stay there.

Staying in Kellys Inn, a couple of miles out the road from Ballygawley, fulfilled one of my great travel ambitions. I've always wanted to stay in a motel and, though Kellys is a bit more up-market that the kind of Alabaman establishment I was thinking of, it did have that motel feature of having a row of rooms set apart from the premises with their front doors facing the road. When you'd got your key, you didn't have to go back into the hotel and you could lie on the bed and listen to Merle Haggard if you had any of his tapes handy. Only I didn't, so I went back into the hotel to talk to Cathal and to the boundlessly enthusiastic Seamus Horisk who was a past-chairman of the club. A family were eating at the table next to us, the kids wearing Tyrone jerseys. Kellys was quiet as hotel-type establishments tend to be in the evening but they sponsored the team and this seemed to be where the club conducted official interview business.

The first question was fairly obvious. 'I was talking to his mother this morning and she said it was a pity after all these years he won't be 100 per cent on the day,' said Horisk.

'But he'll play, he'll definitely play,' McAnenly said urgently before explaining exactly what a tragedy it would be if that didn't happen.

'People outside don't know how much he's put into the game. Peter has managed his life around football. He has never let us down once. If his holidays are booked and they clash with a match, it's the holidays that'll lose out. In February of 1994, we were beaten in an All-Ireland club semi-final replay in Newbridge on a Saturday afternoon by Nemo Rangers. It was a terrible bus journey back, the atmosphere wasn't good because we should have won the first day. But he got up at six on the Sunday morning and went all the way down to Ennis to play for Ulster in the Railway Cup final. He'd have been excused if he hadn't, but that's the kind of commitment he has.'

It's almost impossible to imagine the status that Canavan has within his own club. County players generally stand out on club teams anyway, but Canavan is the most gifted footballer in the game. He stands out on an inter-county side, at club level he must look almost superhuman. There was a certain awe in the tone of his fellow clubmen as they talked about him.

'We'll only appreciate him fully, you know, when he stops playing football. We'll think that we didn't appreciate him enough when he was playing. Everyone is born with a talent and Peter's is football. He was one of those kids who always had a football in his hand when he was five or six and he worked at it and kept at it till he got to be as good as he could be.'

Horisk concurred.

'Sometimes I think that people outside Errigal Ciarán get more out of watching him than we do. We're always seeing the special things he can do, we've become kind of case hardened. I remember when he played in a Vocational Schools final against Kerry in Croke Park, this wee slight 16-year-old tapping over 50s. And the one that sticks with me is an Under-21 game against Dungannon when he pointed a 50 from the right side with his right foot and a 50 from the left side with his left foot. He's the best footballer in Ireland and he's inspired two generations of young people here since he won his first Under-21 title, it must be 15 years ago.'

They idolised Canavan in Errigal Ciarán though it was a peculiar irony that the great man hadn't played underage football with the club. When he first caught the eye as a Tyrone minor, Canavan was notable for not having any club. His part of the parish had refused to play with Ballygawley due to a row over a sending off in a competition held within the club. Thus the renaming of the club as Errigal Ciarán, the adoption of new colours and a relaunch of football in the area in 1991. They made up for lost time by winning their first county title two years later. Horisk described that as the best day ever for the area and revealed himself as a true GAA clubman by admitting that when Tyrone went well, he worried that the club football of the Errigal men would be affected. (The club lost the county final by a point to Killyclogher a few weeks after the All-Ireland. Canavan's ankle injury prevented him from playing.)

'Like, we're happy that Tyrone are doing well but, in the end of the day, there's nothing like club success because it's your own people. If push comes to shove even Peter is a *club* man. Football is a second religion here.'

We talked about the Red-and-White Days in the local school when the kids eschew their uniforms in favour of clothes in the Tyrone colours, and the fact that the shop in Dungannon, which was the main agent for the county team, could hardly keep up with the demand for replica jerseys and all the other manifestations of fandom.

'We'd have 60 youngsters out training at Under-10 and Under-12, not playing matches just getting them used to football. To them it's cool to wear the Tyrone top or the Errigal Ciarán top in a way it wouldn't have been 10 years ago. They all want to be Peter Canavan. You know when you're young and you play the All-Ireland final all over again when the final is over. We all used to want to be Kerry players but now it's all Peter Canavan,' said McAnenly with a grin.

We didn't talk so much about Mickey Harte who'd kept a remarkably low profile throughout the championship, though he made up for that by publishing a book after the final. Harte was both Errigal and GAA through and through. His brothers had played for the club and one of them had become chairman of the

Ulster council. Mickey himself had played on the Tyrone minor team that had reached the 1972 All-Ireland final. He'd had plenty of offers from other clubs, they told me, but he'd never managed any other club team or any other county. They reckoned he never would. He was firmly rooted in his locality. 'Mickey Harte and Peter Canavan were born only two kicks of a ball apart from each other. That'd be on the road out from the town to here,' observed Horisk.

When the subject of the 'other' community came up, Horisk insisted that there were closet GAA fans on the other side of the political fence.

'They wouldn't come to a game around here but there'll be a few of the other community down at the All-Ireland, people from a rugby background who'll be caught up in the excitement of it all. They've started taking notice with all the coverage that there is and they probably see that it's an exciting game and enjoy that.'

At this stage, we entered the realms of multimedia. A man who was making a film about Errigal Ciarán's All-Ireland week arrived and insisted on filming me interviewing the two clubmen. I'd more or less run out of questions by this stage, so we had to go back over everything again while I held the boom mike and the cameraman buzzed around enthusiastically. By the time we were finished, I was well in the mood for diversion.

'Do you want to go into town for a pint?' asked Cathal Mc-Anenly.

Is Peter Canavan the best forward in Tyrone?

So, after Cathal had dropped off his car and got his wife to leave us into town, we arrived in Quinns, a pub owned by the brother of Paudge Quinn, who'd scored Tyrone's first ever All-Ireland final goal in 1985 against Kerry. It would remain their only All-Ireland final goal after Sunday's match though we didn't know that then.

And here is where things get very hazy. I know that I had an enjoyable night in Quinns, but I remember very little of what was said, largely due to a tactical mistake I made at around midnight.

'I think I might as well knock it on the head for tonight, lads.'

'Ah, now, come on. You'll have another drink. You'll have a short.'

'OK, I'll have a short.'

Don't think ordering a short in a pub with a locked door will get you out of there any quicker. People will just think you're a whiskey drinker and keep buying you the stuff.

Which is exactly what happened. Every time I finished one whiskey, there was another in front of me courtesy of the friendly Quinns' customers and the boss man himself. The quicker I drank them, the quicker they kept coming. After a few hours of this, my blood was as full of whiskey as a still in the mountains of North Carolina tended by inbred men wearing beards. The night and early morning in Ballygawley are not coming back to me. I remember just one incident, perhaps because it confirmed my paranoid conviction that you really never do where you're talking.

'Cathal, do you remember when Canavan came through first there were two other brilliant young forwards, Adrian Cush and Eamonn McCaffrey. Whatever happened to them?'

'Well Eamonn, Adrian Cush had a lot of trouble with injury. And Eamonn McCaffrey...' With that Cathal turned to the man sitting next to me.

'What did happen to you McCaffrey?' Everyone in the pub laughed and Eamonn McCaffrey, an outstanding U-21 centre half-forward over a decade ago, seemed to get as much enjoyment out of my faux pas as anyone else. In fact, it was he who dropped me out to Kellys Inn at some hour of the morning. It was the kind of coincidence you couldn't have made up and I said a silent prayer that I hadn't enquired about the whereabouts of some cumbersome full-back or inaccurate wing-forward. When I checked my money the next day, I noticed that I hadn't been allowed buy a single drink. And, once more, I felt a much richer person for having met the people I'd met. In the States, they bang on about Southern hospitality. I don't think I've ever experienced hospitality in this country like I found in Mayobridge and Bally-gawley.

In the morning, I realised how accurate Kingsley Amis's famous line from *Lucky Jim* about hangovers is. 'His mouth had been used as a latrine by some small creature of the night, and then as its mausoleum.'

My small creature of the night seemed to have brought along a few of his friends. I emerged from my motel room and went into the inn in search of a taxi. I don't think they'd ever seen anyone react with such a degree of horror when offered breakfast. In the lobby was a bust and some pictures of a man who looked vaguely familiar.

'That's not John Montague, is it?'

'John Montague the poet, it is. He comes from very close to here.' You can be cynical and think that the notion of Irish respect for poets and writers in general is a bit of a Bord Fáilte fabrication. But I felt moved by the fact that a living poet was getting some recognition here in his home place. I don't think you'd find the same in every country. The memory of staring at that bust of Montague moves me even more now. Of all the books my father read when he was sick, the one he loved most was a big selected poems by Montague. Several times, he told me that he wished he hadn't taken so long to discover a writer so great. He'd wasted so much time on books he didn't like and here was this great Irish poet he was only coming to at this stage.

The time we waste. Fifty-nine is too young for anyone to die. And to go at 18 or 19 is an obscenity, no matter what cause is at issue. There's enough death in the world without adding to its store.

They called me a taxi back to Monaghan and mentioned that the Tyrone players were coming in for breakfast that morning. I was sitting on a bench outside the premises when they began to arrive. And there was the king himself, Peter Canavan. Off the field, he looked so unremarkable, so small and so light that it almost seemed cruel for this man to be carrying the hopes of an entire county. As he walked past me, I did what everyone else in Tyrone had probably been doing when they saw him.

I looked down at his ankle.

The guts of the rest of the day was spent hanging around Monaghan, a town that seemed as obsessed with the All-Ireland final as the neighbouring bailiwicks over the border. There was huge goodwill towards Tyrone and non-stop speculation about the ankle that I'd been fortunate enough to see just a few hours previously. How had he been walking? I didn't know. In a pub, I met a middle-aged woman obsessed with country music who told me of her infatuation with the music of Patrick Feeney, apparently the new sex god of the C&W scene. I didn't tell her that the same man lived next door to my mother because she wouldn't have believed me.

It was in the same pub that the woman of the house played me a couple of the All-Ireland songs doing the rounds. That great country stalwart Philomena Begley, who'd sung 'My Elusive Dreams' with Ray Lynam and got mentioned in the Pogues song 'My Brown Eyes' as a result, had released a Tyrone tribute record. But the one that tickled the customers was entitled 'Living Next Door to Champions' and had the same tune as an old Smokie hit with a similar name. (No, not 'I'll Meet You at Midnight.') Its popularity had much to do with a verse that slagged off Pat Spillane. Ever since he'd claimed that his mother could move faster than the Armagh full-back line, he had become a *bête noir* for Ulster football fans. And the 'puke football' comment ensured there was all-party agreement among the finalists that he should be derided at every opportunity. They were having so much fun with it that, had Pat Spillane not existed it would have been necessary to invent him. Someone showed me a newspaper article about Steven McDonnell's uncle dyeing his sheep orange and white. They were talking about nothing but the final in Monaghan that day.

Cathal McAnenly had told me that people from Aughnacloy

and Ballygawley commuted to jobs in the town. Emyvale had been bedecked with red-and-white flags. During the Troubles, people down here had frequently been exhorted to accept the immutable reality of the border. Up there was a completely different country and we should stay out of it and let them solve their own problems between themselves. But anyone living in a border town must have known that this was nonsense. When you were in Monaghan, Tyrone was just up the road. In political terms it might have been a different country but in emotional terms it wasn't. Actually, the whole island is too small to think in those terms. As the Christy Moore song about the hunger strikes had pointed out, even Belfast is only 'ninety miles from Dublin town'.

One story that caught my eye concerned a group of 15-foot sculptures in Strabane that had been clothed in giant Tyrone jerseys made for the local club by the O'Neills factory in the town. It seemed like another way to show how special All-Ireland final week was, but an Ulster Unionist councillor, Derek Hussey, hit the roof over it. He referred to the 'growing hysteria' and 'over-the-top exhibitionism' of GAA fans and described the dressing of the statues as, 'an outward exhibition of a cultural/political supremacy movement'.

Typical Unionist intransigence you might think but the council chairman, Jim Emery, who was also a UUP member, took a different tack, saying, 'The sculpture site is intended to be more or less neutral but I have no problem with it. I have continued to pledge my support for the members of the Tyrone team, their supporters and management. I hope the Sam Maguire Cup will be displayed proudly in Strabane.'

The future of the North may depend on the Councillor Emerys, on both sides, outnumbering the Councillor Husseys. Here's hoping.

After two enjoyable days of excess in Tyrone and Monaghan, I beat a path back southwards. The first thing I was asked when I got back to base was whether Peter Canavan would be fit for Sunday. I raised my throbbing head, looked out through my bloodshot eyes and groaned a reply, 'Will Peter Canavan be fit for Sunday? Fuck that. Will I be fit for Sunday?'

I was.

There was a tremendous atmosphere that Sunday. It was as though the fans of Tyrone and Armagh, aware of the scurrilous whispers predicting trouble, were going out of their way to prove the doubters wrong. Even by the high standards of the GAA, it was a uniquely good-humoured throng that trooped past the African shops and international call centres of Parnell Street and the flat blocks of Summerhill to embrace their teams' destiny. A huge sense of appreciation reigned. The supporters knew they were making history. This was a special day, the first All-Ireland final between two Ulster teams, something that might not happen again for a long time. And, even if it did happen again next year, this was the first. You wouldn't want a final between two neighbouring teams every year because part of the fun of All-Ireland day is in the contrast between counties but, just this once, it was no harm at all. The Northern counties had come through years unimaginable to their counterparts in the Republic. If the final was a celebration of Ulster football, it also seemed to tell a story of a newly confident community coming into its own.

In the Shakespeare and in Gills and all the other pubs on the route from city centre to stadium, Canavan's ankle was the *topic de jour*. One fan knew for sure he wouldn't even tog out, another reckoned they'd send him around in the parade and not start him, another reckoned he'd start and be taken off early on. A couple of Armagh fans even wondered if it might not all be a devious Mickey Harte mind-game.

Canavan togged out all right and kicked around as Tyrone warmed up. Armagh went down the same end as Tyrone initially and started bumping into the opposing players in what they undoubtedly saw as another masterpiece of psychological warfare. But it just looked silly, so they quit quickly enough.

Peter the Great marched in the parade and showed no sign of

withdrawing when the music was over. He was going to play in the All-Ireland final, regardless of his bad ankle. It must have given the Tyrone youngsters a tremendous boost and deprived Armagh of a nice gee-up at the beginning. Whatever happened now, he'd made it to the starting line.

From the start, it was obvious that Canavan was seriously hampered. He wasn't able to make those darting off-the-ball runs and, as a result, couldn't take his usual place as leader of the attack. But he was able to take frees and converted a couple as Tyrone once more left the blocks like a sprinter on steroids. Gerard Cavlan lashed over a glorious point from 50 yards which was hit so well it would probably have gone over from 70. For a few minutes, it looked as though he'd finally have the dominating game his talent made him capable of, but soon he fell quiet.

The one forward on top of his game was the one you'd expect. Stevie from Killeavy kicked his first point despite having three defenders swarming all over him. His second point, a snapshot kicked back over his shoulder as he moved away from goal, was the kind of score forwards often essay in training and rarely achieve in a big match. But McDonnell was surviving on a frugal diet because Tyrone were on top, their expected edge in pace being aided by the superior hunger only a team that has never won the All-Ireland can really summon.

Earlier in the championship, Owen Mulligan would have made hay from the kind of possession that was coming his way in Croke Park. But he got no change from that unlikeliest of heroes, Francie Bellew. Bellew even got an early booking, which ensured that he had to be careful about committing another foul. If he had been merely the puller and dragger of popular myth, that yellow card would have been disabling. Instead Bellew kept playing sensible, tight and unruffled defence and finally convinced everyone that he was a defender of a high order. Mulligan lacked nothing in huffing and puffing effort, but his team would have to look else-where for heroes.

Seán Cavanagh, whose Moy origins meant he probably had more riding on this game than anyone else in terms of local rivalry, was as adventurous as ever in midfield, but Armagh covered his runs forward and delivered some punishment. None of it looked deliberate, but Cavanagh was down a couple of times and it took its toll on a boy still young enough to play U-21.

The player who had the biggest game for the Ulster champions was an unlikely hero cut from the same kind of cloth as Francie Bellew. Kevin Hughes had been one of those players who must have waited nervously every time Mickey Harte announced a team. He hadn't made the starting 15 for the first round game against Derry. He was at left half-forward in the replay before graduating to midfield for the provincial semi-final against Antrim. Yet he was back at Number 12 for the drawn final against Down. Returned to midfield for the replay, he'd remained there probably because of Cormac McAnallen's move to full-back. One of the last Tyrone players you'd think of, Hughes is one of those hard-working players seemingly condemned to toil at the level below stardom. He is an awkward mover, an infrequent scorer and has the kind of haircut much beloved by inter-county minors but usually shed once they leave school.

However, no one did more for Tyrone on All-Ireland final day than Hughes. While flair players sputtered and played in fits and starts, he was consistently on top of his game. An amount of ball fell his way and he moved it on with simple passes. When a linkman was needed between defence and attack, Hughes was there. And when the ball was loose in the crowded midfield jungle, he swooped on it more often than anything else. He did nothing spectacular but it was a supreme display of competence.

Tyrone kept looking on the verge of breaking away, and might have done when Brian McGuigan opened up the Armagh full-back line by the strange expedient of tunnelling forward, like Brian O'Driscoll making for the line. Two passes later and Cavanagh had only Paul Hearty to beat. He calmly made space and sliced the ball horribly wide of a gaping goal. It was strangely reminiscent of the way Cork had cocked up their goal chance in the first half of the hurling final. Yet Tyrone were taking more of their chances than the Rebels, and there was a significant moment when Brian McGuigan left Kieran McGeeney sprawling on the ground before kicking a point. McGeeney was such a good defender that it was hard to remember the last time he'd been beaten one on one let alone left sprawling on his arse like a fall guy in a *Home Alone* film. But McGuigan was replaced by Stephen O'Neill shortly afterwards. It was an odd, uncomfortable half, and Tyrone missed another goal chance just before the whistle when Enda McGinley's shot was pushed over the bar by Hearty, one of the few players who looked like he was enjoying himself out there.

It was 0–8 to 0–4 at half-time and Armagh were hanging on. But they'd hung on before and chiselled out wins. The mystique that had been built up around the team's supposed invincibility in tight games had been summed up when Joe Brolly had commented, after the Donegal match, that no team of ordinary human beings could beat Armagh. If Tyrone were spooked by this kind of chat, then they might be dwelling on the missed chances in the dressing room.

Peter Canavan bowed to the inevitable at half-time and bowed out. Brian McGuigan replaced him in what must have been the quickest ever return to action for a subbed player. Once more, the apprentices would have to prosper without the sorcerer. The second half followed more or less the same pattern at first with Tyrone on top but Armagh sticking at it. Every time Tyrone threatened to move sufficiently far ahead to allow their fans an exhalation of breath, Armagh came back with a score. Armagh were like that car that appears in your rear-view mirror late at night and never draws nearer nor falls farther behind. They were just there.

Yet they didn't look as threatening as they had against Laois or Donegal. The quiet Gavin Devlin and the novice full-back

Cormac McAnallen once more shored up the middle and Hughes continued to thrive at midfield. Yet Tyrone could never relax because McDonnell, starved of possession but obviously sharp, still stalked around in search of the one opportunity that was all he needed to change the game, which seemed to be getting away from Armagh.

Early in the second half, Tyrone had their second nailed-on goal chance that might have enabled them to relax. O'Neill put Cavlan clean through but the big wing-forward dragged his shot wide of the far post. And when Mulligan broke through and put a miserable effort wide, it seemed as though we were watching a new kind of performance, the neurotic triumph. The game was there for Tyrone, but they seemed determined to make this as hard a day as possible for themselves and their fans, who bore the looks of nervous flyers hitting an air pocket as the chances went astray.

Coming into the third quarter, Armagh looked to have been comprehensively banjaxed when Diarmaid Marsden was sent off. If decisions had gone their way in the semi-final, this one went against them and proved that a kind of karma obtains over the course of a GAA season. Tyrone's All Star to be wing-back Philip Jordan ran at Marsden off the ball and, when the Armagh man raised his arm to protect himself, Jordan toppled spectacularly. Brian White gave Marsden the line, a decision so bad that the Games Administration Committee, who usually stand up for referees, ruled that no suspension should be served. I was very fond of this Tyrone team, but they were mighty fond of hitting the deck. It was ironic that, when White finally got fed up of the diving and urged Brian Dooher to get to his feet late in the game, the Tyrone wing-forward had genuine cause for complaint as he had been hit by an elbow. It remains to be seen whether it will become a feature of Gaelic football or whether the GAA will act to stamp it out. To further spur Tyrone on, Canavan came back on for the final ten minutes.

But, even with a man extra, Tyrone seemed reluctant to close out the game. They stayed between two and four points ahead and Armagh never enjoyed anything like dominance. But, with just a few minutes to go, the nightmare vision began to unfold for the Tyrone fans. A hopeful ball bobbed around between a couple of defenders and a quick pass put Steven McDonnell racing clear. The best forward in the country, the man who finished goal chances better than anyone else and all he could see in front of him were the goals and John Devine. Armagh would be suddenly in the driving seat, the force would be with them. They had saved their biggest miracle comeback of all for their neighbours.

Then, as McDonnell cocked the gun and drew back the trigger, Tyrone's left half-back Conor Gormley launched himself into a desperate dive. Gormley was behind and to the side of McDonnell when he made his move. If he had mistimed his dive, he could easily have got a boot in the face. More seriously for Tyrone, even the slightest miscalculation could have resulted in the ball deflecting off Gormley and flying into the net past a wrongfooted Devine. He had set himself an almost impossible task but, as the ball left McDonnell's boot, it met the outstretched arm of Gormley and flew wide.

Blocking down a kick was perhaps the least glamorous skill in Gaelic football, but Gormley had just done wonders for its profile. In terms of difficulty and timing, he had executed probably the greatest block ever seen in Croke Park. The match-winning move in this All-Ireland final would not be a goal or a point but a piece of defensive play. All the football played from May to September had led to this moment. Had Conor Gormley not made up the ground and been inch perfect with that block, McDonnell would probably have scored the goal and Armagh would have been very hard to beat. On instants like this do whole seasons depend. All Tyrone's preparations and everything that had brought them this close to making history would have counted for nothing had it not been for one man doing the right thing at the right time.

The road that had started with Waterford scoring a first-minute penalty against Tipperary more or less came to an end when Gormley denied McDonnell. That was the winning of the All-Ireland there and then. Stephen O'Neill wrapped it up with a late point. With Canavan injured and Mulligan fazed by the big occasions, the sub had turned out to be Tyrone's best forward in their last two games. You never do know where your hero is going to come from. The final pass before that final score came from the slight Brian Dooher who was still chugging away as though somewhere along the line in his work as a vet, he'd arranged for the heart and lungs of a racehorse to be transplanted into his frail form.

There were ironies about the denouement. Gormley came from Carrickmore, Errigal Ciarán's fiercest rivals and the team who'd been involved in the brawl that had embroiled Canavan in controversy a few years back. But it was his intervention that had secured the win for the captain.

And what if Brian White had made the right call and left Marsden on the field? As McDonnell homed in on goal and Gormley dived towards the ball, might the corner-forward not have spotted Marsden coming through the middle and passed the ball inside to him? Perhaps Gormley would have had one eye on Marsden and the block wouldn't have come off. We'll never know.

In reality, it had been a hugely dominant performance by Tyrone. They had been nervy, they had missed at least three good goal chances and they had done it with Peter Canavan effectively reduced to passenger status. At the start of the year, no one would have dared suggest they could win an All-Ireland without a major input from their star player. To put it in context, had Armagh been forced to play 60 minutes of the semi-final without McDonnell, they wouldn't have reached the final. Over the next week, there would be some sour talk about Tyrone's victory being bad for the game and talk of yet another crisis in Gaelic football. But they had played superb football up until the second half of the semi-final and only deserted their best instincts when history seemed to weigh down on them. Their team was full of richly talented young-sters – McMenamin, McAnallen, Cavanagh, Jordan, Hughes, Mulligan, O'Neill – and there were other tyros energised by underage success eager to come in. With the monkey of championship failure off their back, they might relax and play the expansive football that would mark them out as a truly great team. They had the ability to be the most exciting team since the great Kerry teams of Mick O'Dwyer.

But they might decide that the percentage, take-no-risks approach, which they'd employed in their last three halves of football, had worked and should be followed from here on in. It depended on Tyrone. A lot would depend on Tyrone in the future because All-Ireland champions set the standard. They could be a force for good or bad.

Not that these musings would have meant anything to the Tyrone fans who followed the lead of Laois and Armagh and invaded the pitch. When the victory was big enough, the sup-porters found a way on to Croke Park and the sky didn't fall down. Perhaps it's only those teams whose supporters are keen enough to disregard the GAA ordinance and make it on to the pitch who deserve ultimate success. The boys from Ballygawley were somewhere out there.

We all stood around and watched Peter Canavan lift the Sam Maguire. And, just as I was preparing to revel in his triumph and experience a moment of transcendent joy, he had to go and spoil it all by saying 'There was another Mickey Harte who sang 'We've got the World Tonight' well this Mickey Harte…'

Peter, Peter, Peter. I'd spent the start of the summer being haunted by Mickey Joe Harte but, lately, he'd been banished from my mind. I thought I'd got the better of him but now, right at the end of the season in front of 80,000 people, here was my favourite footballer giving him a plug. Mickey Joe I surrender. You win.

But it was hard to stay cross with Canavan, who was so

overcome with joy that his speech was as disjointed and incoherent as Kieran McGeeney's had been stately and brilliant the year before. I thought of Cathal McAnenly saying how Canavan had fitted his life around football and about the ferocious hunger so evident every time he played. There must have been times when he thought he would retire without this moment ever coming to pass and the anticipation of that must have been dreadful to him. His father had died not long ago as well. He'd come through a lot before getting his hands on the Sam Maguire. There was a photo in the next day's paper of Canavan shaking his fists in joy as he caught the eye of someone in the crowd. He looked like a mystic visited by the divine. The county of Tyrone had come through a lot, too. Folk had to watch their neighbours in Donegal, Derry and Armagh win the Sam Maguire by producing the kind of performances Tyrone had never been able to summon in Croke Park. And off the field, there had been so much suffering. The county town of Omagh had suffered the greatest loss of the Troubles and the cruellest, in that it came when peace seemed to have arrived. The days when young men had been gunned down in Cappagh, in Coagh and in Ardboe seemed a long way away now.

For the next week, the Tyrone fans would wake up each morning feeling that much better about the world. Old men would forgive past defeats because they'd led to this day, youngsters wouldn't yet realise that they'd be thinking about this moment when they were old. Tyrone people in Australia and the United States would have grins so wide that strangers would be alarmed when passing them on the streets. The video of the game would be watched in the pubs as the winter nights drew in and Gormley's block cheered as though it was just happening for the first time. The cup would go to every small village in the county and thousands of photos would be taken of families touching the Sam Maguire with wonder in their eyes. There is no greater machine for the production of mass happiness in this country than the GAA.

Perhaps I should have gone to Ballygawley and seen what the celebrations were like. But, to be honest, that lock-in whiskey wasn't long out of the system. I hadn't been able to stick with the Ballygawley boys before the final, so I didn't reckon much on my chances of hanging in there when they were in celebration mode. Instead, I went to the Hideout, a pub in the Portland Place estate near Croke Park. You go down a quiet street and turn down a lane to get to the Hideout and this makes it sufficiently remote to be not too crowded on a match day. The first time I ever drank there was the day of the 1987 All-Ireland hurling final, the night after we'd met the transvestite from Tipperary.

I sat down, had a contemplative pint and thought of the journey since I'd set off for Dungarvan on May 24th. Transported with joy, a group of Tyrone fans were discussing their chances in next year's championship.

'Like I'd say that team, once they'll win one they might win three or four.'

'I suppose, but Kerry will bounce back mind.'

'Cork will have Billy Morgan back in charge. And I wouldn't say Meath are finished yet.'

'Armagh'll be there again next year and Ronan Clarke will be in better nick. And the Dubs, you know, they'll not be bad.'

When you think that it's over, it's only begun.

Epilogue

The Mighty, Mighty Haven

19 October: Cork Senior Football Championship Final
Páirc Uí Chaoimh, Cork
Castlehaven 1–11, Clonakilty 1–9

I didn't know the GAA until I came to Castlehaven. Sure, I'd gone to plenty of games and followed every championship since I was five years old, but it wasn't till I fetched up in this corner of West Cork, that I saw what the association could mean to a local community, how it could be so embedded in a place that parish identity was based around the club.

I moved here in 1998. Today, it's 2004 and I'm still here. The address has changed but I'm still in Castlehaven parish, the home of one of the most extraordinary clubs in the country.

Haven pick from the villages of Castletownshend and Union Hall and the countryside in between. The pick is small and reduced further because the population of Castletownshend has a high proportion of foreign retirees. The population resources of the club mean that they should logically be playing at junior level. Perhaps it began with the seven Collins brothers – Christy, Dinty, Bernard, Donie, Francis, Anthony and Vincent – who set about making the club a force to be reckoned with and steered it as far as a county senior final in 1979. They lost that to a St Finbarr's team that went on to win an All-Ireland, and everyone reckoned the fairytale was over and Castlehaven would soon resume a station more fitting to a club of their size.

They didn't. They won Cork senior titles in 1989 and 1994 and went on to win the Munster titles in those years. When they lost a county final to a divisional team in 1997, they were nominated to represent Cork in Munster and won the province again. They were aided by the arrival of Larry Tompkins, something that their rivals made great play of while ignoring the fact that the big-city teams Haven were beating often fielded four or five players they'd recruited along the way. The great Haven sides included Niall Cahalane, John Cleary, Mike Maguire and Michael Burns who all won All-Ireland medals, as well as a host of top-class club footballers who delighted in overcoming the odds.

Haven were fiercely proud of the great tradition set by that golden generation of footballers. I learned that the first day I moved into Castletownshend village and went for a pint in Collins' pub (owned by Christy, the best footballer of the seven brothers and a former Cork midfielder). Christy and Batt Maguire (brother of Mike) and Chris O'Brien (who was on the sideline when Haven won the county final) and Tim Joe Regan (who'd scored the winning point in the 1989 final) and John Maguire (who'd been in goals that day) and all the other habitues of Collins' and the village's two other pubs, Lil McCarthy's and Mary Ann's were the most knowledgeable GAA people you could hope to meet.

It is unusual to meet anyone, man or woman, adult or child, who doesn't know about football. It is the number one preoccupation in the area and every game played by the club is analysed and worried over in the following week. In the off-season, the season past and the season to come were scrutinised in detail. When the U-21 games, which heralded the beginning of another year's football, started huge crowds travelled to see this year's crop of youngsters playing. And when the senior league began, we'd all troop up to the pitch at Moneyvoulihane in the wind and the rain, suffering such punishment from the elements that the hot whiskeys and pints back in Collins' seemed less like an indulgence and more like a medical necessity.

The Haven fans were legendary for their fanaticism. There is a story that may be apocryphal but which I've heard so many times I can't resist repeating it.

The rivalry between Castlehaven and O'Donovan Rossa, the club in the nearby town of Skibbereen, is one of the most fervent in the country. And when they met each other in the 1994 final, it reached an almost South-American intensity. The story goes that some Haven folk were in Skibberreen one day when they saw a washing machine in the window of an electrical shop. Tumbling around in the window was a blue-and-white jersey. They couldn't believe their eyes. It was a Haven jersey. The old enemy were deliberately insulting them. One thing led to another and soon the shop was threatened with a boycott by people from the Castlehaven area. The impasse was only ended when an employee of the shop was sent down to Castlehaven creamery with a Manchester City jersey, which he swore was the garment that had been in the washing machine. So the story goes. It may not be true, but the fact that it even exists says a lot about the immense seriousness with which football is taken in this part of West Cork.

I have only one regret about living in Castlehaven. At some point in the football conversation, Christy or Batt or Chris or John will shake their heads and say, 'Ah, you should have been here when we were winning county titles. It was just incredible.'

In the 1998 All-Ireland club semi-final, Haven had contrived to lose a seven-point lead in the last five minutes and that seemed to ring the curtain down on their golden era. Many of the players on that team had retired and there was general agreement that Haven wouldn't see the same kind of success again. It was the same kind of general agreement there'd been after 1979 come to think of it.

So we came to 2003. Nemo Rangers were knocked out by Na

Piarsaigh, which gave the other clubs some hope, but Haven were still outsiders in their quarter-final against Bishopstown, the new favourites for the title. Bishopstown were much bigger than Haven and played them off the field in the first half en route to a five-point lead at half-time. I hoped the final score wouldn't be too cruel. Haven's second-half performance was one like I'd rarely seen. On an emotional high and playing almost entirely on heart and instinct, they got home by two points. One win later, and they were in the final against Clonakilty.

The build-up was like nothing I'd seen before at club level. For weeks beforehand, the streets in Skibbereen were blocked with knots of Haven people who were so obsessed by the match that they had to stop and talk to each other about it. No telephone pole was without its flag and bunting. Haven slogans were painted on the roads into Castletownshend and Union Hall and also on the main Cork–Skibbereen road. Some innovative Havenite painted blue on the white line in the middle of the main road so motorists were travelling on blue and white all the way into Skibb. The council painted over the blue. The blue appeared again. The council took the hint. A giant blue-and-white doll appeared on the roof of Castlehaven creamery. A tailor's dummy in full Haven kit thumbed a lift on the road to Cork.

On the day of the final, the entire parish decamped to Cork. From eight to 80, they were there. Clonakilty were outnumbered and comprehensively outshouted, outsung and outhooted. The *Southern Star* commented that, while the Clonakilty people were going to see a match, the Haven crowd were going on a crusade. It seemed mathematically impossible but most of the 15,000 crowd seemed to come from Castlehaven, a parish whose population is a small fraction of that number. But perhaps that was because the legend of the Haven is so beguiling that they make converts. I travelled up to the game with two people from Cape Clear Island. They were Haven fans. I travelled back with a man from Cork city. He was a Haven fan. And I am a convert too.

The Haven die-hards don't question the presence of these blow-in supporters, they presume that anyone with any sense would want to follow the blue and white.

They won that county final by two points and, at the end, I stood on the pitch with Tim Joe Regan and John Maguire and we watched Liam Collins, Christy's son, lift the cup. His brother Bernie was beside him. I'd been at Bernie's farewell party when he went to Australia to play Rules Football. A report in *The Sunday Times* said that he'd come incredibly close to making the big time there, but had been beaten by injury. Bernie's return to Ireland had been a turning point for the team. Niall Cahalane was there too, 40 years old and playing with a torn muscle in his leg, which meant he could hardly kick the ball. What it must have been like running on that leg doesn't bear thinking about. He was one of the last survivors of the club's golden generation and he'd seen Haven do the unthinkable and produce an almost entirely new team of young players from this small catchment area to win the county title again. Colin Crowley got the Man-of-the-Match award. I'd had a conversation in the street with his uncle, Pat, the day before. Pat, who talked about religious mysticism and life in Spain as fluently as he talked about football, had been nervous about the favourites tag bestowed on Haven. They'd borne it lightly.

Back in Castletownshend, there were fireworks and drinking out of the cup and bar-room replays of Colin Crowley's goal. I headed for home at midnight and was walking up the hill from Mary Ann's when a car stopped.

'Where are you going?'

'Home.'

'We're going to Union Hall, we can drop you near home.'

And when we got to the turn near my house, John Cleary (All-Ireland medal-winner 1989 and 1990, son of Ned who'd been one of the club's great guiding lights, brother of Denis and Edmund who's won county medals with Haven and of Nollaig, who'd score eight points from play when Gabriel Rangers won the All-Ireland junior women's football championship that December and of Eimear who'd played on that team too) said that, seeing as I'd come this far, I might as well see what the crack was like in Union Hall.

It was five in the morning. The streets were full, the pubs were packed and everyone was so high on the moment that nobody seemed drunk. For about the 100th time, people were up on tables and chairs in Nolan's, jumping up and down with their arms around each other and singing. Who's your man with the baseball cap over there lepping around the place? Oh yeah, it's the parish priest, another convert and a selector on the team. It's that kind of night. And then they began to sing the club's theme song.

Everywhere we go, everywhere we go,
People always ask us, people always ask us,
Who we are, who we are,
And we tell them, and we tell them,
We're from the Haven, we're from the Haven,
The mighty, mighty Haven, the mighty, mighty Haven.

And, right at that moment, while I was still jumping up and down on a wobbly table, it struck me that they had summed up the essence of the GAA's appeal.

It is a haven.

A mighty, mighty haven.

A haven for Waterford footballers who hope someday their team will win a match, for Celtic fans on Hill 16, for Dublin surgeons dedicating themselves to the cause of Cuba, for financial advisers who'd wanted justice for players, for time-defying forwards in the Down jersey, for falsetto singers on the Thurles–Cork train, for quietly spoken managers living in clock towers, for schoolteachers coaching youngsters in the Kerry Gaeltacht, for chatty wee barmaids from Tempo, for Laois footballers wary of persecution by mystery callers from Meath, for legendary veterans with footballs hanging over the counter of their pub, for website sheepstealers from Roscommon, for club officers from the northside of Cork city, for reporters waiting outside dressing-room doors, for commentators who decried 'puke football', for referees from Kildare who got things wrong because they were only human, for clubs whose triumph had been to just keep going, for lads from Tyrone villages who'd nearly poison you with whiskey out of pure generosity, for a man from Kilkenny who knew he was dying but managed to see one last All-Ireland final.

A mighty, mighty haven. For all of them and many more.

Over the next few weeks, Haven's neighbours enjoyed great success. Ilen Rovers won the intermediate title to go senior for the first time. Carbery Rangers won their first ever county junior title, Muintir Bháire of Durrus won their first ever county junior B title. There would have been jubilation, drinking from the cup and dancing on the tables in all those places too. In every county, the scenes would be the same as the club honours were decided, hundreds of celebrations, hundreds of nights when a local community could be unreservedly happy.

Every week in the summer, I look at the GAA notes in the *Southern Star* and at the mind-boggling number of games that will be played at all levels and think of the astounding amount of hard work and goodwill that keeps the show on the road. It has no parallel in this country.

There is nothing like the GAA because, in the end, the association is not the Croke Park hierarchy or even the star inter-county players, it's everyone, it is the people who dance on the tables. They own it and it owns them. That will never change.

Final whistle.

In Memoriam, Cormac McAnallen

I thought I'd look back on the championship in years to come and think of it as the one I wrote the book about. Now last year will always be the year my father died and the games will be tied in with that.

When I wrote those words in December, I had no idea that after 2 March 2004, the football championship of 2003 would take on a different meaning for everyone who followed the GAA. It would be remembered as the last one before Cormac McAnallen died of a rare heart condition.

We live in a hyped-up world where round-the-clock news channels are constantly exhorting people to feel shock, to fake empathy, to be profoundly moved by today's headlines. The result of all this is that the disasters, which appear on our screens, can seem as unreal as images from a video game.

Cormac McAnallen's death, on the other hand, was genuinely shocking. Someone rang me at half-nine that morning to tell me about it. They weren't a GAA fan and my first thought was that they'd got it wrong. Perhaps it was an elderly relation of McAnallen's or some Tyrone star of the past who he'd been compared to. And then there was another phone call, and another. One of the game's young stars, an athletic 24-year-old, had died suddenly after being taken ill at his home in Eglish, just a few months after playing on Tyrone's All-Ireland winning team. It seemed impossible to credit.

The news was sudden, it was senseless and it was true. I can't remember a death outside my family and friends that left me with the same feelings of sadness. There is something terrible about the death of a young person but there's an added poignancy when that youngster is an athlete, someone who has risen to prominence because of the fitness and strength of their body. Cormac McAnallen was the greatest Irish sportsman to be cut off in his prime since Liam Whelan of Manchester United had died in the Munich air crash.

And, as had been the case when Whelan and the other Busby Babes died, part of the sensation of tragedy stemmed from the feeling of things left undone. McAnallen had achieved a huge amount in a brief senior career but, when you watched him, you also saw the things he would do in the future. Great midfielders got better as they became more experienced. McAnallen had perhaps another 10 years when he could be one of the finest footballers in the game. We imagined him at 27 or 28, completely commanding in the centre of the field. We had already awarded him those years, projected his inevitable future triumphs.

In the days following his death, it was obvious, even making allowances for the custom of speaking well of the dead, that McAnallen was a person of rare quality. A teetotaller, he was dedicated to his work as a teacher and had spent his last bus trip with the team revising the lesson he was to teach his pupils the next day. The evening before he died, he'd gone to the gym and then settled down to watch *University Challenge*, boning up on his general knowledge for a forthcoming quiz. He was engaged to be married. The affection with which these facets of his character were dwelt upon is telling about the values that, deep down, are really held dear in Irish society. Underneath all the beer-ad bravado and bluster, which were held to characterise the Tiger nation, what people really admired are gentler qualities redolent of a more old-fashioned decency. The sense of loss among those who knew him was almost unbearable to witness. When Mickey Harte was interviewed, he sounded like a man in deep shock, struggling to make sense of the world.

McAnallen's decency was also obvious on the pitch. It was impossible to remember any incident of bad sportsmanship involving him. On a team that was prone at times to narkiness and which had been involved in many ferociously competitive matches, he was a calming influence, often breaking up arguments. His status as a natural leader had been recognised by his appointment as county captain for 2004.

Without McAnallen, Tyrone wouldn't have won their first All-Ireland. Thrown in at the deep end in a position he had little experience of, the big man played three flawless games at full-back and completed the final piece in the Tyrone jigsaw by giving them a watertight defence. With him at full-back, Tyrone conceded a scarcely believable average of just over seven points a game. Prior to the move, they'd been letting in 13 a game. Like Seamus Moynihan before him, he had curbed his attacking instincts to serve the team and had been rewarded.

A couple of weeks after his funeral, McAnallen's team-mates played Longford in a National League match and won by a big margin. Football, being part of life, had to carry on. But it was a much sadder game without Cormac McAnallen. All championship games will be sadder from now on. May he rest in peace.

Acknowledgements

A book of this sort is necessarily dependent on the goodwill and help of many people and I would like to apologise for omitting anyone who should be thanked.

Thanks to Batt Maguire, Tim Joe Regan, Christy Collins, Gerry O'Sullivan, Dermot and The Group, John Dowd, Tommy Conlon, Adhamhnan O'Sullivan, Tony Leen, Dermot Crowe, Kieran Shannon, Johnny Murphy, Gary Hurney, Cathal McAnenly, Seamus Horisk, James Gallagher, Joseph Gallagher, Tom O'Hare, Mickey Linden, Pat Brennan, Joe Drury, John O'Mahony, Geraldine O'Mahony, Liam O'Rócháin, David Hickey, D.J. Linehan, Tom Kenny, Paddy Connery, Mark Landers and Damien Irwin.

The book would not have been written without the contribution of my agent Pat Kavanagh who was her usual supportive self. I'd also like to thank Ciara Considine of Hodder Headline for giving me the chance to write a book which has been on my mind for a long time. Claire Rourke's work on the manuscript was also a great help.

I'd like to thank my daughter Emily for being a constant delight and massively improving my life. Sometime in the future she may hopefully get the same enjoyment from this book as she currently derives from *Bear in the Big Blue House*. Emily's mother, Siobhan, and my friends Ronnie Bellew and Mike McCormack were a great support throughout the writing of the book and the other events of the past year.

I hope that this book would have earned the approval of

my father Joe Sweeney (1943–2003) and that he has fetched up in an afterlife where every day is a Kilkenny hurling final victory. My mother, Evelyn, and my sister, Maura, provided all kinds of practical help and emotional support far beyond the call of duty and I can't thank them enough.

Finally, thanks to Michael Cusack and the six other men who on 1 November 1884 turned up in the billiard rooms of Hayes's Commercial Hotel, Thurles, to found the GAA. Irish life might be a lot less exciting today had they opted to stay in that night.